ADVANCES IN PERSONALITY ASSESSMENT
Volume 9

ADVANCES IN PERSONALITY ASSESSMENT
Volume 9

Edited by
Charles D. Spielberger
University of South Florida

James N. Butcher
University of Minnesota

LEA LAWRENCE ERLBAUM ASSOCIATES, PUBLISHERS
1992 Hillsdale, New Jersey   Hove and London

Lawrence Erlbaum Associates, Inc. Publishers
365 Broadway
Hillsdale, New Jersey 07642

Library of Congress Cataloging in Publication Data

ISSN 0-278-2367
ISBN 0-8058-1226-1

Printed in the United States of America
10 9 8 7 6 5 4 3 2 1

Contents

Preface   ix

1. **The Nature of Perceived Social Support:**
   Findings of Meta-Analysis Studies   1
   Mary E. Procidano

   Reliability   4
   Validity   5
   Construct Validity   8
   Discussion   18
   Summary   21

2. **Assessment of Appreciation of Humor:**
   Studies with the 3 WD Humor Test   27
   Willibald Ruch

   Theory and Research on the Nature and
      Assessment of Humor   28
   Construction and Psychometric Properties of
      the 3 WD   35
   Findings of Published and Unpublished
      Studies Using the 3 WD   45
   Discussion and Conclusion   67
   Summary   72

3. **The Construct of Machiavellianism:**
   Twenty Years Later   77
   Beverley Fehr, Deborah Samsom, and
   Delroy L. Paulhus

   Personality Correlates   78
   Behavioral Validation   88
   Psychometric Issues   100

4. **Personality and Perception: Rorschach and**
   Luescher Correlates of Jungian Types as
   Measured by the Myers-Briggs Type Indicator   117
   Benjamin J. Porter and Samuel Roll

   Method   119
   Results   121
   Discussion   122
   Summary   124

5. **Susceptibility of the Rorschach to Malingering:**
   A Schizophrenia Analogue   127
   Glenn G. Perry and Bill N. Kinder

   Method   128
   Results   129
   Discussion   134
   Conclusions 138
   Summary   139

6. **Empirical Assessment of Marital Distress:**
   The Marital Distress Scale for the MMPI-2   141
   Stephen Hjemboe, James N. Butcher, and
   Moshe Almagor

   Method   142
   Results   145
   Conclusion   148

7. **Angina Pectoris and Personality: Development**
   and Validation of the Anginal Syndrome
   Questionnaire   153
   Anthony F. Greene, Douglas D. Schocken,
   and Charles D. Spielberger

   Anginal Symptoms, Neurotic Traits, and
      Coronary Disease   155

Development of the Anginal Syndrome
   Questionnaire   158
Discussion and Conclusions   164
Summary   166

8. Trait Anger: Theory, Findings, and Implications   **177**
Jerry L. Deffenbacher

Relation of Trait Anger to Style of
   Anger Expression   178
Tests of Trait-State Anger Theory   180
Implications for Anger Theory and
   Future Research   192
Implications for Clinical Assessment and
   Treatment   195
Summary and Conclusions   198

Author Index   **203**

Subject Index   **211**

List of Contributors

Almagor, Moshe, University of Haifa, ISRAEL
Butcher, James N., University of Minnesota, Minneapolis, MN USA
Deffenbacher, Jerry L., Colorado State University, Fort Collins, CO USA
Fehr, Beverly, The University of Winnipeg, Winnipeg, CANADA
Greene, Anthony F., University of Florida, Gainesville, FL USA
Hjemboe, Stephen, University of Haifa, ISRAEL
Kinder, Bill, University of South Florida, Tampa, FL USA
Paulhus, Delroy L., University of British Columbia, CANADA
Perry, Glenn G., University of South Florida, Tampa, FL USA
Porter, Benjamin J., Unversity of New Mexico, Albuquerque, NM USA
Procidano, Mary E., Graduate School of Arts and Sciences, Fordham University, Bronx, NY USA
Roll, Samuel, The University of New Mexico, Albuquerque, NM USA
Ruch, Willibald, Universität Dusseldorf, Dusseldorf, GERMANY
Samson, Deborah, University of British Columbia, CANADA
Schocken, Douglas D., University of South Florida, Tampa, FL USA
Spielberger, Charles D., University of South Florida, Tampa, FL USA

Preface

The resurgence of interest in personality assessment that we noted in our preface to Volume 8 continues unabated as psychologists explore new horizons for their craft in the present information age. Evidence for this Renaissance in personality assessment can be found in the rapid growth of the Society for Personality Assessment whose membership has more than doubled over the past five years, the expanded goals of the Division of Evaluation and Measurement of the American Psychological Association to explicitly encompass psychologists interested in the development and applications of personality assessment, the establishment of several new journals on assessment in the U.S. and Europe, and the founding of the European Association for Psychological Assessment, which held its first meeting in Barcelona in September 1991.

Growth in the field of personality assessment has been stimulated by important new conceptual developments that have contributed to the construction of better measures, and by increasing consumer demand for assessment services in areas in which practitioners of personality assessment were not previously active. The interest of business and industry in so-called integrity tests, sophisticated evaluation of managers and executives for promotion to more senior positions, and recognition of the need to select law enforcement officers who can control impulsive and aggressive behavior under extreme provocation are but a few of the many areas in which the demands for personality assessment have greatly increased.

The present volume, the ninth in this continuing Series on *Advances in Personality Assessment*, reflects the broadening boundaries of our field as well as increasing international interests. A common thread that can be discerned in most of the individual chapters is the inclusion of a comprehensive review of relevant research. This is especially true in Procidano's meta-analytic studies of the nature of perceived social support (Chapter 1) and in Ruch's examination of previous research on humor and his construction and validation of new tests to assess manifestations of this important personality characteristic (Chapter 2). The work reported by Procidano and by Fehr, Samsom and Paulhus (Chapter 3) who examine the evolution and predictive validity of the construct of Machiavellianism, contribute scientific light to the frontier between personality assessment and the fields of personality and social psychology.

Although Chapters 4, 5 and 6 examine applications of more traditional personality assessment techniques such as the Rorschach and the MMPI, they report applications of these techniques to relatively unexplored topics. Porter and Roll's (Chapter 4) analysis of Rorschach correlates of Jungian types as measured by the Meyer-Briggs Type Indicator provides a unique integration of these very different methods of personality assessment, and Hjemboe, Almagor and Butcher (Chapter 5) report impressive evidence of the utility of the MMPI-2 in the empirical assessment of critical dimensions of marital distress. Perry and Kinder (Chapter 6) draw interesting inferences from the application of the Rorschach to the detection of malingering and the diagnosis of schizophrenia.

In Chapter 7, Greene, Schocken and Spielberger review epidemiological and clinical studies of angina pectoris, a form of chest pain that is critical in the diagnosis of underlying cardiovascular disease, and describe the construction and validation of the Anginal Syndrome Questionnaire, a new instrument for assessing angina. In the final chapter, Deffenbacher reports the results of a series of studies on the assessment of anger and its correlates, with findings that have great import for psychodiagnosis and treatment planning.

As the importance of psychosocial factors in physical disorders such as heart disease and cancer are more generally recognized and the costs of health services continue to escalate, the need and corresponding demand for more efficient and effective psychodiagnostic procedures will continue to grow. Thus, the continued growth of personality assessment and the potential of our field to significantly contribute to theory, research and the effective practice of psychology seems assured.

Charles D. Spielberger
James N. Butcher

1 The Nature of Perceived Social Support: Findings of Meta-Analytic Studies

Mary E. Procidano
Fordham University

Early conceptualizations of social support as being of direct benefit to psychological adjustment (Antonovsky, 1974; Caplan, 1974), and expectations that social support might interact with or buffer the effects of stress (e.g., Cobb, 1976; Rabkin & Struening, 1976), have led to the development and utilization of several social support measures, and to a concomitant refinement of our definition of social support. According to Barrera (1986), it is accepted widely that "social support" itself is a "meta-construct" (p. 413), consisting of social embeddedness, supportive transactions, and subjective appraisal, or perception, of support (Sarason, 1988; Vaux, 1987). Most available instruments purport to measure one or more of these particular constructs. This chapter is based mostly on a compilation of meta-analytic data relevant to the validity of measures of perceived social support from family (PSS–Fa) and from friends (PSS–Fr) that were originally developed and validated on college students (Procidano & Heller, 1983). This information is intended to contribute to our growing understanding of the perceived social support construct, and to document the utility of the PSS measures.

There are different rationales and benefits associated with assessing each of the three widely recognized support constructs. Hirsch and Rapkin (1986) stated that social embeddedness, or social network characteristics, although virtually always assessed via subjects' self-reports, is believed to possess ecological validity in reflecting peoples' "personal communities" (p. 395). Network characteristics, such as size and presence of family members and friends, have been found to correlate with adjustment but often have no direct or stress-buffering effect on symptomatology. Furthermore, knowing structural characteristics of individuals' support networks does not help to clarify the processes by which supportive transactions occur and consequently might aid in coping and adjustment (Barrera, 1986; Cohen & Wills, 1985).

Assessing supportive transactions also is believed to have particular advantages. Again, virtually always obtained via self-report, as opposed to behavioral observation (Barrera, 1986), this type of measure affords specificity and precision in delineating the supportive functions that network members might serve, by "gauging the responsiveness of others in rendering assistance when subjects are confronted with stress" (p. 417). The most widely used measure of supportive behaviors, the Inventory of Socially Supportive Behaviors (ISSB; Barrera, Sandler, & Ramsay, 1981), has been found to reflect meaningful categories of supportive transactions (Barrera & Ainlay, 1983; Stokes & Wilson, 1984; Walkey, McCormick, Siegert, & Taylor, 1987). However, the expectation that such specificity would aid in the prediction of positive adjustment to stress has generally not received empirical verification (e.g., Cohen & Wills, 1985; Sandler & Barrera, 1984; Tetzloff & Barrera, 1987). One explanation for this lack of confirmation is that behaviors that are designated a priori as supportive may not be subjectively desirable to the recipient, perhaps because they are performed begrudgingly, or by persons not otherwise perceived as supportive. At issue is the distinction between overt behaviors performed by social network members and their subjective impact on the recipient.

The PSS–Fa and PSS–Fr scales (Procidano & Heller, 1983) were designed to assess such subjective impact, guided in part by theoretical statements regarding the nature and potential outcomes of social support. Cobb (1976) described social support as "information leading the subject to believe that he is cared for and loved . . . esteemed and valued . . . and belongs to a network of communication and mutual obligations" (p. 300). Similarly, Cassel (1976, p. 107) used the term *feedback* in describing social support. This cognitive or attributional definition of social support is also consistent with current conceptualizations of coping as including an appraisal component (e.g., Folkman, Schaefer, & Lazarus, 1979). The PSS measures are composed of 20 declarative statements each, regarding the extent to which subjects believe that their needs for support, information, and feedback (Caplan, 1974) are being fulfilled by family or friends, respectively. Each instrument includes some items reflecting provision of support by the subject to others, consistent with findings of a relationship of reciprocity and bidirectional support-provision to adjustment (Maton, 1987; Tolsdorf, 1976). Original validation studies with college students (Procidano & Heller, 1983) indicated that the measures reflected related but separate constructs. This differentiation has been supported by Sarason and her colleagues (B. R. Sarason, Shearin, Pierce, & Sarason, 1987), who found different patterns of correlations for the two scales.

Additional empirical evidence is available to indicate the particular advantages associated with assessing perceived social support. Perceived support has been found to correlate with social-network characteristics (Procidano & Heller, 1983; Stokes, 1983; Vaux & Athanassopoulu, 1987; Vaux & Harrison, 1985) and with supportive transactions (Vinokur, Schul, & Caplan, 1987; Wethington & Kessler, 1986). It has been suggested that the beneficial influence of received support is mediated by perceived support (Wethington & Kessler, 1986). Many investigators have found that, compared to social embeddedness and receipt of supportive transactions, subjective appraisal of support is more likely to predict well-being and/or to buffer stress (e.g., Barrera, 1986; Wethington & Kessler, 1986; Wilcox, 1981). Consistent with the original speculations regarding the nature of social support (Caplan, 1974; Cassel, 1976; Cobb, 1976), Sarason and her colleagues (B. R. Sarason et al., 1987) concluded recently that, essentially, social support involves the feeling "that we are loved and valued, that our well-being is the concern of significant others" (p. 830). Of the three social-support constructs, perceived support seems closest to this definition (I. G. Sarason, 1988).

The principal argument against such measures is that they may be confounded with other variables, particularly antecedent adjustment and stress (e.g., Barrera, 1986; Eckenrode & Gore, 1981). The specific rival hypotheses are: (a) that the apparently beneficial effects of support may be attributable to individual difference variables, such as social competence (Procidano & Heller, 1983); (b) that the negative association of social support to symptomatology may be attributable to conceptual overlap between the two construct domains (e.g., Dohrenwend, Dohrenwend, Dodson, & Shrout, 1984); and, (c) that the apparent stress-buffering or interaction effect of support may be an artifact of its correlation with stress measures, such that stress by support interaction terms are not composed of independent components.

The available responses to these concerns are incomplete. First, it still is unclear to what extent antecedent personality characteristics contribute to variance in social support or, more seriously, account for its apparent effects. Cutrona (1986), for instance, found that network characteristics accounted for only about 30% of the variance of perceived support and suggested that future research examine other determinants of support perception, including personality characteristics. Regarding possible confounding of support with symptomatology, some evidence suggests that the two domains are distinct. Turner (1983) made such a conclusion on the basis of factor analytic studies. Vinokur et al. (1987) found in a longitudinal study that perceived support was influenced by supportive transactions, as reported by social network members; but only "moderately" by subjects' own negative outlook bias, and "weakly" by antecedent anxiety and depression (p. 1137). Procidano and Heller (1983) found, in an experimental study involving college students, that PSS–Fa was unaffected by positive or negative mood inductions, but PSS–Fr was lowered by a negative mood induction. Finally, Cohen and Wills (1985) investigated potential confounding between support and stress. After reviewing the available published studies that tested the buffering hypothesis, they concluded that the support by stress interaction was not an artifact of correlations between the two variables, because of the frequency with which the buffering effect still was observed in the absence of such a correlation.

More information is needed to help clarify the issue of confounding. There is still little consensus regarding the constructs to which support dimensions, including perceived support, "should" or "should not" be related. Thus, it is not surprising that Heitzmann and Kaplan (1988) observed that discriminant-validity information for social support measures is lacking. Barrera (1986) suggested a seemingly balanced approach to this matter, suggesting that "concern for confounding [might] discourage the scrutiny of legitimate relationships between social support concepts and measures of stress and distress" (p. 434).

The purpose of this chapter is to summarize reliability and validity information regarding the PSS measures across a reasonably wide range of populations. Some reviewers of social support instruments have commented that such data are very limited (House & Kahn, 1985; Tardy, 1985) but would be valuable in helping to clarify the nature and potential outcomes of social support (Heitzmann & Kaplan, 1988). Toward these ends, all available published and unpublished findings regarding the PSS measures were collected and submitted to several sets of meta-analyses. The inclusion of unpublished material minimizes the "file-drawer problem" in meta-analytic research, whereby the apparent magnitude of effects is inflated because nonsignificant results are less likely to be accepted for publication (Wolf, 1986). The findings were organized into categories relevant to specific aspects of reliability (internal consistency and test–retest) and validity (content, contrasted groups, and construct), as reflected in the current literature.

RELIABILITY

Internal Consistency

Estimates of the internal consistency of the PSS instruments were available for four samples, including college students (Ferraro & Procidano, 1986;

Procidano & Heller, 1983), high school girls (Procidano, Guinta, & Buglione, 1988), and male multiple sclerosis patients (Louis, 1986). Cronbach alphas ranged from .88 to .91 for PSS-Fa and from .84 to .90 for PSS-Fr, and thus the instruments appear to be internally consistent.

Test-Retest Reliability

Test-retest reliabilities were available for four samples of subjects, including college students (Ferraro & Procidano, 1986), adolescents and adolescents with alcoholic fathers (Clair, 1988), and high school girls (Procidano et al., 1988). The test-retest reliabilities for PSS-Fa over a 1-month period ranged from .80 for high school girls to .86 for college students. The average correlation based on z transformations, as recommended by Wolf (1986), was .82. The reliability for PSS-Fr for the same period of time ranged from .75 for adolescent offspring of alcoholic fathers to .81 for adolescent offspring of nonalcoholic fathers (Clair, 1988), $r = .79$.

There was no evidence of testing effects (over a 1-month period) in the instruments. Pre-post comparisons (based on t tests for correlated means) of data from college students (Ferraro & Procidano, 1986) were nonsignificant for both PSS-Fa [t (112) = .41, n.s.] and PSS-Fr [t (112) = −.60, n.s.]. Results based on high school girls were similar: t (88) = .25, n.s., for PSS-Fa; and t (88) = .46, n.s., for PSS-Fr.

VALIDITY

Norms and Contrasted-Groups Validity

Table 1.1 provides normative information (means and standard deviations) of the PSS instruments for 24 samples. For the meta-analysis, the samples were categorized a priori as nonclinical or clinical (i.e., all or most subjects carrying diagnoses and/or receiving psychological or psychiatric treatment). There are 13 nonclinical samples (from Procidano & Heller, 1983, through Lyons, Perrotta, & Hancher-Kuam, 1988). Samples receiving medical treatment, including multiple sclerosis patients (Louis, 1986; McIvor, Riklan, & Reznikoff, 1984) and diabetics (Lyons et al., 1988), were classified as nonclinical. As it was not clear whether or not Clair's sample of adolescent offspring of alcoholic fathers should be considered clinical by virtue of the father's status (as well as the possibility that the subjects themselves might be involved in treatment), or nonclinical, that sample was not included in the classification. The remaining 10 samples from Procidano and Guinta (1988) through Grey, Osborn, and Reznikoff, 1986,

TABLE 1.1
Means and Standard Deviations of PSS Measures

Source	Sample	N	Age Range	Age M	Age SD	PSS-Fa M	PSS-Fa SD	PSS-Fr M	PSS-Fr SD
Procidano & Heller (1983)	College students	66	—	19	—	13.40	4.83	15.15	5.08
Ferraro & Procidano (1986)	College students	114	17–22	19.50	—	14.28	5.10	15.81	4.30
Arsuaga (1988)	College students	214	—	19.72	—	12.68	2.68	12.74	1.86
Lyons, Perotta, & Hancher-Kuam (1988)	College students	92	—	—	—	11.90	6.40	13.90	5.00
Ford & Procidano (1987)	Nontraditional college students	106	18–81	36.80	—	11.60	6.40	14.70	4.90
Clair (1988)	Adolescents	50	13–19	—	—	11.62	5.33	12.50	4.78
Procidano et al. (1988)	High school girls	90	14–17	14.82	1.26	11.71	5.50	13.56	4.41
Wade & Procidano (1986)	Expectant mothers	33	—	27.39	3.73	17.15[a]	4.57	12.67	5.74
Wade & Procidano (1986)	Mothers of young children	26	—	32.46	3.88	15.15[a]	4.28	12.88	4.54
Zelles (1988)	Male partners of abortion patients	127	18–35	—	—	—	—	12.66	4.60
McIvor, Riklan, & Reznikoff (1987)	Multiple sclerosis (MS) patients	120	23–71	45.24	10.73	13.43	5.63	13.45	5.37
Louis (1986)	Male MS patients	60	34–72	54.25	10.43	15.20[b]	5.10	13.45	5.22
Lyons et al. (1988)	Diabetics	53	—	—	—	13.10	5.20	12.90	4.50
Clair (1988)	Adolescents with alcoholic fathers	40	13–19	—	—	9.03	5.78	12.33	4.79
Procidano & Guinta (1988)	Young adult psychiatric inpts.	30	15–23	—	—	10.33	5.40	10.20[c]	6.06
Frigon (1986)	Hospitalized suicide attempters	32	—	37.94	12.30	7.19	5.85	10.09	4.80
Frigon (1986)	Hospitalized depressed patients	39	—	34.03	9.53	7.26	5.13	10.74	5.86
Wolff, Procidano, & Raps (1983)	Vietnam veterans	90	—	34	—	7.61	6.17	9.78	5.60
Crits-Christoph & Procidano (1988)	Chronic schizophrenic outpatients	75	19–72	43.7	15.8	11.28	5.75	12.01	4.94
Lyons et al. (1988)	Chronic psychiatric patients	74	—	—	—	9.60	6.10	10.90	6.20
Procidano & Crits-Christoph (1988)	Elderly psychiatric day patients	30	—	62.2	7.7	10.16	7.34	11.94	5.43
Procidano & Crits-Christoph (1988)	Elderly nursing home patients	21	—	68.0	—	7.19	6.39	9.90	5.71
Grey, Osborn, & Reznikoff (1986)	Methadone treatment patients	30	23–46	32.2	5.4	11.37	6.69	—	—
Grey et al. (1986)	Naltrexone[d] treatment patients	30	23–46	32.2	5.4	10.40	5.83	—	—

[a,b,c]Alternate forms used: PSS-Spouse, PSS-Immediate family (i.e., spouse and children), PSS-Friends outside the hospital, respectively. Not included in meta-analysis.

[d]Naltrexone treatment is an alternative to methadone maintenance.

including the samples of Vietnam veterans (Wolff, Procidano, & Raps, 1983) and elderly nursing home patients (Procidano & Crits-Christoph, 1988), met the criteria for clinical status.

For PSS-Fa, means of the nonclinical samples ranged from 11.60 to 14.28, compared to 7.19 to 11.34 for clinical samples. The distributions of nonclinical versus clinical means approached each other but did not overlap. (Obviously, the same was not true of the respective distributions of scores.) Pooling all the nonclinical and clinical samples into two groups yielded a nonclinical grand mean of 12.70, compared to 9.25 for the clinical group. A comparison of these two groups was highly significant: t (1354) $=$ 12.32, $p < .001$.[1] It can be seen post hoc that Clair's sample of adolescent offspring of alcoholic fathers falls in the range of the pooled clinical group with respect to PSS-Fa, in fact, very close to the grand mean.

For PSS-Fr, the individual means ranged from 12.50 to 15.81 for nonclinical samples, and from 9.78 to 12.01 for clinical samples. Again, the two sets of group means did not overlap. The respective grand means were 13.62 (nonclinical) versus 10.74 (clinical), t (1510) $=$ 9.76, $p < .001$. Interestingly, Clair's sample of adolescent offspring of alcoholic fathers, not previously classified, fell between the two grand means, implying that having an alcoholic father has clearer effects on PSS-Fa but may also lower PSS-Fr.

The Role of Age

The potential relationship of age to PSS was examined by correlating subjects' mean ages (in samples for whom such data were available) with the PSS means. Both relationships approached significance: r (15) $= -.40$, $p < 10$; r (16) $= -.41$, $p < 10$, for PSS-Fa and PSS-Fr, respectively. However, age and clinical status also covaried, r (18) $= .41$, $p < .10$, such that clinical samples were composed of slightly older individuals. Controlling for age did not attenuate the relationship between clinical status and PSS-Fa (partial r (10) $= -.79$, $p < .001$) or PSS-Fr (partial r (10) $= -.77$, $p < .002$); however, controlling for clinical status substantially reduced the relationship of age to PSS-Fa [partial r (10) $= -.18$, n.s.] and PSS-Fr [partial r (10) $= -.12$, n.s.].

To summarize, this meta-analytic contrasted-groups procedure supports

---

[1]Grand means were calculated from $\dfrac{\Sigma N_i \bar{X}_i}{\Sigma N_i}$

pooled variances from $\dfrac{\Sigma df_i S_i^2}{df_i}$

the validity of the PSS instruments, in that nonclinical and clinical groups differed significantly. There was no evidence from these data that PSS diminishes with age.

CONSTRUCT VALIDITY

The Relationship of PSS–Fa to PSS–Fr

An important question regarding the meaning of perceived social support, and the validity of the PSS measures, is the extent of overlap versus distinction between different sources of support—in this case, between PSS–Fa and PSS–Fr. Correlations between the two indices, obtained from 12 nonclinical and 4 clinical samples (Arsuaga, 1988; Crits-Christoph & Procidano, 1988; Ferraro & Procidano, 1986; Louis, 1986; Lyons et al., 1988; Procidano & Crits-Christoph, 1988; Procidano & Guinta, 1988; Procidano & Heller, 1983; Procidano et al., 1988; Sarason et al., 1987; Wade & Procidano, 1986), ranged from $-.11$ to $.53$. The average correlation (r) was $.31$, indicating a medium effect size. The PSS–Fa–PSS–Fr correlations did not differ between nonclinical and clinical subgroups: $z = .72$, n.s.

Relationships to Other Social-Support Indices

The relations between PSS–Fa and PSS–Fr, and other social-support indices, perhaps most central to the issue of their construct validity, are presented in Table 1.2. The first four sections of the table refer to an aspect of structural support-network characteristics, namely, size. Network size is defined as the number of family-member providers of intangible and tangible support, and friend providers of tangible and tangible support, respectively. The studies reported here all used a modification (Procidano & Heller, 1983) of the Social Network Questionnaire (Liem & Liem, 1977).

Summing across the studies (via z transformations), PSS–Fa was related moderately to the number of family members reported to provide intangible support $(r = .30)$; and more modestly to the number of tangible-support providers in the family $(r = .22)$. Somewhat similarly, PSS–Fr was related moderately to the number of friend intangible-support providers $(r = .31)$ and more weakly $(r = .16)$ to friend tangible-support providers.

The relationships between PSS–Fa and the size of the friend network, and vice versa, provide some evidence for discriminant validity for the measures and further basis for distinguishing between different networks as sources of support. Summing across the studies again, PSS–Fa was unrelated to the size of intangible $(r = .01)$ and tangible friend support networks $(r = .03)$, and PSS-Fr was similarly unrelated to intangible ($r = .05$) or tangible family support ($r = .11$). Thus, perceptions of support appear to be related specifically to the number of support providers in the corresponding network.

The relationships of PSS-Fa to family environment characteristics, as measured by the subscales of the Family Environment Scale, or FES (Moos, 1974), were fairly high: $r = .67$ for Cohesion, $r = .51$ for Expressiveness, and $r = -.44$ for Conflict. The relationships between PSS-Fr and the same family environment characteristics were of moderate magnitude for Cohesion ($r = .29$) and for Expressiveness ($r = .27$), and low for Conflict ($r = -.14$). The magnitude of the cumulated (averaged via z-transformations) relationship between PSS-Fa and these family environment indices exceeded that between PSS-Fr and the same indices [$t (19) = 4.76, p < .01$], based on a t test for independent rs (Cohen & Cohen, 1975). In contrast to the relations of support perceptions to characteristics of social networks, perceptions of different networks are not independent of each other. However, perceptions of the same network measured in different ways (i.e., PSS-Fa and FES) seem to converge more than perceptions of different networks.

Information regarding some additional relationships was available for single studies. Interestingly, PSS-Fr but not PSS-Fa was found to be related negatively to FES Independence (Procidano & Heller, 1983). Arsuaga (1988) found that both PSS-Fr and PSS-Fa were related moderately to received support, as measured by the Inventory of Socially Supportive Behaviors (Barrera et al., 1981). B. R. Sarason et al. (1987) reported fairly substantial correlationships between both PSS-Fr and PSS-Fa and subscales of the Social Support Questionnaire (I. G. Sarason, Levine, Basham, & Sarason, 1983) and the Interpersonal Support Evaluation List (Cohen & Hoberman, 1983). Finally, Zelles (1988) found a moderate relationship between PSS-Fr (he did not study PSS-Fa) and the Empathy and Congruence subscales of the Barrett-Lennard Relationships Inventory (Barrett-Lennard, 1962).

Relationships to Personality and Social Competence

Some limited information is available regarding relationships between the PSS indices and measures of personality and social competence. Unfortunately, the number of studies that are informative in this regard are few, and all based on college students (including one sample of nontraditional college students). In the original validation of the instruments, five measures believed to measure social competence were chosen for examination. PSS-Fr was correlated with the three subscales of the California Psycho-

TABLE 1.2

Correlations of PSS with Other Social Support Variables

Support Variable	PSS-Fa	PSS-Fr
Support Network Characteristics		
Family Relationships–Intangible Support		
Source / Sample		
Procidano & Heller (1983) — College students	.34**	.13
Ferraro & Procidano (1986) — College students	.05	.09
Louis (1986) — Male MS patients	.39**[a]	–
Louis (1986) — Male MS patients	.33**[b]	–
Procidano & Guinta (1988) — Young adult psychiatric inpatients	.15	–
Wolff et al. (1983) — Vietnam veterans	.35***	–
Crits-Christoph & Procidano (1988) — Chronic schizophrenic outpatients	.24*	.00
Procidano & Crits-Christoph (1988) — Elderly chronic psychiatric day patients	.59***	.15
Procidano & Crits-Christoph (1988) — Elderly nursing home patients	.26	–.11
Family Relationships–Tangible Support		
Source / Sample		
Procidano & Heller (1983) — College students	–.11	–.10
Ferraro & Procidano (1986) — College students	–.02	–
Louis (1986) — Male MS patients	.37**[a]	–
	.44***[b]	–
Procidano & Guinta (1988) — Young adults psychiatric inpatients	–.13	–
Crits-Christoph & Procidano (1988) — Chronic schizophrenic outpatients	.37***	.16
Procidano & Crits-Christoph (1988) — Elderly chronic psychiatric day patients	.53**	.28
Procidano & Crits-Christoph (1988) — Elderly nursing home patients	.10	.09
Friend Relationships–Intangible Support		
Source / Sample		
Procidano & Heller (1983) — College students	.04	.14
Ferraro & Procidano (1986) — College students	.12	.21*

Study	Group		
Wade & Procidano (1986)	Expectant mothers	.16[c]	.44**
Wade & Procidano (1986)	Mothers of young children	−.02[c]	.26
Louis (1986)	Male MS patients	—	.36**[a]
			.38*[a]

Friend Relationships–Tangible Support

Study	Group		
Procidano & Guinta (1988)	Young adult psychiatric inpatients	—	.32*
Wolff et al. (1983)	Vietnam veterans	—	.35***
Crits-Christoph & Procidano (1988)	Chronic schizophrenic outpatients	.01	.06
Procidano & Crits-Christoph (1988)	Elderly chronic psychiatric day patients	.27	.28
Procidano & Crits-Christoph (1988)	Elderly nursing home patients	−.37*	.57**
Procidano & Heller (1983)	College students	−.12	−.01
Ferraro & Procidano (1986)	College students	.11	.06
Louis (1986)	Male MS patients	—	.21
Procidano & Guinta (1988)	Young adult psychiatric inpatients	—	.33**
Procidano & Guinta (1988)	Young adult psychiatric inpatients	—	.23
Crits-Christoph & Procidano (1988)	Chronic schizophrenic outpatients	−.13	.13
Procidano & Crits-Christoph (1988)	Elderly psychiatric day patients	.01	.17
Procidano & Crits-Christoph, 1988	Elderly nursing home patients	.00	.24

Family Environment Measures

Cohesion

Study	Group		
Procidano & Heller (1983)[f]	College students	.64***	.28**
Clair (1988)	Adolescents	.72***	.36*
Clair (1988)	Adolescents with alcoholic fathers	.65***	.25

Expressiveness

Study	Group		
Procidenao & Heller (1983)[f]	College students	.45***	.28**
Clair (1988)	Adolescents	.47**	.31*
Clair (1988)	Adolescents with alcoholic fathers	.61***	.21

Conflict

Study	Group		
Procidano & Heller (1983)[f]	College students	−.26**	−.06
Clair (1988)	Adolescents	−.63***	−.18
Clair (1988)	Adolescents with alcoholic fathers	−.38**	−.19

(continued)

11

TABLE 1.2 (continued)

Support Variable	PSS-Fa	PSS-Fr
Procidano & Heller (1983[f])		
Independence		
College students	-.00	.19*
Receipt of Socially Supportive Behaviors (ISSB)		
Arsuaga (1988)		
College students	.27***	.36***
Social Support Questionnaire		
Sarason et al. (1987)		
Number College students		
Number	.38	.44
Family	.49	.27
Satisfaction	.56	.57
Interpersonal Support Evaluation List		
Sarason et al. (1987)		
Total College students	.47	.61
Appraisal	.51	.58
Belonging	.35	.57
Tangible	.33	.40
Self-esteem	.38	.49
Barret-Lennard Relationship Inventory (form MO)		
Empathy		
Zelles (1988) Male partners of pregnant women	—	.31**
Congruence		
Zelles (1988) Male partners of pregnant women	—	.31**

[a,b] Alternate forms used: PSS-Immediate family, extended family, respectively. The average of these correlations was used in the meta-analysis.
[c] Alternate form used: PSS-Spouse. This correlation was not included in the meta-analysis.
[d,e] Alternate forms used: PSS-Friends outside the hospital, friends in the hospital, respectively. The average of these correlations was used in the meta-analysis.
[f] These data are not included in the published version.
*$p < .05$; **$p < .01$; ***$p < .001$.

logical Inventory, or CPI (Gough, 1969), including Good Impression ($r =$ .23, p < .05), Social Presence ($r = .51, p < .001$), and Sociability ($r = .33$, $p < .01$), a "Lacks Self-Confidence" measure (Hirschfeld et al., 1977), $r = -.45$, $p < .001$, and a measure of Dating and Assertiveness Skills (Levenson & Gottman, 1978), $r = .40, p < .01$. PSS–Fa was related to Dating and Assertiveness Skills ($r = .35, p < .001$), but not to the other four dimensions.

Subsequently, Arsuaga (1988) examined potential relationships between PSS–Fa and PSS–Fr and an omnibus personality inventory (Jackson, 1984) that includes social competence as well as other dimensions. Using $p < .05$ as a criterion (because of the number of simultaneous tests), PSS–Fa had five personality correlates, including Affiliation, Autonomy (negative correlation), Dominance, Exhibition, Nurturance, and Desirability. Of these, two (Affiliation and Exhibition) were related to PSS–Fr, and four (Affiliation, Dominance, Exhibition, and Nurturance) to support receipt (ISSB; Barrera et al., 1981). Thus, it appears that personality characteristics do not account for a large proportion of the variance of perceived support, and that the extent to which they might play some role is not disproportionate to their relationship to receipt of supportive transactions.

Finally, Ford and Procidano (1987) found that Self-Actualization (Shostrom, 1963) was related to both the PSS–Fa ($r = .27$) and the PSS–Fr ($r = .41$) in nontraditional college students. The relationship between Self-Actualization was not more strongly related to PSS–Fr than it was to PSS–Fa [t (103) $= 1.11$, n.s.].

Relationships to Symptomatology

The "main effect" hypothesis of social support predicts a negative relationship between social support and symptomatology. A compilation of data relevant to this hypothesis is presented in Table 1.3. Several outcome measures are reflected in these analyses: an abbreviated MMPI (Faschingbauer, 1974); the MMPI (Hathaway & McKinley, 1967); the BSI, an abbreviated form of the SCL–90 (Derogatis, Rickels & Rock, 1976); the SCL–90 (Derogatis, 1977); a symptom screening inventory (Langner, 1962); a measure of PTSD (Egendorf et al., 1981); the Beck Depression Inventory (Beck, 1967); State and Trait Anxiety (Spielberger, Gorsuch, & Lushene, 1970); and State Anxiety and Anger (Spielberger, 1979). Note that in each instance that multiple symptomatology indices were reported on a single sample the average of the correlations (based on z-transformations) was used in the meta-analysis, so that no sample made a disproportionate contribution to the result (see Rosenthal, 1984; Wolf, 1986).

Summing across all the studies, symptomatology was related to both PSS–Fa ($r = .40$) and PSS–Fr ($r = .32$). These two correlations differed

TABLE 1.3
Correlations with Symptomatology

Source	Sample	Symptom	PSS-Fa	PSS-Fr
Procidano & Heller (1983)	College students	MMPI D[a]	-.43***	-.12
		MMPI Pt[a]	-.33***	-.23*
		MMPI Sc[a]	-.33***	-.20*
Procidano & Guinta (1988)	Young adult psychiatric inpts. (N = 23)	MMPI Pd	-.33	.02
				-.15
Louis (1986)	Male MS patients	MMPI Pt	-.37*	-.31[b]
				-.35*[c]
		BSI	-.50***[d]	-.11
			-.26*[e]	
Crits-Christoph & Procidano (1988)	Chronic schizophrenic outpatients	BSI	-.12	-.32*
Procidano & Crits-Christoph (1988)	Elderly chronic psychiatric outpatients	SCL-90	-.44**	-.47**
Procidano & Crits-Christoph (1988)	Elderly nursing home patients	SCL-90	-.16	.04
Procidano & Heller (1983)	College students	Langner 22-item Screening Inst.	-.29**	-.27***
Wolff et al. (1983)	Vietnam veterans	PTSD	-.33***	-.33***
Ferraro & Procidano (1986)	College students	Beck Depression Inventory	-.51***	-.61***
Ford & Procidano (1987)	Nontraditional college students	BDI	-.40**	-.40**
McIvor et al. (1984)	MS patients	BDI	-.60***	-.71***
Clair (1988)	Adolescents	Trait Anxiety[f]	-.48***[f]	-.12
Clair (1988)	Adolescents with alcoholic fathers	Trait Anxiety[g]	-.68***[g]	-.54***
Clair (1988)	Adolescents	State Anxiety[f]	-.40*[f]	-.17
Clair (1988)	Adolescents with alcoholic fathers	State Anxiety[g]	-.59***[g]	-.28
Procidano et al. (1988)	High school girls	State Anxiety[h]	-.36***[h]	-.22*
Procidano et al. (1988)	High school girls	State Anger[h]	-.36***[h]	-.16

[a] Abbreviated form.
[b,c] Alternate forms: PSS-Friends outside the hospital, in the hospital, respectively. Averaged in meta-analysis.
[d,e] Alternate forms: PSS-Immediate and extended family, respectively. Averaged in meta-analysis.
[f,g,h] Averaged in meta-analysis, [g] not included in nonclinical/clinical classification.

*$p < .05$; **$p < .01$; ***$p < .001$.

significantly, t (944) = 2.34, $p < .05$, indicating a stronger relationship of PSS–Fa to symptomatology. Furthermore, nonclinical versus clinical status appeared to mediate the PSS–symptomatology relationships. For PSS–Fa, there was a higher correlation with symptomatology ($r = .43$) in the pooled nonclinical than in the pooled clinical group ($r = .28$; $z = 1.73$, $p < .05$). The difference in PSS–Fr's relations to symptomatology is that nonclinical ($r = .35$) versus clinical groups ($r = .26$) approached significance: $z = 1.27$, $p < .10$. (See Wolf, 1986, for a discussion of this procedure of examining mediating effects.) The potential role of age in moderating the relationship between PSS and symptomatology was examined by correlating each sample's mean age (when available) with the respective PSS–symptomatology correlation (Rosenthal, 1984). Neither relationship achieved significance: r (11) = $-.31$, n.s., for PSS–Fa, and r (12) = $-.03$, n.s., for PSS–Fr. Thus, PSS, particularly PSS–Fa, was more strongly related to symptomatology in nonclinical samples, and this result was not attributable to age differences.

The Role of Response Bias

One way of investigating the nature and validity of the PSS–symptomatology relationship is to ask whether that relationship is accounted for by some aspect of response bias. Data from four studies were informative in this regard, including three samples of college students (Arsuaga, 1988; Procidano & Heller, 1983 – two independent samples included), and one of male MS patients (Louis, 1986). In each case, PSS–Fa was related to the index of response bias (Byrne, Barry, & Nelson, 1963; Crowne & Marlowe, 1964; Faschingbauer, 1974; Jackson, 1984). The average correlation ($r = .30$) indicates a moderate effect size. However, in each of the three studies in which symptom measures were used (all but Arsuaga, 1988), controlling for response bias (via partial correlation) did not attenuate the relationship between PSS–Fa and symptoms. Thus, there is no evidence that response bias is a confound in the PSS–Fa–symptom relationship. In each of the studies, and across the studies, ($r = .13$), response bias was unrelated to PSS–Fr.

The Buffering Hypothesis

Results of investigations of the potential stress-buffering role of PSS are presented in Table 1.4. Three of the studies (Ferraro & Procidano, 1986; Ford & Procidano, 1987; Procidano et al., 1988) involved nonclinical samples; of these two, the first and third used longitudinal designs. Two other studies (Crits-Christoph & Procidano, 1988; Wolff et al., 1983) involved clinical samples. Wolff et al. used current and retrospective

TABLE 1.4
Tests of the Buffering Hypothesis

Source	Sample	DV	Stress Measure	Main Effects			Buffering Effects	
				Stress	PSS–Fa	PSS–Fr	PSS–Fa	PSS–Fr
Ferraro & Procidano (1986)	College Students Time 1	BDI	Life Events	Yes	No	Yes	No	Yes
			Daily Hassles	Yes	–	–	Yes	Yes
	Time 2		Life Events	No	No	Yes	No	No
			Daily Hassles	Yes	–	–	Yes	Yes
	Across Time		Life Events	No	No	Yes	No	No
			Daily Hassles	Yes	–	–	Yes	Yes
Ford & Procidano (1987)	Nontrad. college students	BDI	Life Events	Yes	Yes	Yes (females only)	No	No
Procidano et al. (1988)	High-school girls							
	Time 1	State Anxiety	Life Events	Yes	Yes	Yes	No	No
		State Anger		No	Yes	No	No	No
	Time 2	State Anxiety		No	Yes	Yes	No	No
		State Anger		No	Yes	Yes	No	No
	Across Time	State Anxiety		No	Yes	No	No	No
		State Anger		Yes	Yes	Yes	No	No
Wolff et al. (1983)	Vietnam veterans Post-discharge Current	PTSD	Combat Index	Yes	Yes	Yes	No	Yes
				No	No	Yes	No	No
Crits-Christoph & Procidano (1988)	Chronic Schizophrenic outpts.	BSI	Life Events	No	No	Yes	No	No
			Daily Hassles	Yes	–	–	No	Yes

assessments, in which all measures were obtained under a "current" instructional condition and a "retrospective" condition. In the latter, subjects were directed to think back to the 6 months following their discharge from service.

Several stress measures were used in these studies. Life Events (under "Stress Measure") was measured by the Life Experiences Survey (I. G. Sarason, Johnson, & Siegel, 1978), except in Procidano et al., where life events was measured by the Adolescent Life Events Scale (Yeaworth, York, Hussey, Ingle, & Goodwin, 1980). The measure of Daily Hassles was that developed by Kanner, Coyne, Schaefer, and Lazarus (1981). The Combat Index (Boulanger, 1980) was used by Wolff et al. to reflect level of combat experiences during the Vietnam War.

Some inferences can be made regarding the buffering hypothesis with respect to perceived social support. First, the hypothesis failed to be confirmed more often than it was confirmed. Second, buffering effects were observed twice as often for PSS–Fr (six times) as for PSS–Fa (three times); and somewhat more consistently for hassles than for major life events. All four tests (three in Ferraro & Procidano, one in Crits-Christoph & Procidano) of a PSS–Fr by hassles interaction were confirmed. PSS–Fa buffered hassles in the former but not the latter study (i.e., for college students but not for chronic schizophrenics). Frequently, stress by support interactions generally were not observed in the absence of main effects for stress and/or the relevant PSS measure. (The one exception to this occurred in Ferraro & Procidano, in which PSS–Fa buffered the effects of hassles, in the absence of a main effect for PSS–Fa.) In Wolff et al.'s study of Vietnam veterans, PSS–Fa did not buffer the effects of combat stress on post-traumatic stress disorder symptoms. PSS–Fr did buffer combat stress, but only after an intervening time period (i.e., in the current but not postdis-charge assessment). This may suggest that veterans' friend networks were not well formed soon after discharge, or that severe stressors are more difficult to buffer without some intervening passage of time.

In summary, it appears that the extent to which buffering effects are observed for PSS depends on several factors, including the definition of stress that is applied, the variance in the measures involved in the interaction term, and numerous other contextual factors that are suggested by differences in types of samples.

Relationships to Measures of Stress

It has been suggested that the apparent buffering effect of support may be an artifact of its correlation with stress measures, such that stress by support interaction terms are not composed of independent components. Multiple relevant tests were available from studies of college students

(Ferraro & Procidano, 1986; Procidano & Heller, 1983), nontraditional college students (Ford & Procidano, 1987), high school girls (Procidano et al., 1988), and chronic schizophrenic outpatients (Crits-Christoph & Procidano, 1988). In general, the life events–PSS relationships were nonsignificant, and the overall effect sizes ($r = .10$ for PSS–Fa; $r = .11$ for PSS–Fr) were weak. Most of the buffering effects observed in Table 1.4 occurred in the absence of corresponding significant correlations, suggesting further that such effects are not artifacts of a PSS-stress correlation.

DISCUSSION

This chapter was intended to summarize available information regarding measures of perceived social support from family and from friends. Reviewers of support instruments, including the PSS measures, have noted that often reliability and validity data are limited, particularly on noncollege populations; they have called for such information to indicate the instruments' utility and to help clarify the nature of social support (Heitzmann & Kaplan, 1988; House & Kahn, 1985; Tardy, 1985).

Both the internal consistency and test–retest reliability estimates of the instruments were fairly high, based on studies of mostly nonclinical groups, including college and high school-aged students, adolescents with and without alcoholic fathers, and adult male MS patients. Collectively, these data serve as cross-validations of the reliability data originally reported for the measures (Procidano & Heller, 1983), and as indications of their generalizability across groups.

The normative data provided in this chapter should be useful to investigators who contemplate using the PSS measures in studies of various nonclinical or clinical groups. This type of information has been called for by reviewers of social support measures. The fact that the pooled nonclinical and clinical groups differed on both measures attest to their validity across broad groups, particularly as that result was not attributable to variation in subjects' ages. It is interesting that Clair's (1988) sample of adolescent offspring of alcoholic fathers, not originally classified, fell into the clinical range with respect to PSS–Fa; and between the two groups for PSS–Fr. This suggests that parental diagnostic status is a useful risk indicator for studies of the nature of social support among offspring, an approach used by Hirsch (Hirsch, Moos, & Reischl, 1985) in studies of the social networks in offspring of depressed and arthritic parents. Studies of this type might answer many questions about the development and effects of support, such as how might family support and perceptions of it be enhanced. For members of very dysfunctional families, to what extent can enhanced friend support substitute in preempting symptom formation?

Does this apply equally to naturally occurring friend networks as well as to "special" friend networks, such as self-help groups, or peer participants in groups for individuals at risk? It should not be concluded prematurely that stability in some aspect of support is inconsistent with providing such complementary support. Sarason and Sarason (I. G. Sarason & Sarason, 1986), for instance, found that experimentally provided support contributed to performance for "low-support individuals," despite such stability in overall social support.

It should be noted that the magnitude of the nonclinical–clinical group differences (i.e., high t values) were, no doubt, partially attributable to the rather large Ns that emerged from the pooling process. The actual mean differences of 3.45 for PSS–Fa and 2.23 for PSS–Fr suggest that there may be limited practical utility in using the PSS (or any other social-support) instruments in a "diagnostic" way (e.g., via cutting scores) to infer clinical status. Rather, the measures appear to have reliable diagnostic as well as intrapersonal, interpersonal, and other contextual correlates.

Several important findings emerged with respect to the construct validities of the PSS–Fa and PSS–Fr measures that help to specify and delineate the meaning of perceived social support. Perceptions of the same social networks covary more than perceptions of different networks. Although separate but related constructs (Procidano & Heller, 1983), PSS–Fa and PSS–Fr are related to the structure of the respective network, and both are related to receipt of supportive behaviors. Specifically, PSS–Fa was related strongly to other family-based perceptions; and moderately to PSS–Fr, receipt of supportive behaviors, number of family intangible-support providers; somewhat less so to the number of family tangible-support providers; and weakly to the number of friend intangible-and tangible-support providers. PSS–Fr was related moderately to PSS–Fa, receipt of supportive behaviors, the number of friend intangible-support providers; somewhat less so to friend tangible-support providers; and weakly to other family-based perceptions and to family-based provision of tangible and intangible support.

Information about the relationships of PSS to personality factors is, unfortunately, still based on a few studies of college students. It appears that PSS–Fa may have numerically more personality correlates than PSS–Fr (but about the same number as receipt of supportive behaviors), but social competence dimensions may be more related to friend support. This is in keeping with notions that family experience contributes to personality development, and that separation and development of peer relationships depends on outgoingness and other social skills. Social desirability was consistently related to PSS–Fa but never accounted for the relationship between PSS–Fa and symptomatology, whereas PSS–Fr was not related to social desirability.

Of perhaps more relevance, the number of personality correlates of PSS were small and inconsistent with notions that the apparent effects of social support might be artifacts of the "true" contributions of personality predispositions. It would be useful to incorporate some key personality dimensions, particularly affiliation and exhibition, into future examinations of the main and buffering effects of social support in order to continue to refine our knowledge about the development, nature, and effects of social support.

The strong relationship of PSS–Fa to symptomatology was greater than that of PSS–Fr. Thus, the "main effect" hypothesis was confirmed for both dimensions, but more so for family support. These findings do not in themselves indicate causality, but in the two longitudinal investigations (Ferraro & Procidano, 1986; Procidano et al., 1988), perceived social support was found to contribute to subsequent symptomatology controlling for initial symptom levels, but not vice versa. Unfortunately, no such longitudinal data are available for clinical groups. Indeed, the present meta-analytic study found that the PSS–symptomatology relationship was significantly stronger within the nonclinical group than in the clinical group, particularly for PSS–Fa. It is possible that different causal models are appropriate for nonclinical and clinical groups. In the former, social support might contribute over time to symptom variation more than vice versa. However, in the context of relatively severe and stable psychopathology, any contribution of social support on symptom variation might be dampened. This might need to be incorporated into models of support–symptom relationships in clinical groups.

It is quite possible that the greatest promise for social-support enhancement and its beneficial effects are in the context of preventive interventions that focus on enhancing support perceptions directly, perhaps through cognitive-behavior modification, or indirectly by providing positive social interactions (Barrera, 1986). More caution may be appropriate for intervention with clinical groups, where the PSS–symptomatology relationship was significant but weaker. Nonetheless, it may be possible that social-support interventions might reduce the likelihood of symptom onset or exacerbation even in clinical groups, following the logic and findings of studies of expressed emotionality (e.g., Miklowitz et al., 1986).

Investigations of the relationships of support to antecedent and subsequent personality, coping, and adjustment dimensions would help to specify further the "ecological niche" (or, nomological net) into which dimensions of social support fit. Utilizing this approach with groups at varying degrees of antecedent adjustment also would help to clarify the potentials and limitations for the effects of social support.

One of the clearest results in this study was the distinction between family and friends as sources of support. Differentiating between different networks as support providers and assessing embeddedness and support provision and perceptions of all relevant networks may increase both validity and explanatory power in social-support research. It also might help to clarify the roles of "special" social networks, such as fellow members of risk or self-help groups. Toward these ends, the validation and use of alternate forms of the PSS instruments, in which the directions and item contents are modified to refer to members of other specific networks, might be helpful. Some evidence suggests the utility of such a procedure in studying, for instance, friends in and outside a hospital, and treatment team (Procidano & Guinta, 1988). The potential "edge" that perceived friend support may have in buffering stress (which was not attributable to a PSS-stress correlation) raises the possibility that supportive interventions involving friendship formation for groups experiencing some discrete normative or nonnormative stress may be effective in reducing the impact of the event. At the same time, more information is needed regarding conditions under which stress buffering is more likely, because the present study indicated that such an effect was at best inconsistent. Furthermore, this difference may apply only to young adults and adults, because no buffering effect was observed in the study of adolescents (Procidano et al., 1988).

Differentiating among components of support (i.e., embeddedness, provision, and perception) and among sources of support may be more useful than differentiating among particularly supportive services that network members might provide (see also Gottlieb, 1988; I. G. Sarason, 1988). The latter approach seems to come from an expectation that types of stresses and supports fit together in a kind of "lock and key" fashion. Although such an expectation is logical, it has not received empirical support in studies of the buffering hypothesis (see Cohen & Wills, 1985). Perhaps support recipients do not make their own cognitive distinctions among types of support, but rather from subjective appraisals that others care about them, hold them in esteem, and love them (see also Vaux, 1987).

Finally, toward the ends of obtaining longitudinal and experimentally derived formulation about the effects of social-support, as well as providing service to the community, more systematically obtained information is needed regarding the effects of social-support interventions (Gottlieb, 1988). Hopefully, the conceptual clarity that is emerging in the area of social-support measurement might continue to make some contribution to the design, implementation, and outcome evaluation of support interventions.

SUMMARY

Available reliability, normative, and validity data for measures of Perceived Social Support from Family (PSS–Fa) and from Friends (PSS–Fr) were compiled and submitted to some meta-analyses. The measures were found to be internally consistent and stable. Pooled nonclinical and clinical groups differed on both measures. PSS-Fa was related primarily to other family-based perceptions, PSS-Fr, receipt of support and family-network size; PSS-Fr to PSS-Fa, receipt of support and friend-network size. PSS-Fa was related to more personality dimensions (but to only a few) and more strongly to symptomatology than PSS-Fr. PSS-Fr may be more effective in buffering stress for adults. Implications for the validity of distinguishing among different networks as sources of support, the need for more studies of the development of social support, and implications for supportive interventions were discussed.

ACKNOWLEDGMENTS

This research was partially supported by Fordham University Biomedical Research Grants. Dr. Warren Tryon provided helpful suggestions regarding data analysis. I thank those authors who permitted their data to be used in this study.

REFERENCES

Antonovsky, A. (1974). Conceptual and methodological problems in the study of resistance resources and stressful life events. In B. S. Dohrenwend & B. P. Dohrenwend (Eds.), *Stressful life events: Their nature and effect* (pp. 1–43). New York: Wiley.

Arsuaga, E. N. (1988). *The relationship of perceived social support and socially supportive behaviors to individual personality characteristics.* Unpublished doctoral dissertation, Fordham University, Bronx, NY.

Barrera, M. Jr. (1986). Distractions between social support concepts, measures and models. *American Journal of Community Psychology, 14,* 413–446.

Barrera, M. Jr., & Ainlay, S. L. (1983). The structure of social support: A conceptual and empirical analysis. *American Journal of Community Psychology, 11,* 133–141.

Barrera, M., Sandler, I. N., & Ramsay, T. B. (1981). Preliminary development of a scale of social support: Studies on college students. *American Journal of Community Psychology, 9,* 435–447.

Barrett-Lennard, G. T. (1962). Dimensions of therapist response as causal factors in the therapeutic change. *Psychological Monographs, 76,* (43, whole # 562).

Beck, A. T. (1967). *Depression: Causes and treatment.* Philadelphia: University of Pennsylvania Press.

Boulanger, G. (1980). *A measure of traumatic stress reaction developed on a probability sample of Vietnam veterans, era veterans, and nonveterans.* Unpublished manuscript, Center for Social Research, Graduate Center, City University of New York.

Byrne, D., Barry, J., & Nelson, D. (1963). Relation of the revised Repression-Sensitization scale to measures of self-description. *Psychological Reports, 13,* 323–334.

Caplan, G. (1974). *Support systems and community mental health.* New York: Behavioral Publications.

Cassel, J. (1976). The contribution of the social environment to host resistance. *American Journal of Epidemiology, 104,* 107–123.

Clair, D. (1988). *Stressors, social support, and coping behaviors of children of alcoholics.*

Unpublished doctoral dissertation, University of Waterloo, Waterloo, Ontario.

Cobb, S. (1976). Special support as a moderator of life stress. *Psychometric Medicine, 38,* 300–314.

Cohen, J., & Cohen, P. (1975). *Applied multiple regressional/correlation analysis for the behavioral sciences.* Hillsdale, NJ: Lawrence Erlbaum Associates.

Cohen, S., & Hoberman, H. (1983). Positive events and social supports as buffers of life change stress. *Journal of Applied Social Psychology, 13,* 99–125.

Cohen, S., & Wills, T. A. (1985). Stress, social support and the buffering hypothesis. *Psychological Bulletin, 98,* 310–357.

Crits-Christoph, K., & Procidano, M. E. (1988). *Dimensions of social support, stress, and symptomatology among chronic schizophrenics: An examination of the buffering hypothesis.* Manuscript submitted for publication.

Crowne, D. P., & Marlowe, D. (1964). *The approval motive.* New York: Wiley.

Cutrona, C. E. (1986). Objective determinants of perceived social support. *Journal of Personality and Social Psychology, 50,* 349–355.

Derogatis, L. R. (1977). *The SCL manual I: Scoring, administration, and procedures for the SCL-90.* Baltimore: John Hopkins University School of Medicine, Clinical Psychometrics Unit.

Derogatis, L. R., Rickels, K., & Rock, A. F. (1976). The SCL-90 and the MMPI: A step in the validation of a new self-report scale. *British Journal of Psychiatry, 128,* 280–298.

Dohrenwend, B. S., Dohrenwend, B. P., Dodson, M., & Shrout, P. E. (1984). Symptoms, hassles, social supports, and life events. Problem of confounded measures. *Journal of Abnormal Psychology, 93,* 222–230.

Eckenrode, J., & Gore, S. (1981). Stressful life events and social support: The significance of context. In B. H. Gottlieb (Ed.), *Social networks and social support* (pp. 43–68). Beverly Hills, CA: Sage.

Egendorf, A., Boulanger, G., Kadushin, C., Laufer, R., Sloan, L., & Smith, J. (1981). The combat index. In A. Egendorf, C. Kadushin, R. S. Laufer, G. Rothbart, & L. Sloan (Eds.), *Legacies of Vietnam: Comparative adjustment of veterans and their peers* (pp. 223–250). Washington, DC: U.S. Government Printing Office.

Faschingbauer, T. R. (1974). A 166-item written short form of the group MMPI: The FAM. *Journal of Consulting and Clinical Psychology, 42,* 645–656.

Ferraro, L., & Procidano, M. E. (1986, August). *A longitudinal examination of the buffering hypothesis.* Paper presented at the annual meeting of the American Psychological Association, Washington, DC.

Folkman, S., Schaefer, C., & Lazarus, R. S. (1979). Cognitive processes as mediators of stress and coping. In V. Hamilton & D. M. Warburton (Eds.), *Human stress and cognition: An information-processing appraisal* (pp. 265–298). New York: Wiley.

Ford, G. G., & Procidano, M. E. (1987, August). *The relationship of self-actualization to perceived social support, coping, and adjustment.* Paper presented at the annual meeting of the American Psychological Association, New York City.

Frigon, M. J. (1986). *Perceived social support in suicide attempters versus depressed inpatients.* Unpublished masters thesis, University of Utah, Salt Lake City.

Gottlieb, B. H. (1988). Marshaling social support: The state of the art in research and practice. In B. H. Gottlieb (Ed.), *Marshaling social support: Formats, processes and effects* (pp. 11–51). Newbury Park, CA: Sage.

Gough, H. G. (1969). *California psychological inventory.* Palo Alto: Consulting Psychologists Press.

Grey, C., Osborn, E., & Reznikoff, M. (1986). Psychosocial factors in outcome in two opiate addiction treatments. *Journal of Clinical Psychology, 42,* 185–189.

Hathaway, S. R., & McKinley, J. C. (1967). *The Minnesota Multiphasic Personality Inventory Manual* (rev). New York: The Psychological Corporation.

Heitzmann, C. A., & Kaplan, R. M. (1988). Assessment of methods for measuring social support. *Health Psychology, 7,* 75–109.

Hirsch, B. J., Moos, R. H., & Reischl, T. M. (1985). Psychosocial adjustment of adolescent children of a depressed arthritic, or normal parent. *Journal of Abnormal Psychology, 94,* 154–164.

Hirsch, B. J., & Rapkin, B. D. (1986). Social networks and adult social identities: Profiles and correlates of support and rejection. *American Journal of Community Psychology, 14,* 395–412.

Hirschfeld, R. M., Klerman, G. L., Gough, H. G., Barrett, J., Korchin, S. J., & Chodoff, P. (1977). A measure of interpersonal dependency. *Journal of Personality Assessment, 41,* 610–618.

House, J. S., & Kahn, R. K. (1985). Measures and concepts of social support. In S. Cohen & S. L. Syme (Eds.), *Social support and health* (pp. 83–108). New York: Wiley.

Jackson, D. N. (1984). *Personality Research Form Manual* (3rd ed.). MI: Research Psychologists Press.

Kanner, A. D., Coyne, J. C., Schaefer, C., & Lazarus, R. S. (1981). A comparison of two modes of stress measurement, daily hassles and uplifts versus major life events. *Journal of Behavioral Medicine, 4,* 1–19.

Langner, T. S. (1962). A twenty-two items screening score of psychiatric symptoms indicating impairment. *Journal of Health and Human Behavior, 3,* 269–275.

Levenson, R. W., & Gottman, J. M. (1978). Toward the assessment of social competence. *Journal of Consulting and Clinical Psychology, 46,* 453–462.

Liem, J. H., & Liem, G. R. (1977, September). *Life events, social supports, and physical and psychological well-being.* Paper presented to the annual meeting of the American Psychological Association, Montreal, Canada.

Louis, E. (1986). *The relationship between social support and group participation to psychosocial adjustment in multiple sclerosis.* Unpublished doctoral dissertation, Fordham University, Bronx, NY.

Lyons, J. S., Perrotta, P., & Hancher-Kuam, S. (1988). Perceived social support from family and friends: Measurement across disparate samples. *Journal of Personality Assessment, 52,* 42–47.

Maton, K. I. (1987). Patterns and psychological correlates of material support within a religious setup. The bidirectional support hypothesis. *American Journal of Community Psychology, 15,* 185–208.

McIvor, G. P., Riklan, M., & Reznikoff, M. (1984). Depression in multiple sclerosis as a function of length and severity of illness, age, remissions, and perceived social support. *Journal of Clinical Psychology, 40,* 1028–1033.

Miklowitz, D. J., Strachea, A. M., Goldstein, M. J., Snyder, K. S., Hogarty, G. E., & Falloon, I. R. H. (1986). Expressed emotionality and communication deviance in families of schizophrenics. *Journal of Abnormal Psychology, 95,* 60–66.

Moos, R. H. (1974). *Family Environment Scale: Preliminary manual.* Palo Alto, CA: Consulting Psychologists Press.

Procidano, M. E., & Crits-Christoph, K. (1988). *Social support and symptomatology among elderly psychiatric and nursing home patients.* Unpublished data, Fordham University, Bronx, NY.

Procidano, M. E., & Guinta, D. M., (1988). *The nature of perceived social support in young adults during psychiatric hospitalization.* Manuscript submitted for publication.

Procidano, M. E., Guinta, D. M., & Buglione, S. A. (1988, August). *Perceived social support and subjective states in urban, adolescent girls.* Paper presented at the annual meeting of the American Psychological Association, Atlanta, GA.

Procidano, M. E., & Heller, K. (1983). Measures of perceived social support from friends and from family: Three validation studies. *American Journal of Community Psychology, 11,* 1–24.

Rabkin, J. G., & Struening, G. L. (1976). Life events, stress, and illness. *Science, 194,* 1013-1020.

Rosenthal, R. (1984). *Meta-analytic procedures for social research.* Beverly Hills, CA: Sage.

Sandler, I. N., & Barrera, M., Jr. (1984). Toward a multimethod approach to assessing the effects of social support. *American Journal of Community Psychology, 12,* 37-52.

Sarason, B. R., Shearin, E. N., Pierce, G. R., & Sarason, I. G. (1987). Interrelations of social support measures: Theoretical and practical implications. *Journal of Personality and Social Psychology, 52,* 813-832.

Sarason, I. G. (1988, August). *The sense of social support.* Paper presented at the annual meeting of the American Psychological Association, Atlanta, GA.

Sarason, I. G., Johnson, J. H., & Siegel, J. M. (1978). Assessing the impact of life changes: Development of the Life Experiences Survey. *Journal of Consulting and Clinical Psychology, 46,* 932-946.

Sarason, I. G., Levine, H. M., Basham, R. B., & Sarason, B. R. (1983). Assessing social support: The Social Support Questionnaire. *Journal of Personality and Social Psychology, 44,* 127-139.

Sarason, I. G., & Sarason, B. R. (1986). Experimentally provided social support. *Journal of Personality and Social Psychology, 50,* 1222-1225.

Shostrom, E. L. (1963). *Personal Orientation Inventory.* San Diego: Educational and Industrial Testing Service.

Spielberger, C. D. (1979). *Preliminary manual for the State-Trait Personality Inventory (STPI).* Unpublished manuscript.

Spielberger, C. D., Gorsuch, R. C., & Lushene, R. E. (1970). *Manual for the State-Trait Personality Inventory.* Palo Alto, CA: Consulting Psychologists Press.

Stokes, J. (1983). Predicting satisfaction with social support from social network structure. *American Journal of Community Psychology, 11,* 141-152.

Stokes, J. P., & Wilson, D. G. (1984). The inventory of socially supportive behaviors: Dimensionality, prediction, and gender differences. *American Journal of Community Psychology, 12,* 53-70.

Tardy, C. H. (1985). Social support measurement. *American Journal of Community Psychology, 13,* 187-202.

Tetzloff, C. E., & Barrera, M. Jr. (1987). Divorcing mothers and social support: Testing the specificity of buffering effects. *American Journal of Community Psychology, 15,* 419-434.

Tolsdorf, C. C. (1976). Social networks, support, and coping: An exploratory study. *Family Process, 15,* 407-417.

Turner, R. J. (1983). Direct, indirect and moderating effects of social support on psychological distress and associated conditions. In H. B. Kaplan (Ed.), *Psychological stress: Trends in theory and research* (pp. 105-155). New York: Academic Press.

Vaux, A. (1987). Appraisals of social support: Love, respect and involvement. *Journal of Community Psychology, 15,* 493-502.

Vaux, A., & Athanassopoulu, M. (1987). Social support appraisals and network resources. *Journal of Community Psychology, 15,* 537-556.

Vaux, A., & Harrison, D. (1985). Support network characteristics associated with support satisfaction and perceived support. *American Journal of Community Psychology, 13,* 265-268.

Vinokur, A., Schul, Y., & Caplan, R. (1987). Determinants of perceived social support: Interpersonal transactions, personal outlook, and transient affective states. *Journal of Personality and Social Psychology, 53,* 1137-1145.

Wade, L. N., & Procidano, M. E. (1986, August). *The effects of childrearing on mothers' social support.* Paper presented at the annual meeting of the American Psychological Association, Washington, DC.

Walkey, F. H., McCormick, I. A., Siegert, R. J., & Taylor, A. J. W. (1987). Multiple replication of the factor structure of the Inventory of Socially Supportive Behaviors. *Journal of Community Psychology, 15,* 513-519.

Wethington, E., & Kessler, R. (1986). Perceived support, received support, and adjustment to stressful life events. *Journal of Health and Social Behavior, 27,* 78–89.

Wilcox, B. L. (1981). Social support, life stress, and psychological adjustment: A test of the buffering hypothesis. *American Journal of Community Psychology, 9,* 371–386.

Wolf, F. M. (1986). *Meta-analysis: Quantitative methods for research synthesis.* Beverly Hills, CA: Sage.

Wolff, B. M., Procidano, M. E., & Raps, C. (1983, August). *Perceived social support and post-traumatic stress syndrome among Vietnam veterans.* Paper presented at the annual meeting of the American Psychological Association, Anaheim, CA.

Yeaworth, R. C., York, J., Hussey, M. A., Ingle, M. E., & Goodwin, T. (1980). The development of an adolescent life change event scale. *Adolescence, 15,* 91–97.

Zelles, P. (1988). *Empathy and social support as predictors of couvade syndrome in male partners of abortion patients.* Unpublished doctoral dissertation, California School of Professional Psychology, Berkeley.

2 Assessment of Appreciation of Humor: Studies With the 3 WD Humor Test

Willibald Ruch
University of Düsseldorf

Humor tests have a long tradition in psychology and have served different functions. First, it was recognized that humor is an important part of the human personality, and instruments measuring this trait had to be constructed. A second use emerged after discovering the close connection between an individual's humor and personality. In this tradition, appreciation of humor served as an "objective" test of personality. Under the guise of assessing one's sense of humor, the scores were also used to draw inferences about an individual's location on personality dimensions like intelligence, extraversion, or anxiety. Third, tests were used to establish taxonomies of humor and to test their validity. For example, it was investigated whether the categories used are exhaustive and stable across cultures. Fourth, humor inventories were constructed to test existing theories of humor. For example, if a theory assumes that repressed drives find relief in humor, typically the constructed inventories contain categories of sexual and aggressive humor. Studies then examined whether arousal of the motive leads to enhanced appreciation of the respective humor category, or whether appreciation of humor of a certain category leads to reduction of the respective drive. Fifth, humor inventories were used to test theories of personality or of other factors influencing appreciation of humor. If one, for example, assumes that sensation seeking predicts the liking of stimuli of different intensity, complexity, novelty, or incongruity in general, the validity of the model underlying this trait is tested in the realm of humor by choosing humor categories that vary along these parameters. Sixth, humor inventories were used to test general theories in the field of humor appreciation. In this context, humor tests served to examine the roles of

27

autonomic arousal and cognition in the genesis of emotions, the functional specialization of the hemispheres, or the effects of crowding on mood. Finally, humor tests were used in emotion research as induction methods for studying smiling–laughter and positive emotions, such as exhilaration or joy. In this approach the emotional responses to humor are the main focus, and items from humor tests are used in order to have a representative set of stimuli.

THEORY AND RESEARCH ON THE NATURE AND ASSESSMENT OF HUMOR

Despite the wide use of humor tests, the state of the art of assessment of humor appreciation has not developed very far. In most of the investigations, the "humor test" used is an ad hoc measure of unknown psychometric properties. Most frequently, a couple of jokes and cartoons was employed, which were selected by several "experts" as being representative for certain theoretical humor categories. Neither an empirical test of the homogeneity of these scales was applied nor an investigation of the validity or the comprehensiveness of the categories used was undertaken. Most frequently, the Freudian categories of harmless, sexual, and aggressive humor were used. Some of these humor measures were employed by one author only, or, even worse, by one author in one study only. Consequently, results obtained in different studies were not comparable, and thus this approach did not lead to much accumulation of knowledge on the nature of humor.

A Pioneer

Other instruments are based on more careful and solid work. In this tradition, factor analysis was used to derive an exhaustive taxonomy of humor. Next, guided by psychometric principles, scales were designed and validity studies were undertaken. As an example of this approach, the IPAT Humor Test of Personality (Cattell & Tollefson, 1966) deserves to be mentioned. This humor test is based on factor analytic studies of humor by Cattell and colleagues as well as by other researchers (Andrews, 1943; Cattell & Luborsky, 1947; Eysenck, 1942, 1943; Yarnold & Berkeley, 1954). Cattell arrived at a taxonomy of humor consisting of 12 factor analytically derived categories that should not only provide a profile of an individual's humor but also an assessment of dynamic or temperamental dimensions. For example, humor factor 1 ("anxious considerateness vs. debonair sexual and general uninhibitedness") is considered to be synonymous with the second-order questionnaire factor of extraversion. This assumption is based on the correlation of this scale with the 16PF markers of extraversion, A (cyclothymia), F (surgency), and H (venturesomeness). In addition to the 12 humor factors, a further scale (Factor 13: dullness vs. general intelligence) was added to measure, roughly, general intelligence. These items were initially selected on the basis of their correlation with intelligence measures.

The final version of the IPAT humor test consists of two forms: Form A, employing eight pairs of jokes for each of the 13 factors (104 items) and utilizing a "forced choice" design; and Form B, comprised of 10 items per factor to be rated individually (130 items). Whereas in Form A subjects indicate which of the pair is *funnier,* in Form B they mark whether they consider the joke or cartoon as *funny* or *dull* (i.e., above or below their average) after being instructed to use each of the two labels about equally frequently. For both forms there is a test booklet containing the jokes and cartoons and a separate answer sheet. Separate norms for male and female high school and college students are added. The test is considered to be suitable for individual and group administration. For the latter there is the instruction not to disturb others by laughing aloud or attempting to share a joke. Split-half coefficients are between .18 and .50, stability coefficients for an interval of 2 weeks are between .20 and .58, and the correlations between the two forms range between .19 and .43.

Despite the efforts spent for the construction of the test, the IPAT humor test today plays a minor role in contemporary research on both personality and humor. Although the humor test was used in several studies (e.g., Breme, 1976; Carroll, 1989; Mones, 1974; Saper, 1984), its overall impact is low and seems to be obsolete. Considering contemporary knowledge on the assessment of humor, one can assume that the selected "forced choice" answer format is responsible for the problems with the IPAT humor test, such as the apparent overextraction, preoccupation with minor sources of variance, neglect of structural characteristics in humor, lack of reliability, or unproved validity. Cattell and Tollefson applied these answer formats because they assumed that the shape of the profile (i.e., the preference for certain humor categories) already contains the relevant information, whereas the interindividual differences in the level of the profile are irrelevant. However, this format eliminated the strong factors and thus probably hindered the discovery that the first factors appearing in factor analysis of jokes and cartoons are characterized by the items *structure* and not by their *content.* Ruch (1981, 1984) as well as Herzog and Larwin (1988) reported the existence of one or two factors appearing that deal with a variety of themes but are characterized by similar structure. The common denominator of these jokes and cartoons refers to similar cognitive processes rather than to thematic content. Whereas the format hindered the extraction of major humor factors, it raised the relative importance of minor sources of variance, which apparently are less reliable as reflected in the coefficients reported earlier. The absence of strong factors impaired the distinction in major and minor sources of variance. The overextraction can be seen in the facts that in subsequent studies between three and four meaningful factors were extracted and that, with the possible exception of the sexual humor category, no other of Cattell's factors was replicated. The answer format also seems to be responsible for a further specifity of the IPAT humor test, the bipolarity of the humor dimensions. There is a convergence in the results of the studies from Andrews (1943) onward. Whenever there is no restriction in the number of items one is allowed to find funny, the overwhelming majority of the intercorrelations between pairs of jokes or cartoons are positive, and negative coefficients seldomly exceed the value of − .20. As a consequence, only unipolar factors appear and tend to be orthogonal or positively correlated but never negatively correlated.

Despite the persuasive arguments favoring humor tests as a means for the objective assessment of personality, the IPAT humor test has not found widespread use in personality research. Maybe this is due to the failure of Cattell and Tollefson to present convincing tables of correlation coefficients showing that the relationship between humor and personality is strong and replicable. From the perspective of humor research, the explicit link to theory is also lacking. The work of Cattell and colleagues was stimulated by the Freudian (1905) hypothesis that repressed needs find relief in jokes. Thus, they expected that application of factor analysis will help to find such repressed areas in the realm of humor. Whereas some factors (e.g., Factor 5: urbane pleasantness vs. hostile derogation) relate to sex or aggression and thus have face validity, others (e.g., Factor 10: cheerful independence vs. mistreatment humor) are less easily integrated in taxonomies of needs. Thus, there are no apparent links between humor categories measured by the IPAT humor test and general humor theories, especially because influence of Freudian thinking on humor research ceased and alternative theories were developed (see McGhee, 1979).

The Current Standard in the Assessment of Appreciation of Humor

Although the IPAT humor test now seems to be obsolete, its basic ideas have been taken up and pursued by more recent humor tests. The use of factor analysis to derive a taxonomy of humor and the belief that the appreciation of humor reflects aspects of personality continues to inspire research. However, the investigation of individual differences in humor is presently more integrated into general humor research than in the pioneer years. There is a fruitful mutual exchange between general humor theories and taxonomic studies of humor.

Ruch (1980) proposed that a comprehensive assessment of humor should not only cover a taxonomy of humor stimuli but also an investigation of the dimensionality of the responses to humor. The taxonomy of humor stimuli was achieved by a set of factor analytic studies of differing but overlapping sets of jokes and cartoons. In order to get a robust taxonomy, samples differing with regard to sex, age, occupation, health status, and other variables were used. Most importantly, the first construction samples covered Austrian as well as German subjects. After establishing the taxonomy, the items were translated into English, French, Hebrew, Russian, and Turkish in order to be able to test its cross-cultural stability. Similarly, the dimensions of appreciation were obtained by correlational and factor analytic studies of several rating scales covering different aspects of the responses to humor.

A Taxonomy of Jokes and Cartoons

Structure and Content as Ingredients in Humor.   Factor analytic studies showed that structural properties of jokes and cartoons are at least as important as their content. Two of the three factors extracted consistently are based on the structure of cartoons and jokes, not on their content (Ruch, 1981, 1984; Ruch & Hehl, 1984, 1986b). These two factors are defined as *incongruity-resolution* (INC-RES) humor and *nonsense* (NON) humor. The jokes and cartoons of these two factors deal with a variety of topics (except sex), but they are similar to each other with respect to the cognitive processes involved. The third factor, *sexual* (SEX) humor, may be based on one structure or the other but is homogeneous with respect to the sexual content involved.

The extraction of an *incongruity-resolution* structure factor is a noteworthy finding, because it confirms the significance of both incongruity and resolution information in humor as stressed in theoretical models of humor (Bariaud, 1983; Schiller, 1938; Shultz, 1972; Suls, 1972). There is general agreement about the existence of this two-stage structure in the process of perceiving and understanding humor (McGhee, Ruch, & Hehl, 1990). Jokes and cartoons of this humor category are characterized by punchlines in which the surprising incongruity can be completely resolved. The common element in this type of humor is that the recipient first discovers an incongruity that is then fully resolvable upon consideration of information available elsewhere in the joke or cartoon. Although individuals might differ with respect to how they perceive and–or resolve the incongruity, they have the sense of having "gotten the point" or understood the joke once resolution information has been identified.

The other consistently emerging structural factor is *nonsense* humor, which also has a surprising or incongruous punchline, exactly as in incongruity-resolution humor. However, according to McGhee et al.

(1990), "the punchline may (1) provide no resolution at all, (2) provide a partial resolution (leaving an essential part of the incongruity unresolved), or (3) actually create new absurdities or incongruities" (p. 124). In nonsense humor the resolution information gives the appearance of making sense out of incongruities without actually doing so (see also Rothbart & Pien, 1977). Nonsense humor should not be confused with the so-called "innocent" humor, because it refers to the typical structure of humor rather than to a harmless content. Both the incongruity–resolution and the nonsense structure can be the basis for harmless as well as tendentious content (as in the case of sexual humor).

The *sexual humor* category was initially the easiest to identify due to its salient content. Furthermore, it was the only one of the three factors that was expected to appear, because a factor of sexual humor has been found in all factor analytic studies from Eysenck (1942) to Herzog and Larwin (1988). Subsequently, however, sex jokes and cartoons typically have two loadings: one on the sexual humor factor and a second one on one of the two structure factors. The size of this second loading seems to depend on the degree of the theme's salience. In very explicit items (mostly cartoons) the loading on the structure factor is very low, whereas in less salient items the loadings on the content and structure factor can be of about equal size. Thus, one has to distinguish between a *factor of sexual humor,* which is composed of the content variance of the sexual jokes and cartoons only (bereft of the structure variance), and the *sexual humor category* (as used in humor tests), in which both content *and* structure are involved. Whereas a sexual humor factor usually is orthogonal to the two structure factors, the sexual humor category correlates with nonsense and incongruity–resolution humor due to the structure overlap.

According to their loading patterns, the items of the general sexual humor category roughly can be subdivided into three classes of "pure" sexual humor (in which the content largely overpowers the structure), incongruity-resolution-based sexual humor, and nonsense-based sexual humor. The validity of the separation of the two structure-based subgroups of sexual humor is supported by their different correlational profiles, not only with the general structure categories but also with personality dimensions.

These three humor factors are considered to provide an exhaustive taxonomy in classifying jokes and cartoons at a general level. They consistently explain approximately 40% of the total variance (Ruch, 1981, 1984; Ruch, Accoce, Ott, & Bariaud, 1991).

Dimensions of Appreciation

Factor analysis has also been used to investigate the dimensionality of the responses to humor (Ruch, 1981; Ruch, Rath, & Hehl, 1988). The results suggest that the appreciation of humor is defined by two nearly orthogonal components of *positive* and *negative* responses that are best represented by ratings of "funniness" and "aversiveness" (in former studies called *rejection*). Maximal appreciation of jokes and cartoons consists of high funniness and low aversiveness, whereas minimal appreciation occurs if the joke is not considered funny but is found aversive. However, a joke can also be considered not funny but be far from being aversive; or it can make one laugh although there are certain annoying aspects (e.g., one can consider the punchline original or clever but dislike the content of the joke).

The necessity of an empirical separation of positive and negative responses first emerged from a three-mode factor analysis in which ratings of the degree of funniness, induced exhilaration, laughter, and liking formed one factor and the rating of the degree of rejection of the jokes and cartoons formed the other (Ruch, 1980). In a subsequent study (Rath, 1983), it turned out that all positively toned ratings tended to intercorrelate highly positive, independently of whether they referred to the perceived properties of the stimuli (funny, witty, original) or to the recipients feelings (exhilarated, amused). Negative ratings also intercorrelated. A factor analysis of these data (Ruch et al., 1988) yielded a strong "funniness" factor covering all eight positive response scales but not the nine negatively toned scales. The latter tended to fall into two clusters, representing milder (e.g., plain, feel bored) and stronger (e.g., tasteless, feel angered) forms of aversive reactions. Because they were highly correlated, it was not considered necessary to separate them. Therefore, the negative responses are represented in the humor test by one negative scale only.

Development of the Taxonomy of Humor

There were several stages in the construction of the taxonomy that finally led to the 3 WD *(Witz-Dimensionen)* humor test (Ruch, 1983). The initial sample of jokes and cartoons comprised 600 items selected from very different sources in order to obtain a representative pool. Some were recruited to represent humor categories discussed in the literature, others were selected randomly. For a first-factor analytic study, every sixth was chosen on a random basis (Ruch, 1980). These 100 jokes and cartoons were given to 156 subjects who were asked to rate them on a 7-point scale ranging from "not at all funny" to "very funny," and to mark whether the cartoons and jokes were already known or not. This pool of items was subsequently reduced to 48 on the basis of the factor analytic results. Widely known jokes were deleted, too. The subsequent main study used a fairly representative sample of 110 Austrian adults, who rated each of these 48 jokes and cartoons on 7-point scales according to five criteria (degree of funniness, rejection, exhilaration, laughter, and liking). A three-mode factor analysis was performed and yielded the three orthogonal humor stimulus factors described earlier, two humor response factors of funniness and aversiveness, and four bipolar person factors (Ruch, 1981).

In order to test whether additional dimensions needed to be extracted, a new large pool of humor items was assembled that consisted of jokes and cartoons expected to be either good or poor representatives of the three categories. A third experimental version of the humor test was created consisting of 46 of the 48 items from the previous study and 74 drawn randomly from the newly established pool. This version with 120 jokes and cartoons was administered to four German and Austrian samples containing approximately 700 subjects altogether, who were tested individually in order to avoid social influences (Ruch & Hehl, 1984). In order to prevent overstimulation and boredom, the 120 items were distributed among six test booklets and administered on different occasions. Each set of 20 items was preceded by three "warm-up" items, which were not considered in the analyses.

The same three humor categories emerged again in these four samples, and serial rotations with 4 to 10 factors confirmed that it was not necessary to expand the 3 WD test to include new factors (Ruch, 1984). Pairwise comparison of the factor loadings for these samples revealed a highly replicable structure. The cosines between the varimax matrices of two German samples suggested identity of the corresponding factors (coefficients of > .998), and Tucker's congruence coefficient, a further measure of stability of factor patterns, yielded high coefficients too: .97 for incongruity–resolution, and .94 for nonsense and sexual humor.

Cross-National Stability of the Humor Factors.   When comparing the varimax rotated loading matrices of one German and two Austrian samples of young adults, the cosines between the factor patterns suggested high cross-national stability for the humor factors of incongruity–resolution (.99, .99), nonsense (.98, .97), and sexual (.97, .97) humor (Ruch & Hehl, 1984). Evidence for cross-national stability of this humor taxonomy was later also found in samples of 115 German and 139 French students using the final humor test (Accoce, 1986; Ruch et al., 1991). The cosines for the respective factors in German and French adults were .98, .98, and .99; Tucker's congruence coefficient yielded coefficients of .88, .91, and .93. It is possible that additional factors might appear in humor material in the countries investigated. The intrinsic structure in this set of jokes and cartoons, however, is essentially identical in the European countries investigated hitherto. Support for the significance of these factors has also been obtained in a sample of 260 Turkish subjects (Ciftci, 1990) and in an American sample (McGhee, unpublished results).

State Variance in Appreciation of Humor?   There is evidence that situational factors and mood contribute to the responses to humor.

However, they only explain between 5% and 7% of the variance, and this variance can be reduced by suitable precautions. In the factor analyses of the 120-item pool, two additional factors appeared that altogether explained 6.6% of the total variance. Whereas the loadings on the "warm-up" factor decreased from the first to approximately the tenth joke, the "end of test" factor was loaded by the last 15 items only (again with increasing size of the loadings). The factor pattern of these items with respect to the first three factors was clearly interpretable albeit lower in size. These sources of variance were eliminated in the final humor test by raising the number of practice items to 5 and by reducing the total number of items.

Furthermore, "testing time" factors were extracted from funniness (explaining 5.30% of the variance) and aversiveness (6.21%) ratings of two sets of 10 items administered to 4,292 subjects approximately 1 month apart (Ruch, McGhee, & Hehl, 1990). Independent of their category, the jokes and cartoons administered at the first testing time loaded negatively, and the items of the second set loaded positively on the testing time factor. These effects might be specific for the circumstances of that study, because only one warm-up item was employed and no experimenter was present to assure equal testing conditions between occasions. Finally, a cheerfulness scale administered immediately before presenting the items of the humor test (via slides) correlated consistently positive (.20) albeit nonsignificant with the funniness rating in two samples (Ruch, 1990). Whereas the correlations with facial responses were higher, they were significant only when a further subject or the experimenter was present under mere presence conditions.

Thus, in order to eliminate the state variance, it is important to administer the 3 WD humor test under standardized testing conditions: Subjects are tested individually, and during the administration of the 3 WD the experimenter is either absent or, for the subjects visible, engaged in other activities and not paying attention to the subjects.

CONSTRUCTION AND PSYCHOMETRIC PROPERTIES OF THE 3 WD

The 3 WD Humor Test

The 3 WD ("3 Witz–Dimensionen") humor test (Ruch, 1983) was designed to assess funniness and aversiveness of jokes and cartoons of the three humor categories of incongruity–resolution humor, nonsense humor, and sexual humor.[1] Three versions of the test (3 WD-K, 3 WD-A, and 3 WD-B) exist. They contain 50 (Form K) or 35 (Forms A and B) jokes and cartoons, which are rated on "funniness" and "aversiveness" using two 7-point scales. The

---

[1]Copies of international versions of this test may be obtained by writing to the author.

funniness rating ranges from *not at all funny* = 0 to *very funny* = 6, and the aversiveness scale ranges between *not at all aversive* = 0 to *very aversive* = − 6. Forms A and B are parallel tests. They are used together as a long form (with 60 items scored) when reliable measurement is needed, or as parallel versions before and after an intervention whose effects have to be evaluated. Form A and B do not overlap, but their purest items form the 3 WD-K, which is a short form. The first five items of each form are used for "warming up" and are not scored. The jokes and cartoons are presented in a test booklet with two or three items on a page. The instructions are typed on the separate answer sheet that also contains the two sets of rating scales.

Six scores can be derived from each form of the test: three for funniness of incongruity–resolution, nonsense, and sexual humor (i.e., $INC\text{-}RES_f$, NON_f, and SEX_f) and three for their aversiveness (i.e., $INC\text{-}RES_a$, NON_a, and SEX_a). These six scores describe an individual's sense of humor at a general level.

As mentioned previously, sometimes the three subcategories of "pure" sexual humor (PURE SEX), incongruity–resolution-based sexual humor (INC-RES SEX), and nonsense-based sexual humor (NON SEX) are used in addition to the general sexual humor category. Other indices have been derived as well and were validated in several studies (Ruch, 1988; Ruch & Hehl, 1988; Ruch et al., 1990). For example, a *structure preference index* was obtained by subtracting $INC\text{-}RES_f$ from NON_f. Similarly, the funniness and aversiveness scores of a humor type could be combined to form a more general *appreciation* score.

Construction of the 3 WD Humor Test

The 3 WD humor test (Ruch, 1983) was constructed on the basis of the factor analytic and item analytic results obtained for the four Austrian and German samples described earlier. Those of the 120 jokes and cartoons that showed a stable factor pattern across the four samples were selected for the final version of the test. Furthermore, in order to obtain parallel forms, an attempt was made to get pairs of jokes and of cartoons matched for content, mean funniness, loading pattern, and style (verbal or pictorial with or without caption). Then one of the pair was used in Form A and the other in Form B.

Psychometric Properties of the 3 WD

A first evaluation of the psychometric properties was done on the data used in the factor analysis (Ruch & Hehl, 1984). Since then, the different forms of the 3 WD were used in several studies with Austrian and German samples, and therefore information regarding the inventory's psychometric properties is available.

Characteristics of the Scales.   Table 2.1 presents the means and standard deviations of the six scales obtained for Form K and the parallel Forms A and B separately and combined. With the exception of one Turkish sample (Ciftci, 1990), all subjects were Austrian or German.

Table 2.1 shows that, whereas the three humor categories are roughly comparable with respect to funniness, the sexual humor category is much higher in aversiveness than the two structure-based humor categories. Analysis of the distribution of the scores reveals that there is no deviation from normality for all three funniness scales and for aversiveness of sexual humor. Because many subjects do not find the structural humor categories aversive at all, there is a skewness in these distributions that is significant in some samples (especially when Forms A and B are studied separately).

Review of several studies (Ruch & Hehl, 1985) and the results of a large-scale study (Ruch et al., 1990) unequivocally reveal that there are no sex differences in funniness or aversiveness of incongruity–resolution or nonsense humor. There is, however, a tendency for males to give higher funniness and lower aversiveness ratings to sexual humor (Ruch & Hehl, 1985). Whereas this difference can be found consistently, the effect is small and the coefficients are not always significant. It can be assumed that this difference is due to the sexual content of the jokes and cartoons of this category rather than to its structural basis. There are no data from the 3 WD humor pool allowing for an estimate of whether this effect holds for all types of sexual themes or only for those that involve sexism. The difference is in agreement with the sex differences found for predictors of sexual humor (see following).

There was no detailed study of age differences in appreciation of sexual humor. A review of correlation coefficients obtained for several samples suggests no such effect (Ruch & Hehl, 1985). Age differences in appreciation of the structural humor categories were studied more extensively (McGhee et al., 1990; Ruch et al., 1990). Although the age differences of the 11 age groups studied cannot be described by only linear trends, one roughly can say that $INC-RES_f$ increases with increasing age, whereas NON_f and aversiveness of both structure dominated humor categories tends to decrease during the life span.

Reliability of the 3 WD Scales.   Reliability estimates are available from several samples (see Table 2.2). Information exists on internal consistency (based on Cronbach's alpha) for the short form (3 WD-K), the parallel Forms A and B separate and together, and on the parallel test reliability of the Forms A and B. No retest study was undertaken (due to the nature of

TABLE 2.1
Means and Standard Deviations of the 3 WD Scales

	N	Sex	Age	$INC\text{-}RES_f$		NON_f		SEX_f		$INC\text{-}RES_a$		NON_a		SEX_a	
				M	SD	M	SD	M	SD	M	SD	M	SD	M	SD
Form A															
Hehl & Ruch (1985)	92	M, F	18–41	22.50	12.91	25.70	11.30	17.52	12.82	9.22	11.80	7.58	8.92	19.79	15.92
Jansa (1990)	102	M	19–35	21.44	11.60	26.19	9.32	21.17	11.87	3.93	5.66	5.77	6.98	10.28	10.97
Ruch & Hehl (1985)	120	M, F	18–37	21.50	12.90	23.32	12.14	14.81	11.55	5.15	7.84	7.39	9.02	17.38	14.41
Ruch & Hehl (1986a)	115	M, F	18–32	23.46	11.50	25.99	11.22	17.67	11.69	6.72	7.69	9.42	8.85	19.98	15.94
Ruch et al. (1984)	50	M	19–30	20.30	13.48	24.06	12.54	18.84	13.87	6.22	9.37	6.78	7.57	11.16	12.77
Form B															
Hehl & Ruch (1985)	92	M,F	18–41	23.41	12.15	26.33	11.56	18.38	13.51	8.78	11.47	9.34	9.15	20.04	16.43
Jansa (1990)	102	M	19–35	21.32	13.21	26.80	9.76	19.41	12.08	5.31	7.28	4.29	5.29	12.44	13.20
Ruch & Hehl (1985)	120	M, F	18–37	20.60	12.84	24.40	12.28	12.96	10.38	6.99	9.03	5.81	8.16	16.37	13.47
Ruch & Hehl (1985)	144	F	19–43	22.49	11.59	24.60	11.02	14.38	10.33	10.74	8.83	7.06	6.48	26.96	14.75
Ruch & Hehl (1986a)	115	M,F	18–32	23.15	12.15	27.01	11.91	17.38	11.23	8.76	9.84	7.57	8.15	21.16	15.68
Ruch et al. (1984)	50	M	19–30	22.92	12.45	23.74	11.33	19.88	12.55	8.56	8.12	7.68	9.25	16.78	13.69

Form K

Busse (1987)	68	M	20–31	31.21	16.77	36.91	17.68	26.50	15.84	9.60	14.14	10.37	11.85	22.50	21.23
Ciftci (1990)	260	M, F	18–58	47.67	18.04	36.04	15.32	43.57	18.02	28.38	20.55	35.27	20.92	36.05	22.16
Regul (1987)	160	M,F[1]	19–67	44.42	20.62	29.47	18.06	36.16	21.74	14.10	15.55	22.28	20.46	27.07	22.04
Ruch (1988)	160	M, F	18–55	43.43	17.46	34.22	17.63	29.08	16.54	8.46	11.49	15.05	15.89	24.56	21.01
Ruch & Hehl (1985)	159	M,F	20–69	37.16	19.04	32.56	16.78	27.77	17.73	11.18	13.72	15.75	15.76	29.68	22.08
Ruch & Hehl (1985)	51	M	19–30	31.00	17.29	39.48	17.07	28.20	16.89	9.60	11.38	11.64	11.31	27.84	22.18
unpublished data	86	M[2]	36–56	47.66	18.13	27.79	16.22	38.94	17.30	6.98	11.96	16.33	18.92	17.79	16.74
unpublished data	137	M,F[3]	20–85	48.97	18.66	28.39	17.25	34.71	20.18	8.25	11.46	17.86	20.05	28.08	23.04
unpublished data	110	M,F[4]	19–45	47.50	17.58	32.45	15.92	31.90	18.07	8.18	11.10	17.31	15.00	33.57	23.06
Form A + B															
Jansa (1990)	102	M	19–35	42.91	23.86	53.07	17.96	40.75	22.84	9.19	12.03	10.02	11.57	22.72	23.73
Hehl & Ruch (1985)	92	M, F	18–41	54.91	22.53	52.02	20.41	35.90	24.03	18.00	21.54	16.91	15.84	39.83	30.22
Ruch & Hehl (1987)	115	M, F	18–32	46.60	22.43	53.00	21.46	35.05	21.67	15.47	16.57	16.99	15.52	41.15	30.68
unpublished data	121	M, F	15–28	42.48	24.33	37.17	20.17	39.79	24.31	16.93	19.15	23.93	23.67	32.88	24.73

[1] psychiatric patients;
[2] "young" CHD-patients;
[3] psychosomatic patients;
[4] Austrian school teacher.

TABLE 2.2
Reliability Measures of the 3 WD

Sample	N	Sex	Age	INC-RES$_f$	NON$_f$	SEX$_f$	INC-RES$_a$	NON$_a$	SEX$_a$	rel
Form A										
Hehl & Ruch (1985)	92	M,F	18–41	.90	.81	.90	.91	.82	.91	IC
Jansa (1990)	102	M	19–35	.87	.69	.87	.79	.78	.91	IC
Ruch & Hehl (1985)	120	M,F	18–37	.90	.84	.87	.87	.83	.89	IC
Ruch & Hehl (1986a)	115	M,F	18–32	.83	.77	.84	.76	.76	.91	IC
Ruch et al. (1984)	50	M	19–30	.89	.85	.91	.90	.77	.93	IC
Form B										
Hehl & Ruch (1985)	92	M,F	18–41	.88	.81	.91	.90	.80	.93	IC
Jansa (1990)	102	M	19–35	.91	.73	.89	.82	.68	.91	IC
Ruch & Hehl (1985)	120	M,F	18–37	.90	.83	.87	.85	.82	.88	IC
Ruch & Hehl (1985)	144	F	19–43	.83	.77	.82	.70	.59	.86	IC
Ruch & Hehl (1986a)	115	M,F	18–32	.85	.79	.85	.82	.74	.90	IC
Ruch et al. (1984)	50	M	19–30	.84	.78	.88	.74	.82	.82	IC
Form K										
Busse (1987)	68	M	20–31	.89	.86	.88	.92	.86	.94	IC
Ciftci (1990)	260	M,F	18–58	.86	.79	.85	.90	.89	.90	IC
Joachim (1986)	73	M,F	19–35	.93	.72	.87	.88	.60	.92	IC
Rath (1983)	100	M,F	17–37	.71	.68	.65	–	–	–	IC
Regul (1987)	160	M,F	19–67	.90	.87	.91	.88	.91	.91	IC
Ruch & Hehl (1985)	159	M,F	20–69	.91	.86	.90	.88	.88	.91	IC
Ruch & Hehl (1985)	51	M	19–30	.91	.87	.90	.87	.82	.95	IC
unpublished data	137	M,F	20–85	.91	.88	.91	.88	.93	.93	IC
unpublished data	121	M,F	20–85	.90	.87	.92	.88	.93	.93	IC
unpublished data	86	M	36–56	.92	.88	.90	.92	.93	.90	IC
unpublished data	110	M,F	19–45	.90	.85	.90	.89	.86	.93	IC
Unterweger (1983)	104	M,F	19–30	.93	.90	.90	–	–	–	IC

Form A + B

Study	N		Age							rel
Jansa (1990)	102	M	19–35	.94	.84	.93	.88	.85	.95	IC
Hehl & Ruch (1985)	92	M,F	18–41	.93	.88	.94	.94	.88	.95	IC
Ruch & Hehl (1987)	115	M,F	18–32	.91	.87	.91	.88	.85	.95	IC
unpublished data	121	M,F	15–28	.91	.85	.91	.91	.91	.91	IC
Hehl & Ruch (1985) (4 weeks)	92	M,F	18–41	.62	.60	.67	.71	.54	.74	PR
Hehl & Ruch (1985) (no time lag)	96	M	18–32	.91	.86	.90	.90	.82	.93	PR
Jansa (1990) (2 hours)	102	M	19–35	.83	.74	.81	.71	.76	.89	PR
Ruch & Hehl (1985) (no time lag)	120	M,F	18–37	.90	.87	.86	.72	.86	.89	PR
Ruch et al. (1984) (2 weeks)	50	M	19–30	.78	.83	.83	.63	.85	.76	PR
Ruch & Hehl (1986a) (2 hours)	115	M,F	18–32	.80	.75	.79	.78	.67	.88	PR
Ruch et al. (1990) (1 month)[1]	4292	M,F	14–50	.69	.64	—	.74	.72	—	SHR

Note. rel = type of reliability. M = males. F = females. IC = internal consistency based on Cronbach's alpha. PR = Parallel test reliability. SHR = split half reliability.

[1] abridged forms of the 3 WD pool.

41

the material), and only little is known about long-term stability of the scales.

Table 2.2 shows that, in general, the reliability estimates may be regarded as satisfactory for the scales of all forms of the 3 WD. The internal consistency varies between .68 and .95, mostly exceeding .80. There is also a sufficiently high degree of equivalence between Form A and B. The parallel test reliability of the six scales ranges between .67 and .93 (with a median of .86) when both forms are filled in on the same day. The samples with a time lag between 2 and 4 weeks yield coefficients between .54 and .85 with a median of .73. They seem to be lower, however. It cannot be determined whether the lower coefficients are due to the elapsed time span or to the fact that the latter set of data had unequal testing conditions (Form A was given in a small group pretesting, Form B after a lengthy experiment).

The split half reliability with a time lag of 1 month should also be regarded as conservative estimate of the stability of the 3 WD scales, because in this study only an abridged form with five items (of the 3 WD pool) was administered, and the testing conditions were not optimal (Ruch et al., 1990). More importantly, this study showed that internal consistency, parallel test reliability, and factor structure did not differ as a function of age of the subjects. Thus the 3 WD can be applied equally well to different samples across the adult life span.

Finally, Table 2.2 shows that, independent of the form of the humor test and the type of reliability estimation, there is a tendency for the nonsense category to obtain lower coefficients. This could be expected partly from the smaller variance of these scales as shown in Table 2.1.

Items Statistics.   The distribution of the answers to single items usually shows that all seven steps of both funniness and aversiveness scales are used (i.e., any of the jokes and cartoons is considered extremely funny by at least one person but also extremely aversive by another). Nevertheless, the answer category "not at all aversive" ($= 0$) is the most frequent rating given for nearly all the items. Consequently, mean aversiveness of the items is low (e.g., in the sample studied by Ruch and Hehl, 1986b, the means range between .31 and 1.29 for INC–RES humor, between .19 and 2.70 for nonsense, and between 1.22 and 2.96 for the sexual humor category). Mean funniness is higher, the respective ranges being 1.48 and 3.06 (INC–RES), 1.38 and 4.11 (NON), and .72 and 3.55 (SEX).

Part–whole corrected item-scale correlations turn out to be satisfactorily high for all three forms. The median of the coefficients for the six scales (using all 90 items of Form A and B) in the aforementioned sample is .56 for INC–RES$_f$ (range: .39 to .68), .50 for NON$_f$ (.28 to .60), .61 for SEX$_f$ (.23 to .72), .51 for INC–RES$_a$ (.26 to .65), .48 for NON$_a$ (.24 to .61), and .68 for SEX$_a$ (.43 to .80). As a comparison, the medians for the respective scales in the sample studied by Hehl and Ruch (1985) are .59, .45, .65, .65, .45, and .69. The results of the samples studied by Busse (1987) and Regul (1987) are used to demonstrate the item statistics of Form K; the medians of the part–whole corrected item-scale correlations are .57:.58, .52:.53, and .57:.61 for the funniness scales and .66:.53, .53:.60, and .70:.63 for aversiveness of incongruity–resolution, nonsense, and sexual humor, respectively. Thus, the relatively lower homogeneity of the nonsense scales is reflected in the item-scale correlations, too.

Finally, the number of items correlating higher with another humor category than with the own is low in all samples studied. On the average there is less than one such item in funniness of the three humor categories and in SEX_a. For aversiveness of the other two categories, there are roughly two such items out of the 15, respectively, 20 items of Form K (Busse, 1987; Regul, 1987) and Forms A plus B (Hehl & Ruch, 1985; Ruch & Hehl, 1986b).

Intercorrelation Between the Scales.   Table 2.3 shows the intercorrelation between the 3 WD scales including the three subcategories of sexual humor based on the data presented by Ruch and Hehl (1987). These intercorrelations were obtained for both parallel forms combined in a sample of 115 nonpsychology students. Furthermore, data for the 3 WD-K is added based on a sample of 159 German adults studied by Ruch and Hehl (1985).

Table 2.3 shows that funniness of incongruity–resolution humor and nonsense humor tends to be positively correlated. Indeed a slight positive relationship between the two structural humor categories was found for

TABLE 2.3
Coefficients of Correlations between the 3 WD Scales

3 WD Scales	$INC\text{-}RES_f$	NON_f	SEX_f	$INC\text{-}RES_a$	NON_a	SEX_a
$INC\text{-}RES_f$	—	.38***	.63***	−.18*	.12	−.15
NON_f	.28**	—	.44***	.08	−.24**	−.04
SEX_f	.66***	.28**	—	−.02	.10	−.45***
$INC\text{-}RES_a$	−.26**	.09	−.24**	—	.57***	.50***
NON_a	.12	−.22*	−.05	.58***	—	.41***
SEX_a	−.02	.12	−.40***	.63***	.53***	—
Types of sexual humor						
PURE SEX_f	.63***	.28**	.96	−.26**	−.05	−.39***
INC-RES SEX_f	.68***	.10	.90	−.26**	.04	−.34***
NON SEX_f	.28**	.43***	.66	−.01	−.17	−.26**
PURE SEX_a	−.02	.14	−.39***	.64***	.49***	.97
INC-RES SEX_a	−.10	.13	−.41***	.62***	.44***	.92
NON SEX_a	.16	−.02	−.21*	.31**	.57***	.77

Note: Above the diagonal: Form K, $N = 156$. Below the diagonal: Form A + B, $N = 115$.
*$p < .05$; **$p < .01$; ***$p < .001$.

nearly any sample studied (although mostly nonsignificant), although in the factor analytic studies an orthogonal solution seemed to provide the best fit.

Although it is assumed that enjoyment of sexual content and enjoyment of humor structure are *uncorrelated,* a positive correlation between SEX_f and funniness of the two structural humor categories is expected, due to the fact that subjects respond to the structural basis of sexual humor too. This is confirmed by Table 2.3. Furthermore, because most of the sexual humor in the present pool as well as in general is based on the incongruity–resolution structure, it is not surprising that SEX_f is correlated more highly with $INC-RES_f$ than with NON_f. Whereas the range of the correlations with nonsense humor across the different samples studied is between .19 and .45, the coefficients for incongruity–resolution humor vary between .46 and .80. The higher coefficients were obtained for male samples only. This is a noteworthy finding, because it shows that subjects tend to respond similarly to a "tendentious" humor category and to a category with no salient content.

The separation of the subgroups of sexual humor gives further support for the assumption of a structural basis in sexual humor. As already demonstrated by Ruch and Hehl (1986b), funniness of incongruity–resolution-based sexual humor (INC-RES SEX_f) correlates very highly with humor of other content when based on this structure ($INC-RES_f$; $r = .69, p < .001$), but not at all with humor based on the other structure (NON_f; $r = .10$, NS). Similarly, nonsense-based sexual humor (NON SEX_f) correlates highly with nonsense humor of other contents (NON_f; $r = .43, p < .001$), and the correlation with incongruity–resolution humor ($INC-RES_f$; $r = .28, p < .01$) does not exceed the values of the intercorrelation between the two structural categories. Thus the cross-structure correlations suggest that there is no relationship between funniness of the two structural factors and the sexual content. Furthermore, Table 2.3 shows that similar effects can be found for the aversiveness scores. The subgroups of sexual humor correlate more highly with the same than with the other structure category.

With respect to aversiveness, Table 2.3 shows generally positive intercorrelations between the three categories. This can be found in other samples too (median = .55). This higher intercorrelation might be expected from the fact that appreciation of different humor categories is superimposed by a more general tendency to find humor in general more aversive or not at all aversive (see Table 2.1).

Finally, Table 2.3 shows a negative intercorrelation between the funniness and aversiveness aspect in appreciation of humor. Across 15 samples considered, these coefficients range between .05 and −.27 for the incongruity–resolution and nonsense humor categories and between .01 and −.46 for sexual humor. The medians of −.10, −.15, and −.30 confirm that the aversiveness scales represent sources of variance that are not covered by the funniness scales, and thus their use is justified. In general, the results support the separation of positive and negative responses to humor and the use of two rating scales in the 3 WD humor test.

FINDINGS OF PUBLISHED AND UNPUBLISHED STUDIES USING THE 3 WD

Several studies were conducted in order to validate the ingredients in appreciation of humor as proposed by the preceding model. Given the nature of the key elements in appreciation of humor as identified by factor analysis, any hypothesis set up has to bear in mind the differentiation between content and structure as well as between the funniness and the aversiveness component. The lack of consideration of these elements might be the main reason for the inconsistent findings relating humor appreciation to personality variables in prior research (see Hehl & Ruch, 1985, Nias, 1981, and Ruch & Hehl, 1986a, 1986b, for a review). For example, when studying sexual humor it was implicitly assumed that the whole reliable variance in funniness is due to the content, and structural properties do not contribute to funniness. Similarly, in other studies hypotheses assuming that some type of humor might be found *aversive* by certain subjects was tested with funniness scales only (i.e., a scale that does not cover negative responses).

Thus, the following review tries to reveal the different elements that are involved in the concepts assessed by the 3 WD scales. In detail, it evaluates whether there are individual differences in appreciation of humor per se (i.e., independent of the type of humor involved). It examines whether there exist general tendencies to find humor more or less funny, or more or less aversive. Furthermore, it reviews whether the nature of the two proposed types of structures involved in humor can be substantiated. Finally, the significance of the content in appreciation of sexual humor, isolated, and in context with structure is discussed. The evaluation of the contribution of structure and content to appreciation of humor covers both components involved, funniness and aversiveness.

Individual Differences in Degree of Appreciation

The nature of the model of humor under discussion does not suggest by itself the existence of general factors affecting the degree of appreciation irrespective of the humor category. The factor analytic results clearly contradict the assumption of a general factor in both, analysis of the stimuli material and of the response scales. There is, however, a consistent positive intercorrelation between appreciation of the three humor categories that is low for funniness but relatively high for aversiveness (see Table 2.3). Thus, there is some room left for the assumption of stable individual differences in the tendencies to find humor generally more aversive or generally funnier. Because the differences between the categories were more obvious than their possible similarities, no study was conducted testing such hypotheses.

Recent developments in emotion research, however, reintroduces this question. There is increasing evidence that separate factors of *positive affect* and *negative affect* can be extracted from different materials (see Diener & Emmons, 1984; Watson & Tellegen, 1985). Like funniness and aversiveness, these factors are orthogonal. Moreover, extraversion predicts individual differences in positive affect and neuroticism accounts for individual differences in negative affect. Thus, the question arises whether these relationships can be found in the realm of humor appreciation as well. Because funniness represents the positive responses to humor and aversiveness covers the possible negative ones, it could be hypothesized that extraversion correlates positively with funniness of the three humor categories and neuroticism predicts their aversiveness.

Generalized Individual Differences in Funniness?

The data allowing the evaluation of a possible relationship between extraversion and the disposition of finding all types of humor funnier come from studies testing the Eysenckian/Cattellian hypothesis that extraverts prefer sexual humor relative to introverts. Whereas this hypothesis received some support from studies using the 3 WD and other humor tests, the majority of the studies does not show significant relationships (Hehl & Ruch, 1985; Joachim, 1986; Regul, 1987; Ruch & Hehl, 1985). Two peculiarities prevent the abolition of extraversion in the field of humor appreciation. First, in the seven samples using the 3 WD, two yielded a significantly positive correlation between SEX_f and extraversion, and none yielded a negative correlation. Second, all the coefficients for the other two humor categories were positive as well. Thus, although only three correlations exceeded the individual level of significance, all the 21 coefficients were positive. Similar patterns were found in studies of the primary factors of extraversion as contained in several multidimensional personality inventories. The scales of surgency, venturesomeness, need for affiliation and play, sociability, composedness, and energy level yielded generally positive coefficients and thus also support the hypothesis (Hehl & Ruch, 1985; Joachim, 1986).

Thus, the hypothesis that extraverts respond to humor generally more positively than introverts cannot be rejected completely on grounds of the existing data; however, the zero-order coefficients obtained generally lack both statistical and practical significance.

Generalized Individual Differences in Aversiveness?

The data collected also allow evaluation of the hypothesis that neuroticism is a predictor of negative responses to humor. Although only 5 of the 21 correlations between the neuroticism scales of the EPQ or EPI and aversiveness of the humor categories are significant, all except 2 are positive. Similarly, variables associated with N were predictive too, like trait–anxiety (measured via three different scales; i.e., STAI, STPI, and JPI), depressivity, nervousness, guilt proneness, or low ego strength (Hehl & Ruch, 1985; Joachim, 1986). Anxiety and depressiveness scales yield higher coefficients than neuroticism, and extraversion also tends to be negatively correlated with aversiveness. Therefore, the hypothesis could be refined by stating that *introverted* neurotic (i.e., anxious, depressive) individuals tend to respond to humor more negatively in general. Support for the involvement of negative affectivity in generally negative responses to humor comes from a study of sexual attitudes (Ruch & Hehl, 1988); subjects high in sexual prudishness and low in sexual satisfaction found humor of all categories aversive (see also Hehl & Ruch, 1990).

There is a second cluster of variables involved in the general rejection of humor. Whereas the preceding variables share an element of negative affectivity, the second cluster relates to tendermindedness. Humor of all categories is found more aversive by tender than by tough subjects. This could be demonstrated for factors of tendermindedness extracted from personality scales (Ruch & Hehl, 1986b), as well as attitude inventories (Ruch, 1984; Ruch & Hehl, 1986b). Results falling in line with the tendermindedness hypothesis relate to the finding that intraceptive (social, religious, and aesthetic) values go along with high aversiveness, and extraceptive (political, economical, and theoretical) values go along with low aversiveness (Ruch & Hehl, 1987; Study I). Similarly, high interest in technical matters is also a predictor of low aversiveness of humor (Hehl & Ruch, 1990). Furthermore, using the Rokeach Value Survey (Rokeach, 1982), it was found that, whenever an instrumental value was significantly correlated with aversiveness, moral or interpersonal values correlated positively and competence or self-actualization values correlated negatively with aversiveness of humor of all three factors (Ruch & Hehl, 1987; Study II). Finally, the disinhibition subscale of the sensation-seeking scale (Zuckerman, 1979), which is located on the toughmindedness axis, also predicts low aversiveness of humor in four samples (Ruch, 1988).

It was argued that the two groups of predictors might relate to different aspects of aversiveness (Ruch & Hehl, 1988). The tendermindedness complex might refer to the easiness with which feelings are hurt or subjects feel offended by humor, whereas the neuroticism complex determines the threshold for a negatively toned response and its intensity.

Thus, whereas there are only spurious effects of extraversion on generalized positive responses to humor, marked effects can be found for aversiveness. Tenderminded neurotics tend to find humor aversive throughout.

Appreciation of Humor Structure

Much more effort was spent in verifying the existence of the two structures involved in humor. It is assumed that, in jokes and cartoons of the two structure-dominated humor categories (INC–RES and NON), the content plays a minor role. This is inferred from the heterogeneity of the themes involved. These factors of humor emerged because of individual differences in the subjects' responses to the different structural properties of these jokes and cartoons.

Evidence from several sources led to the hypotheses that appreciation of the incongruity–resolution structure is a manifestation of a broader need of individuals for contact with structured, stable, unambiguous forms of stimulation, whereas appreciation of the nonsense structure in humor reflects a generalized need for uncertain, unpredictable, and ambiguous stimuli. First, interpretation of the factors suggests that the two structures mainly differ with respect to the degree of resolution obtained. In incongruity–resolution humor a complete resolution of the incongruity is possible, although there are residual traces of incongruity in nonsense humor. Thus, in the first category the resolution of incongruity contributes to appreciation, whereas in Factor 2 appreciation is based on the existence of residual incongruity. Second, correlations between the 3 WD humor scales and a self-report measure of humor (Ruch, 1980) reveal that self-reported preference for complex and unconventional forms of humor go along with appreciation of nonsense humor (high funniness *and* low aversiveness) and with low funniness of INC–RES humor (Ruch & Hehl, 1985). Third, studies analyzing perceived attributes of humor of the three categories come to the conclusion that nonsense is associated with a higher stimulative value than the incongruity–resolution structure (Joachim, 1986; Rath, 1983; Ruch et al., 1988; Schmiedel, 1987). This could be shown for the attributes original, subtle, and puzzling (Ruch et al., 1988), unprobable (Schmiedel, 1987), and perceived difficulty to understand (Joachim, 1986; Schmiedel, 1987). Furthermore, ratings of funniness and being puzzled are significantly positively correlated within nonsense humor but not within incongruity–resolution humor (Rath, 1983). Within-subjects analysis suggests that rank orders of funniness and experienced surprise are correlated in both forms of humor structures; the average size of the correlation is significantly higher for subjects preferring nonsense humor. Furthermore, factor analysis of response scales reveals that the puzzlement rating loads only on the funniness factor (.96) when nonsense humor is analyzed but loads higher on the negative response factor (.63) than on the funniness factor (.51) when incongruity–resolution humor is analyzed (Ruch et al., 1988). Finally, subjects preferring incongruity–resolution humor tend to rank those jokes and cartoons low in funniness that they also consider highly unpredictable and hard to comprehend, whereas this correlation has the reversed sign for subjects preferring nonsense humor (Schmiedel, 1987).

These differences between the two structures as well as hypotheses formulated elsewhere (e.g., Ruch, 1988; Ruch & Hehl, 1985) suggested that certain personality variables are promising predictors of humor that have not been considered previously. The higher degree of stimulation (e.g., unpredictability, unresolved incongruity, complexity, perceived surprisingness, and perplexingness) associated with nonsense humor should lead to higher aversiveness scores by subjects with a general dislike and avoidance of stimulus uncertainty (in information theory sense; e.g., complexity, novelty, ambiguity, incongruity, unfamiliarity, unpredictability). Whereas *tolerance* of high stimulus uncertainty is a necessary prerequisite for low aversiveness of nonsense, it is questionable whether *mere* tolerance is sufficient for deriving pleasure from it. Therefore, it was argued that high funniness of nonsense humor requires an active pursuit of high levels of stimulation (Ruch, 1988; Ruch & Hehl, 1983a). Conversely, the lower degree of stimulation (e.g., completely resolvable incongruities, lower degrees of unpredictability and complexity) associated with incongruity–resolution humor should appeal to those who generally avoid high levels of stimulation and seek out simpler and safer forms of stimulation. Whereas this allows for the predictions of funniness of INC–RES humor, it is questionable whether the characteristics of this structure can produce high levels of aversiveness (as confirmed by low means in Table 2.1). Jokes and cartoons of this structure can be considered to be below the optimal level of cognitive challenge (see McGhee, 1979), resulting in judgments of being boring, which is halfway between low funniness and aversiveness (Ruch et al., 1988).

Intolerance of ambiguity, conservatism, and sensation seeking were the personality variables considered to provide the clearest conceptual links to appreciation of structural properties in humor, and thus their ability to predict interindividual differences in appreciation of humor structure was investigated in several correlational and experimental studies. The existing data regarding these variables is reviewed next.

Besides mere preference for different degrees of stimulation, it has to be considered that comprehension of the punchline is a prerequisite for appreciation of humor. Because of the fact that this element is also involved, the effects of intelligence are briefly considered too.

Conservatism and Appreciation of Humor Structure

Studies investigating the structure of social attitudes usually extract two bipolar factors of conservatism–radicalism (C) and of tough–tendermindedness (T) (Eysenck, 1954; or conservatism–liberalism and realism–idealism in the terminology of Wilson, 1973). Sometimes a third factor of economic capitalism–socialism is added (Eysenck, 1976). The conservatism factor accounts for most of the variance and was considered to be suited for predicting individual differences in humor because there exists a clear conceptual link between the two basic types of humor structure (Ruch, 1984). According to Wilson's (1973) dynamic theory of conservatism, this trait reflects a *generalized fear of both stimulus and response uncertainty*. This should lead more conservative individuals to show greater avoidance and dislike of novel, complex, unfamiliar, incongruous events and to prefer and seek out stimuli that are simpler, more familiar, and congruent. This model of conservatism received support by successfully predicting preference for structural properties involved in different forms of art (Wilson, 1973), poetry (Gillies & Campbell, 1985), and music (Glasgow, Cartier, & Wilson, 1985).

The relationship between conservatism and the 3 WD humor scales were studied over the last decade. The hypotheses tested in the first studies (Ruch, 1981, 1984) validated that conservative persons find incongruity–resolution humor funnier and nonsense humor more aversive than liberals. Although the basic hypotheses remained stable, the model specifying this relationship was formulated more precisely. One major step was the consideration of the T-factor, which helped to resolve the inconsistencies in the new findings (e.g., Ruch & Hehl, 1986a). The new structural model allowed for the discussion of appreciation of *content* and *structure* of (at least) incongruity–resolution-based humor within a space with two dimensions only (Ruch & Hehl, 1986b). According to this model, conservatism is a predictor of funniness of incongruity–resolution-based humor irrespective of the content, whereas toughmindedness is a predictor of appreciation of sexual content in humor, irrespective of the structural basis of the joke or cartoon. Hence, INC–RES SEX_f is located in the toughminded conservative quadrant (see Fig. 2.1). Because NON_f is only negligibly negatively correlated with conservatism, the location of NON SEX_f is on the T-axis. As discussed earlier, aversiveness of the three humor categories is located on the tenderminded side of this axis. Additionally, according to their structural properties, aversiveness of nonsense-based humor is located on the conservative and aversiveness of incongruity–resolution-based humor is located on the radical side of the C-axis. Thus, whereas nonsense humor

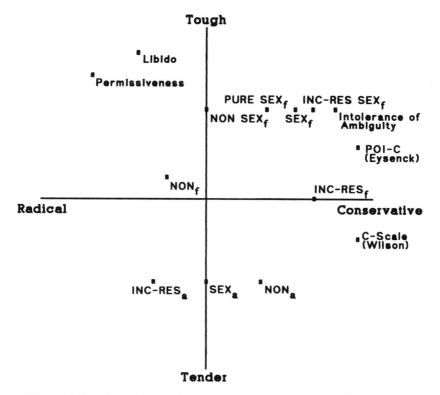

FIG. 2.1   Probable placement of various concepts and the 3 WD humor scales in relation to conservatism and toughmindedness.

should be found aversive by tenderminded conservatives, incongruity-resolution humor should be found aversive by tenderminded radicals.

This location explains the initially perplexing results for different conservatism scales and for several variables associated with conservatism (e.g., superego strength, rigidity, or intolerance of ambiguity). Knowing whether these variables are biased toward tender or toughmindedness allows for the prediction of subtle differences in the profile of correlations with the humor scales. Thus, as compared with pure conservatism measures, scales with a toughmindedness bias will correlate more highly with SEX_f than with $INC-RES_f$ and also more highly negatively with $INC-RES_a$, which is located in the opposite (i.e., tenderminded radical) quadrant (see Fig. 2.1). Scales with a tendermindedness bias will not correlate with SEX_f or at least lower than with $INC-RES_f$, but they will correlate more highly with NON_a, which is located in the same (i.e., tenderminded conservative) quadrant.

Table 2.4 shows the correlation coefficients between different measures of conservatism and the 3 WD humor scales for different samples.

TABLE 2.4
Coefficients of Correlation between Conservatism and Appreciation of Humor

Studies	Sample		Measures		Humor Appreciation					
	m	f	Cons.	3 WD	$INC\text{-}RES_f$	NON_f	SEX_f	$INC\text{-}RES_a$	NON_a	SEX_a
Austrian/German samples										
Busse (1987)	68	– S	WP	K	.30*	-.13	.11	-.03	.19	.16
Hehl & Ruch (1985)	49	56 S	16PF	A + B	.17	-.02	.05	.15	.32**	.27**
Jansa (1990)	100	– S	WP	A + B	.39***	.08	.34***	-.01	.34***	.27**
Joachim (1986)	39	34 S	WP	K	.37***	-.17	.12	-.15	.12	.17
Rath (1983)	50	50 S	WP	A + B[a]	.42***	-.02	.02	–	–	–
Regul (1987)	81	79 P	WP	K	.27*	-.06	.12	.24**	.33***	.17*
Ruch (1984)	55	55 A	WP	A + B[a]	.48***	-.15	-.12	-.09	.33***	.35***
	134	– S	WP	A + B[a]	.46***	-.27**	.28**	-.20*	.19*	-.01
Ruch & Hehl (1985)	–	144 S	WP	B	.39***	.04	.05	-.25**	.03	.06
	44	48 S	WP	A + B	.26*	.00	.20*	.03	.25**	.18
Ruch & Hehl (1986a)	59	56 S	WP	A	.32***	-.21*	.19*	-.06	.22*	.02
			WP	B	.40***	-.12	.25**	-.17	.10	.09
			POI	A	.28**	-.17	.44***	-.10	.10	-.20*
			POI	B	.33***	-.07	.47***	-.23*	.13	-.18*
			MK	A	.24*	-.24*	.28**	-.13	.02	-.21*
			MK	B	.31*	-.13	.29**	-.28**	.15	-.15
			16PF	A	.19*	-.16	.18*	.06	.33***	.13
			16PF	B	.24*	-.13	.27**	.04	.34***	.19*
Ruch & Hehl (1986b)	59	56 S	C'	A + B	.41***	-.17	.39***	-.19*	.20*	-.05
			C''	A + B	.46***	-.18	.42***	-.25**	.13	-.15
French sample										
Accoce (1986)	69	70 S	POI[1]	A + B[a]	.32***	-.13	.04	–	–	–
			POI[2]		-.04	-.22*	.26**	–	–	–
Turkish sample										
Ciftci (1990)	125	135 A	WP	K	.19**	.09	.05	.06	.13*	.15*

Note. m = male, f = female. POI = Public Opinion Inventory (Eysenck, 1976). 16PF = inverted radicalism scale of the 16PF. WP = C-Scale (Wilson and Patterson, 1970). MK = Machiavelianism-conservatism scale (Cloetta, 1983).
C' and C'' = Conservatism factors extracted at scale or item levels.
[a]Humor tests using the 3 WD item pool. [1]Law and Order factor; [2]Right-wing Extremism factor derived from the POI.
*$p < .05$. **$p < .01$. ***$p < .001$.

Conservatism and Funniness of Incongruity-Resolution Humor. Table 2.4 shows the robustness of the relationship between INC-RES$_f$ and conservatism. This main finding was obtained in samples from four different nations (Austria, France, Germany, and Turkey), for both sexes, for students as well as adults, and for normals and psychiatric patients. Furthermore, it was also found for all three forms of the humor test and for four types of conservatism scales. It is likely that the coefficients for French and Turkish samples would be higher, if conservatism scales were used that are standardized for the respective country.

Further support for the hypothesis comes from a study on disparagement humor that was based on a completely different pool of incongruity-resolution jokes and cartoons (Korioth, 1985). Items were selected by judges to be representative for 15 categories. Each category consisted of pairs of "opponents" involved (e.g., husband-wife, teacher-pupil, doctor-patient) with one disparaging the other. For example, there was a category of a teacher disparaging a pupil and another in which the pupil was superior. Factor analysis further helped to subdivide these categories. Finally, a sample of 100 students rated these jokes and cartoons for funniness. Conservatism correlated with *each* of the final 26 categories significantly positive; the coefficients ranged between .31 to .48, with a median of .40. Thus, independently who is disparaging whom in jokes and cartoons, conservative subjects show more appreciation than liberal subjects if humor is based on the incongruity-resolution structure.

The correlation could also be found for an abridged form of the humor test and a conservatism index based on four attitude scales (Ruch et al., 1990). In a sample of 4,292 German subjects between the ages of 14 and 50 (with 37 over age 50), the correlation coefficient was .214, $p < .001$.

Further support comes from the fact that the relationship between conservatism and INC-RES$_f$ could be found at the level of individual jokes and cartoons. In the two samples of the first study, 21 of 48, respectively, 74 of the 120 jokes and cartoons yielded significant ($p < .05$) coefficients (Ruch, 1984). In both samples all items with significantly positive coefficients were based on the INC-RES structure (including sexual humor). In the study by Ruch and Hehl (1986b), all 20 INC-RES jokes and cartoons correlated positively, and 16 of them were significant ($p < .05$; two-tailed). Furthermore, a higher order relationship was verified for these three samples. The higher a joke or cartoon was correlated with conservatism, the higher was its loading on the INC-RES factor. Phi coefficients were computed to determine the strength of the similarity of the two profiles and they turned out to be very high: .90, .91, .95, and .96. Jokes that are more strongly associated with conservatism are also more typical for the first factor. Single conservatism items, on the other hand, correlated with INC-RES$_f$, and the size of these correlations increased with the size of the part–whole corrected item total correlations, again resulting in a high Phi coefficient, .94 (Ruch & Hehl, 1983b).

Further support for the hypothesis comes from studies with personality variables (Hehl & Ruch, 1985; Joachim, 1986; Ruch, 1988; Ruch & Hehl, 1983a, 1985, 1986a, 1986b), values (Ruch & Hehl, 1987), and social (Ruch & Hehl, 1985), sexual (Ruch & Hehl, 1988), and health-related attitudes (Hehl & Ruch, 1990). In these studies, only those variables that correlated with INC–RES$_f$ were also either markers of conservatism or highly correlated with it. There were positive correlations with scales of superego strength, shrewdness, self-sentiment, rigidity, stinginess with money, need for achievement, or value orthodoxy and negative correlations with scales measuring aesthetical interests, complexity, sexual permissiveness, education to autonomy, or bohemian unconcernedness. Among these variables, inhibition of aggression deserves special mention, because computation of partial correlations revealed that conservatism could not fully account for the observed correlations between inhibition of aggression and INC–RES$_f$ in two samples (Ruch & Hehl, 1985). This finding suggests that inhibition of aggression adds to the prediction of INC–RES$_f$.

An independent source of support for this hypothesis was provided by the aforementioned cross-sectional study (Ruch et al., 1990). Trend analyses revealed that age-related differences in conservatism across the sample accounted for 90.5% of the age-related variance in INC–RES$_f$. More importantly, the residual was not significant once the effects of conservatism were partialled out.

Conservatism and Funniness of the Structural Basis in Sexual Humor.
Table 2.4 confirms that conservatism is also a predictor of the *structural basis* of sexual humor. Using a pure measure of conservatism, coefficients around .40 can be obtained. The coefficients are even higher (.44, .47) for INC–RES SEX$_f$ and zero (.02, .05) for NON SEX$_f$ (Ruch & Hehl, 1986b). Consistent with the assumption that conservatism and appreciation of sexual *content* are largely uncorrelated, low or even negative coefficients were obtained when conservatism was related to the *factor* of sexual humor (which consists of content variance only; Accoce, 1986; Ruch, 1984). The finding that the conservatism scale by Wilson and Patterson (1970) is biased toward tendermindedness (due to the idealism items scored for conservatism) additionally accounts for the low size of the coefficients obtained. Whereas this scale is located in the *tenderminded* conservative quadrant, SEX$_f$ is located in the *toughminded* conservative quadrant. Thus, in order to verify the hypothesis that conservatism is a predictor for the structural basis of sexual humor, future studies have to carefully exclude the idealism items from the scale.

Further support for effects of conservatism on the structural basis of sexual humor can be found at the level of individual jokes and cartoons. For incongruity–resolution-based sexual jokes and cartoons, 15 of 17 correlate significantly positively with conservatism (Ruch & Hehl, 1986b). Furthermore, the higher a sexual joke correlates with conservatism, the higher its second loading on the first factor (Phi = .93., .94).

Conservatism and Funniness of Nonsense Humor.   Table 2.4 suggests a slight negative correlation between conservatism and NON_f, the coefficients typically ranging between −.15 to −.20, but they are seldom significant. This finding agrees with the expectations that liberals tend to tolerate unresolved incongruities more than conservatives. However, mere tolerance is not sufficient for finding nonsense funny.

Conservatism and Aversiveness of Humor Structure.   Table 2.4 reveals that correlation coefficients between conservatism and $INC\text{-}RES_a$ are overwhelmingly negative and are significant in the study with the most comprehensive assessment of conservatism (Ruch & Hehl, 1986b). The low size of the coefficients is in accordance with the fact that this scale has the lowest mean and the smallest variance of all 3 WD scales (see Table 2.1). Apart from this, it has to be considered that the orthogonal elements of tendermindedness and neuroticism are involved in general aversiveness, too. Whereas the results suggest that conservatives tend to find incongruity––resolution less aversive than radicals, this effect is small. Thus, replication studies ideally should combine the predictive power of conservatism, neuroticism, and tendermindedness.

At first glance, Table 2.4 clearly seems to support the hypothesis that conservatism predicts aversiveness of nonsense, because all the coefficients are positive and significant in more than half the samples. Nevertheless, the results obtained for the Wilson and Patterson scale might be biased due to its location in the tenderminded conservatism quadrant. Indeed, the factor analytically derived C-axes yield lower coefficients, one being significant, the other not (Ruch & Hehl, 1986b). However, there are two facts contradicting the idea that the results only reflect tendermindedness variance. First, the inverted radicalism scale of the 16 PF correlates significantly positively with NON_a in two samples. Second, the conservatism scales with a toughmindedness bias also correlate *positively* albeit not significantly so. Thus, the results favor the interpretation that conservatives tend to find nonsense humor aversive, although the effect might be lower than suggested by the Wilson and Patterson scale.

With respect to aversiveness of sexual humor, Table 2.4 reveals positive, negative, and nonsignificant coefficients. Assuming that conservatism is unrelated to appreciation of sexual *content* in humor and the dislike of the nonsense structure outweighs the like of the incongruity–resolution structure, one would predict a zero correlation between conservatism and SEX_a. This finding emerged precisely for the conservatism factor (Ruch & Hehl, 1986b). Negative correlations were obtained for the scales biased toward toughmindedness (e.g., Eysenck's POI), whereas positive coefficients seemed to be a function of a tendermindedness bias of the scale (e.g., in the Wilson–Patterson C-scale). Thus, the assumption of no relationship between conservatism and SEX_a still seems valid.

Intolerance of Ambiguity and Appreciation of Humor Structure

Intolerance of ambiguity, introduced by Else Frenkel-Brunswik (1949) as an emotional and perceptual personality variable, overlaps with conservatism both theoretically and empirically. Accordingly, similar hypotheses regarding appreciation of humor were derived, and the first study confirmed the predictions that intolerant individuals give both higher funniness ratings to incongruity–resolution-based humor and higher aversiveness ratings to nonsense humor than do subjects who are more tolerant of ambiguity (Ruch & Hehl, 1983a). Inspection of the correlations between the scale and funniness of each of the 120 jokes and cartoons revealed that, in nearly one half of cases (57 jokes and cartoons), the coefficients were significant. Table 2.5 presents the results of the various replication samples.

It can be seen from Table 2.5 that the correlation coefficients obtained generally support the hypotheses albeit not being significant in each case. Nevertheless, the interest in this variable ceased out of two reasons. First, the German version of the intolerance of ambiguity scale was discovered to have low internal consistency. Second, intolerance of ambiguity correlated positively with conservatism *and* with toughmindedness, which lowered its usefulness as a predictor of humor *structure*. Its location in the toughmindedness–conservatism quadrant explains two anomalies of Table 2.5 not foreseen by the hypotheses. The additional toughness element involved in intolerance of ambiguity is responsible for the generally higher coefficients for SEX_f than for $INC-RES_f$, because it also contributes to the explanation of content variance, which is orthogonal to structure variance. Furthermore, the toughness element is also responsible for the inconsistent results for NON_a, which are lower than expected. Whereas both aversiveness of nonsense and intolerance of ambiguity are correlated with conservatism, the former is located on the tender side of the T-axis whereas the latter is on the tough side and thus suppressed the effects.

Nevertheless, despite its loss as a pure predictor of humor structure, intolerance of ambiguity remains a potent predictor of funniness of sexual humor based on the incongruity–resolution structure.

TABLE 2.5
Coefficients of Correlation between Intolerance of Ambiguity and Appreciation of Humor

Studies	Sample		Measures		Humor Appreciation					
	m	f	INT.A.	3 WD	$INC\text{-}RES_f$	NON_f	SEX_f	$INC\text{-}RES_a$	NON_a	SEX_a
German samples										
Busse (1987)	68	—	BB	K	.02	−.19	.12	.02	.08	.00
	68	—	KI	K	.14	−.13	.15	.00	.13	.00
Jansa (1990)	100	—	BB	A + B	.23*	−.09	.26**	.02	.24*	.04
Ruch & Hehl (1983a)	134	—	BB	A + B[a]	.19*	−.03	.34****	−.06	.19*	−.08
Ruch & Hehl (1985)	—	144	BB	B	.26**	.13	.24**	−.11	.01	−.05
	44	48	BB	A + B	.15	.15	.39****	.20	.28**	−.01
Ruch & Hehl (1986a)	59	56	BB	A	.17*	−.06	.37****	.07	.15*	−.03
			BB	B	.26**	.02	.40****	−.03	.17*	−.04
			BB	A + B	.23*	−.02	.40****	.01	.18	−.04
French sample										
Accoce (1986)	69	70	BB[1]	A + B[a]	.23**	.03	.10	—	—	—
			BB[2]	A + B[a]	.26**	−.25**	.19*	—	—	—

Note: m = male, f = female. BB = Intolerance of Ambiguity (Brengelmann & Brengelmann, 1960).
KI = Intolerance of Ambiguity (Kischkel, 1984).
[1]Uncertainty Avoidance factor;
[2]Authoritarianism factor derived from the BB.
[a]Humor tests using the 3 WD item pool.
*$p < .05$. **$p < .01$. ***$p < .001$.

Sensation Seeking and Appreciation of Humor Structure

Zuckerman (1979) defines *sensation seeking* (SS) as "a trait defined by the need for varied, novel, and complex sensations and experiences and the willingness to take physical and social risks for the sake of such experiences" (p. 10). Thus, whereas intolerance of ambiguity and conservatism emphasize the uncertainty-*avoiding* aspect and thus only allow for the prediction of *tolerance* (i.e., low aversiveness) of nonsense humor, SS also was expected to be involved in *funniness* of nonsense humor.

Ruch (1988) hypothesized that *Experience Seeking (ES)* and *Boredom Susceptibility (BS)* will be related to appreciation of structural properties in humor. ES involves the seeking of stimulation through the mind and the senses, through art, travel, even psychedelic drugs, music, and the wish to live in an unconventional style. There is evidence that ES is closely related to the *novelty* and *complexity* dimension of stimuli (Zuckerman, 1984). BS represents the tendency to avoid repetitive experience and was considered to be sensitive to the differences between incongruity–resolution humor and nonsense humor. Furthermore, ES and BS turned out to be the subscales of sensation seeking most highly correlated with structural properties of different aesthetic objects such as art (Furnham & Bunyan, 1988; Zuckerman, 1979) or music (Glasgow et al., 1985; Litle & Zuckerman, 1986).

Seven hypotheses relating SS to funniness and aversiveness of humor content and structure were derived and tested (Ruch, 1988). The hypotheses relating to the structure of humor predicted that ES and BS, as well as the total score of the sensation-seeking scale, will correlate positively with NON_f, negatively with $INC-RES_f$, and negatively with NON_a. The results of a 448-subject sample are presented in Table 2.6.

Table 2.6 reveals that sensation seeking is an important ingredient in appreciation of humor structure. Like individuals high in conservatism and intolerance of ambiguity, the low sensation seeker dislikes nonsense humor and judges it aversive but gives high funniness ratings to incongruity–resolution humor. Sensation seeking, however, also predicts funniness of

TABLE 2.6
Coefficients of Correlation Between Sensation Seeking and Appreciation of Humor

	$INC-RES_f$	NON_f	SEX_f	$INC-RES_a$	NON_a	SEX_a
Thrill and Adventure Seeking	.02	.09	.11*	− .09	− .13**	− .17***
Experience Seeking	− .24***	.20***	− .03	.01	− .22***	− .15**
Disinhibition	− .18***	.07	.20***	− .11*	− .20***	− .36***
Boredom Susceptibility	− .23***	.15**	− .02	.01	− .22***	− .15**
Total SS	− .20***	.17***	.08	− .06	− .25***	− .28***

*$p < .05$. **$p < .01$. ***$p < .001$.

nonsense humor. The coefficients of correlations are low but reliable, because they are based on a large sample size.

Analyses of the results of subsamples showed that, whereas all the signs were in the expected direction, the correlation coefficients were not significant throughout. Similar inconsistency was found in two recent replication studies. In a sample of 260 Turkish male and female adults, both funniness and aversiveness of nonsense were significantly predicted by ES ($r = .26, p < .001; r = -.25, p < .001$), BS ($r = .24, p < .001; r = -.24, p < .001$), and the total scale ($r = .22, p < .001; r = -.20, p < .01$). However, there was a failure to replicate the results for incongruity–resolution humor (Ciftci, 1990). There was an opposite pattern of results for a sample of 100 male German students. Incongruity–resolution humor was considered funny by subjects low in ES ($r = -.32, p < .001$), BS ($r = -.42, p < .001$), and the total scale scores ($r = -.37, p < .001$). The hypothesis relating to NON_a, however, received only slight support (coefficients of $-.18$, $-.12$, and $-.25$). Furthermore, there was no support at all for the hypothesis relating to funniness of nonsense. This failure is partly explainable by the extraordinarily low variance in the respective humor scales obtained for these samples (see Table 2.1).

This inconsistency led to the hypothesis that sensation seeking (mainly ES and BS) determines the preference for nonsense humor over incongruity-resolution-based humor independent of the degree of enjoyment induced by these two categories (Ruch, 1988). This hypothesis was tested by correlating a Structure Preference Index (SPI; obtained by subtracting $INC–RES_f$ from NON_f) with the sensation-seeking scales (see Table 2.7).

Table 2.7 shows that the SPI score correlates positively with ES, BS, and the total scale in all samples, suggesting that sensation seekers consider humor based on the nonsense structure funnier than incongruity–resolution

TABLE 2.7

Coefficients of Correlation Between Sensation Seeking and Structure Preference

	TAS	ES	DIS	BS	TOTAL
Ruch (1988)					
sample 1	−.19*	.27**	.15	.33***	.18
sample 2	.10	.50***	.23	.37**	.38**
sample 3	.12	.31***	.15	.26**	.29***
sample 4	.09	.30**	.32**	.31**	.33***
sample 1–4	.06	.40***	.23***	.35***	.34***
Replications					
Jansa (1990)	.06	.31**	.18	.45***	.34***
Ciftci (1990)	−.11	.20**	.24***	.12	.13*

Note: TAS = Thrill and Adventure Seeking. ES = Experience Seeking. DIS = Disinhibition. BS = Boredom Susceptibility. Total = Total Sensation Seeking.
*$p < .05$. **$p < .01$. ***$p < .001$.

humor, independent of the absolute degree of appreciation for these two types of humor. This finding is much more stable than the correlations with the funniness scales. Furthermore, the results were obtained in the replication samples too (Ciftci, 1990; Jansa, 1990), suggesting that this finding is valid for Austrian (Ruch, 1988; Sample 3), German, and Turkish (Ciftci, 1990) samples, for students and adults. The preference for nonsense structure could also be extracted from the aversiveness scores. However, the coefficients are lower but still significant (Ruch, 1988).

Further support for a relationship between nonsense and SS comes from the results of variables closely related to sensation seeking, for example, venturesomeness (Hehl & Ruch, 1985) or hedonism (Hehl & Ruch, 1990), as well as from trends in cross-sectional age differences in nonsense and sensation seeking (Ruch et al., 1990).

Seeking-Avoiding Stimulus Uncertainty and Appreciation of Humor Structure

A more direct verification of the nature of the structure elements in humor was undertaken by investigating preference for stimulus properties like symmetry-asymmetry or complexity-simplicity in objects different from humor (Busse, 1987; Ruch, 1986). The experimental tasks covered subjects' exploratory behavior when wearing "prism glasses," judging art postcards placed into four categories (simple-nonfantastic, simple-fantastic, complex-nonfantastic, and complex-fantastic), judging polygons of different complexity, making preference selection of polygons based on symmetry, and producing aesthetically pleasing and displeasing black-white patterns on a square card containing 10 rows and 10 columns.

These studies give strong support for the structural basis of nonsense humor; NON_f correlated positively with the following variables: liking of the "complex-nonfantastic" and "complex-fantastic" art postcards, peer-rated complexity of the "pleasing" pattern, duration of time wearing the prism glasses, and the number of actions designed to increase novel or incongruous visual feedback. On the other hand, $INC\text{-}RES_f$ correlated positively with liking of the "simple-nonfantastic" art postcards, whereas the positive correlation with the category "simple-fantastic" just failed to reach significance. The structure preference score was significantly correlated with preference for asymmetrical polygons: Subjects tending to prefer nonsense humor also more frequently found the asymmetrical alternative polygons more pleasing.

These studies provide stronger tests of the hypothesis that the enjoyment of different forms of humor reflect broader dispositions to seek out and enjoy events that offer more or less stimulus uncertainty, because there is little method overlap. Also such experimental tasks better incorporate the postulated structural properties than do questionnaire assessment of the respective personality traits. Thus, further studies along these lines are recommended.

Intelligence and Appreciation of Humor Structure

The differences between incongruity–resolution and nonsense structure with respect to both difficulty and complexity levels would suggest that general intelligence is a relevant variable in appreciation of humor. The assumption of the importance of a match between level of a person's ability and degree of stimulus challenge as a prerequisite for maximal humor appreciation (as stated by the "optimal level of cognitive challenge" model, see McGhee, 1979) would suggest a positive correlation with NON_f and negative correlations with $INC\text{-}RES_f$ and NON_a. Emphasizing the fact that understanding is a prerequisite for appreciation would lead to the same predictions.

The relationship between intelligence and the 3 WD humor test was studied in three samples employing two different intelligence tests (Ruch & Hehl, 1985) and a replication sample using a third intelligence test (Joachim, 1986). There are converging results showing that positive correlations occurred between intelligence and NON_f only, and negative correlations occurred between intelligence and $INC\text{-}RES_f$ and NON_a only. There was no correlation with $INC\text{-}RES_a$. Because only appreciation (but not comprehension) of humor was investigated, it is not possible to distinguish between the two hypotheses just presented. However, the results show that intelligence has to be considered in the prediction of appreciation of humor structure too. More importantly, partial correlation reveals that intelligence explains variance that is not covered by the other predictors (e.g., conservatism). Thus, its explicit consideration would increase the total amount of variance explained (Ruch & Hehl, 1985).

Appreciation of Humor Content

Although nearly all the studies trying to explain individual differences in appreciation of humor were related to the content aspect, and sexual humor has been the favorite content category, the determinants of appreciation of sexual humor are not known yet in contemporary literature. Whereas several hypotheses have been put foreward (see Hehl & Ruch, 1985; Nias, 1981; Ruch & Hehl, 1986b, 1988, for a review), none of them could be verified unambiguously.

This might be due to two reasons. First, funniness rather than aversiveness scales were employed in cases where the hypotheses explicitly related to the *dislike* (and not reduced funniness only) of sexual humor.

Second, the failure might also be related to the neglect of acknowledging the existence of structure variance in sexual humor and its explicit consideration when testing the hypotheses. Studies investigating individual differences in appreciation of sexual humor have to consider that subjects do not respond to the content of these jokes and cartoons only but also to their structural properties. The sexual humor category is sometimes split up into the three categories of INC-RES SEX, NON SEX, and PURE SEX, and the assumption of a structural basis in sexual humor is validated by the correlation of these categories with predictors of the humor structure, or with the two structure categories themselves. Thus, whereas hypotheses about predictors of sexual humor were nearly exclusively related to the sexual content only, empirical tests of these hypotheses were always based on data containing the structure variance too, thus lowering the power of the test. In other words, whereas the *content factor* of sexual humor is orthogonal to the structure factors, the sexual humor *category* itself is not.

Two simple methods were used to roughly extract structure variance in sexual humor and relate the content to predictors only. First, factor scores of the sexual humor factor were considered to be a relatively pure measure of the appreciation of sexual content, because the structure variance of these jokes and cartoons contributes to the structure factors, as can be seen by their double loadings. Second, partial correlations were used to remove the variance of the structure as represented by the first two humor categories. For example, it was attempted to estimate the correlation between disinhibition and content variance in SEX_f only, by partialling out $INC-RES_f$ and NON_f and thus holding the effects of the structure constant (Ruch, 1988).

Funniness of Sexual Content in Humor

Studies on appreciation of sexual content in humor using the 3 WD converge on the finding that the second dimension in the attitude space, tough-tendermindedness, is the most important predictor. Irrespective of the structure of the joke or cartoon, toughmindedness correlates positively with funniness and negatively with aversiveness of sexual humor (Ruch & Hehl, 1986b). The coefficients of correlation for the three subgroups of sexual humor are significantly positive and range between .28 and .46. This result could be found at the level of individual jokes and cartoons also. The correlation between toughmindedness and the 20 representatives of the sexual humor category were all positive for the funniness scale (with 15 of them being significant) and negative for the aversiveness scale (with 16 reaching significance). Furthermore, a higher order relationship was found. The higher funniness of a sexual joke or cartoon correlated with the two toughmindedness measures used, the higher its loading on the sexual factor.

The Phi coefficients computed turned out to be very high, .98 and .97, respectively. Finally, there was also evidence that toughmindedness is a predictor of contents other than sex. The sign of the loadings of jokes of the first factor (i.e., INC–RES humor) on the sexual factor (approximately 8.4% of variance) tended to correspond with the sign of these jokes' correlation with toughmindedness. In other words, the small amount of content variance in incongruity–resolution humor may be predicted by toughmindedness too.

Evidence for the hypothesis that toughmindedness is a predictor of content of sexual humor can be found in two former studies with the conservatism scale (Ruch, 1984; Ruch & Hehl, 1985). In a factor analysis of items of the German version of the Wilson and Patterson conservatism scale, it was found that the second factor was mainly correlated positively with the funniness and negatively with the aversiveness of sexual humor (Ruch, 1984). Furthermore, it was shown that antihedonism (which is a marker for tendermindedness) was the only subfactor of conservatism that was correlated negatively with the funniness and positively with the aversiveness of sexual humor (Ruch & Hehl, 1985).

Further support for the hypothesis that appreciation of sexual content in humor is located on the T-axis comes from studies with personality variables (Joachim, 1986; Ruch, 1988), sexual behavior and sexual attitudes (Ruch & Hehl, 1988), health-related attitudes (Hehl & Ruch, 1990), and values (Ruch & Hehl, 1987). In these studies, markers of toughmindedness correlated with appreciation of sexual humor. These correlations reflect both content and structure.

There are, however, also results relating to the content only, because the effects of structure were controlled by computing partial correlations. In detail, funniness of content in sexual humor was correlated positively with disinhibition in four samples. These data demonstrate the importance of controlling for the effects of structure, because the correlation with funniness of the sexual humor *category* was not significant in two of the four samples studied (Ruch, 1988). Furthermore, whereas a scale of sexual libido (Eysenck, 1976) was not correlated with funniness of incongruity-resolution-based sexual humor, a significant coefficient emerged after controlling the effects of the structure, which suggests a positive relationship between sexual libido and funniness of sexual content in humor (Ruch & Hehl, 1988).

The relationship between appreciation of sexual humor and disinhibition is especially noteworthy because it allows the derivation of a new hypothesis. Disinhibition is a subfactor of sensation seeking (Zuckerman, 1979). Items of this scale indicate seeking of stimulation through other persons; they express a need for variety in social life and other hedonic pursuits. Zuckerman (1984) suggested that disinhibition relates to the *intensity* dimension of stimulation. Differences between high and low disinhibitors increase with increasing intensity of the stimulation. Sexual content represents one of the most intensive stimulations obtainable in humor. It can be assumed that high disinhibitors tolerate stimulation by highly tendentious humor as they tolerate intensive stimulation by other objects (Litle & Zuckerman, 1986). Thus, one can expect that the size of the correlation between funniness of sexual humor and disinhibition will be higher for highly tendentious material and lower for more veiled forms of sexual humor. This was found to be true for toughmindedness on the higher order relationship aforementioned and should also be verified for disinhibition.

Thus, there is ample evidence for the hypothesis that appreciation of sexual *content* in humor reflects toughminded attitudes. Furthermore, it was argued that the toughmindedness hypothesis is a very parsimonious hypothesis, because it incorporates many other single specific hypotheses set up to explain individual differences in humor (Ruch & Hehl, 1988).

Appreciation of Sexual Humor Based on Different Structures

Sexual content is not funny by itself, because it is embedded in one or the other humor structure. Thus, whereas appreciation of sexual humor is located exactly on the T-axis, appreciation of the different subgroups of sexual humor will not be. Although the matter is far from being settled, there is evidence that content and structure of humor have *additive* influence on its perceived funniness (Ehrenstein & Ertel, 1978; Wilson, 1979). Thus, one could expect that the location of appreciation of the different humor categories can be predicted from the separate locations of their structure and humor content.

Indeed, funniness of *incongruity–resolution-based sexual humor* is correlated positively with both toughmindedness *and* conservatism. Given its location in the toughminded conservative diagonal, one would expect that other variables located in this quadrant are highly predictive of this subgroup of sexual humor (see Fig. 2.1). This could be found for such variables as intolerance of ambiguity, political and economic interests (Ruch & Hehl, 1987), technical interests, support for education toward submissiveness (Hehl & Ruch, 1990), *low* aesthetic and social interests (Ruch & Hehl, 1987), and *low* scores on the 16PF–M scale (bohemian unconcernedness; Ruch & Hehl, 1986b). Variables located in the toughminded *liberal* (or *radical*) quadrant (e.g., sensation seeking, permissiveness) are not expected to correlate with sexual humor based on the INC–RES structure, because appreciation of the content is suppressed by low appreciation of the structure. These variables share the toughmindedness component with INC–RES SEX_f but are on the opposite pole with respect to the conservatism dimension. As shown earlier, disinhibition tends to be *negatively* related with INC–RES$_f$ (see Table 2.6) but *positively* with funniness of sexual content, resulting in only slightly positive correlations with SEX$_f$ (Ruch, 1988).

Funniness of *nonsense-based sexual humor,* on the other hand, also reflects the predictors of funniness of the general nonsense category. Because conservatism is not a potent predictor of funniness of nonsense, within this two-dimensional attitude space, NON SEX$_f$ is located on the T-axis only (see Fig. 2.1), showing no alignment to the conservatism dimension (Ruch & Hehl, 1986b). However, among others, NON SEX$_f$ is more highly correlated with scales of disinhibition and general sensation seeking (Ruch, 1988), hedonism and interest in sex (Hehl & Ruch, 1990), and sexual libido, sexual permissiveness, sexual pleasure, and sexual experience (Ruch & Hehl, 1988). In this subtype of sexual humor, two arousing properties fuse, the sexual content and the nonsense structure. This hypotheses can be confirmed by the fact that NON$_f$ is also correlated to most of the aforementioned variables, albeit lower than NON SEX$_f$. Variables located in the toughminded conservative quadrant (i.e., the predictors of INC–RES SEX$_f$) most frequently are not correlated with funniness of sexual humor based on nonsense (Hehl & Ruch, 1990; Ruch & Hehl, 1987).

None of the variables predicting funniness of incongruity–resolution-based sexual humor has a direct salient link to sex, whereas the predictors of funniness of nonsense sexual humor do relate to positive attitudes to sex and sexual experience. Thus, the various forms of sexual humor differ with respect to their distance to the location of direct expression of sexual impulses. Eysenck and Wilson (1978) summarized that sexual freedom can be reliably located in this two-dimensional attitudes space in the tough-minded radical quadrant. This could be confirmed with the Eysenckian superfactor in sexual attitudes, sexual libido, as well as with scales assessing sexual behavior (Ruch & Hehl, 1988). Whereas sexual libido is more closely related to the T- than to the C-axis, other scales, like sexual permissiveness, correlate with both radicalism and toughmindedness at about an equal size (see Fig. 2.1). None of the scales reflecting positive sexual attitudes was located outside this quadrant. Given the facts that scales of sexual freedom are located in the toughminded radical quadrant exclusively but none of the sexual humor categories are, it has to be stated that funniness of sexual humor does not directly reflect sexual freedom. Nonsense sexual humor is located closest (approximately 30° away) and thus is correlated with scales of sexual freedom. Sexual humor based on incongruity–resolution is very distant (approximately 80° away) and thus is not correlated. Personality variables located there do have relationships to sex albeit not to sexual freedom. The authoritarian personality as introduced by Adorno, Frenkel-

Brunswik, Levinson, and Sanford (1950) is located in the toughminded conservatism quadrant too. Among other components (e.g., conventionalism, authoritarian submission, authoritarian aggression, anti-intraception, power and "toughness," projectivity), authoritarians are characterized by an "exaggerated concern with sexual goings-on" (p. 157). According to the authors, the responses to the authoritarianism items relating to sex indicate the strength of the subject's unconscious sexual drives; scoring in the authoritarian direction reflects that the sexual desires are suppressed and in danger of getting out of hand. Maybe the observation of toughminded conservatives and their appreciation of sexual humor (based on incongruity--resolution) inspired Freud (1905) to put foreward his repression theory of jokes.

Whereas the results for appreciation of sexual humor based on nonsense totally contradict Freudian theory of repressed sexuality, they also do not suggest that finding this humor funny is a sign of *mere* sexual libido or permissivity. More research is definitely needed on this problem. One shortcoming of the 3 WD is that there are only three sexual cartoons with a high nonsense loading included. Thus, the relationship between nonsense sexual humor and sexual attitudes and behavior should be investigated using a broader sample of jokes and cartoons. This should lead to a more stable location of this subgroup of sexual humor. However, the main findings obtained for nonsense sexual humor seem to be solid because the general nonsense humor category (which consists of 20 items) yielded similar patterns (i.e., the correlations with sexual libido, experience, and pleasure obtained for NON_f were only slightly lower than the coefficients of NON SEX_f).

Aversiveness of Sexual Content in Humor

Given the fact that the two components of appreciation of humor, funniness and aversiveness, are substantially negatively correlated in sexual humor only (see Table 2.3), one can expect that predictors of funniness of sexual humor will also tend to predict its aversiveness (with a reversed sign). This was found for most of the predictors (e.g., toughmindedness, disinhibition, extraceptive values). In general, the coefficients tended to be even higher for aversiveness than for funniness. Furthermore, whereas SEX_f is related to the superfactor sexual libido only, SEX_a is related to low libido *and* low sexual satisfaction.

Finally, it should be mentioned that structure also codetermines the results of *aversiveness* of the subgroups of sexual humor. The predictors of aversiveness of sexual humor based on nonsense are quite different from the predictors of aversiveness of sexual humor based on incongruity–resolution (Ruch & Hehl, 1987, 1988).

DISCUSSION AND CONCLUSION

This review shows that the 3 WD humor test fulfills the criteria for several of the functions of humor tests described in the introduction. With respect to the first function, serving as a diagnostic tool for the assessment of appreciation of humor, the application of the 3 WD can be recommended on grounds of the satisfactory psychometric properties. Analyses of the test statistics on the scale and item level yield results comparable to other personality questionnaires. The validity studies confirm the significance of the proposed structure and content elements in the stimulus material and show the usefulness of the consideration of the negative responses to humor on a separate scale.

The differentiation between the two structures is validated by analyses of the ratings of perceived attributes as well as the correlations with predictor variables. Subjects scoring high in $INC\text{-}RES_f$ appreciate the resolution element in the processing of the punchline. For them it is important that the initial discrepance or incongruity can be resolved completely and that no traces of residual tension/incongruity are left over. The existence of residual incongruity, however, plays a crucial role in the appreciation of humor of the nonsense type. For subjects scoring high in NON_f, the residual traces of incongruity enhance enjoyment of humor, whereas the high scorer in NON_a is characterized by low tolerance for unresolved incongruity in humor and a negative response to it. The results of the present review provide ample support for the view that appreciation of the structural basis of humor is embedded into a more general response pattern to simple–complex, incongruent–congruent, familiar–novel, predictable–unpredictable, consistent–varied, unambiguous–ambiguous, and other stimuli not limited to the realm of humor. It can be concluded that the tendency to seek out certain degrees of stimulus uncertainty and to avoid others as observable in general life extends to humor appreciation.

This chapter also validates the significance of the content in sexual humor; however, it also confirms the existence of structure variance in appreciation of this content-dominated humor category. Appreciation of the sexual content seems to reflect the *degree* and *valence* of salience of this theme (i.e., strength of positive salience contributes to funniness and strength of negative salience contributes to aversiveness of sexual content in humor). Thus, the degree of appreciation of the sexual content in humor varies *directly* with one's attitudes to sex and sexual behavior rather than *inversely,* as deducible from Freudian theory. However, there is little understanding of the differences in the functions of the incongruity–resolution structure and the nonsense structure in which the sexual content can be embedded.

Finally, the review supports the validity of the separation of positive and negative responses to humor. The funniness scale covers the degree of positive responses to the stimulus, ranging from no positive response elicited to strong enjoyment. The aversiveness scale covers the responses ranging from tolerance to explicit dislike of the stimulus. Whereas there is no evidence for a strong generalized proneness to find all types of humor funny, such individual differences exist with respect to aversiveness. General proneness to negative affectivity and tenderminded attitudes are factors associated with a low threshold for negative responses to all forms of humor.

Whereas the psychometric properties of the 3 WD humor tests are satisfactory in general, attention should be given to the problems relating to the skewness of the aversiveness scales, the unequal distribution of structure among the sexual items, and the potential involvement of state variance. The skewness of the aversiveness scale is based on the low rate of negative responses that, however, seems to be inherent in the nature of the stimuli. Humor is invented for the amusement or exhilaration of individuals, not for their displeasure. Whereas the funniness rating reflects the more common response to humor, the aversiveness aspect is considered to be an important supplement. One peculiarity of humor tests is that the items cannot be changed in order to get better statistics. Whereas in items measuring personality traits the endorsement frequency can easily be influenced (e.g., by making statement more or less extreme), such manipulations are hardly effective with humor items because one can assume that the joke is already in the shape that assures maximum funniness. An effective reduction of the skewness would be obtained by raising the number of items, including more aversive items, or replacing "aversiveness" by a less negative term. However, all three changes would impose new problems and hence the scales are left as they are.

A possible revision of the 3 WD should take into account the structural basis of sexual humor more explicitly, which, in the present versions, is not balanced. There are more items based on incongruity–resolution than on nonsense. Whereas this reflects the distribution frequency of the two structures in humor in general, the resulting score in the 3 WD is biased toward INC–RES SEX humor. Thus, if a study demands explicit consideration of the structural basis, the use of separate scores for the three subcategories of sexual humor is recommended.

Finally, doubts remain whether the precautions made did lead to a *complete* elimination of the state variance. These doubts are based on the somewhat lower parallel test reliability coefficients for samples with a longer time lag as compared to those with no time lag, and on the varying size of the mean intercorrelation among the three funniness and aversiveness scales. This problem needs a thorough consideration. Future investigations should try to estimate the amount of state variance in humor appreciation, to figure out their causes, and finally to test how state influence could be minimized or eliminated. Studies should be carried out exploring the effects of situational factors (e.g., alone vs. group administration, experimenter present or not). Special attention should also be given to the type of instruction; given that an explicit variation of state–trait instructions (how funny/aversive *at the moment* vs. *in general*) would yield strong effects, the state elements in the current instruction should be eliminated completely. However, remember that the aforementioned problems are not reflecting particular weaknesses of the 3 WD but the lack of knowledge with respect to optimal administration conditions for humor tests in general. Furthermore, there exist alternative explanations (e.g., the positive intercorrelations among the funniness scales might also be related to sample selection; i.e., there were lower intercorrelations in the more representative samples).

None of the studies carried out with the 3 WD directly dealt with the second function of a humor test, the potential use of humor appreciation as an objective test of personality. A necessary prerequisite for serving this function is the proof that there are not only consistent but also substantial correlations between humor and personality, evidence that Cattell and Tollefson (1966) failed to give for their IPAT Humor Test of Personality. According to the present review, conservatism–radicalism might be such a dimension that could be assessed via a humor test. Whereas the zero-order coefficients between conservatism and INC–RES$_f$ do not exceed .50, the size of the coefficients increases to .60 (Ruch, 1984; Sample II), if funniness of the nonsense and sexual humor categories are considered too. A coefficient of .65 was obtained in a canonical correlation approach employing four conservatism measures as criterion and the scales of the 3 WD (both forms; including the aversiveness scales) as predictors (Ruch & Hehl, 1986a). The highest coefficient (.79) was obtained in a multiple regression approach, with funniness of *single* jokes and cartoons used as predictors. Thus, whereas conservatism is most highly correlated with INC–RES$_f$, consideration of the other scales would probably yield more substantial coefficients.

The zero-order coefficients between funniness of sexual humor and toughmindedness do not suggest a strong relationship. However, the coefficients would increase once the structural variance is eliminated and the aversiveness scales are employed too. For example, a correlation coefficient of .51 was obtained for a canonical variate, linking SEX$_f$ and general aversiveness (on the predictor side) and the tough–tendermindedness bias of some conservatism scales (on the criterion side; Ruch & Hehl, 1986a). The zero-order coefficients prohibit the use of the 3 WD scales as a diagnostic tool for the assessment of sensation seeking. However, there is increasing evidence that sensation seeking is a predictor of the *relative* preference for nonsense over incongruity–resolution humor, irrespective of the degree of appreciation, and these coefficients are consistently higher.

When evaluating the size of the coefficients, with a few exceptions only, none of the samples was representative. Student samples certainly do not cover the whole range of variance in traits like conservatism, sensation seeking, or toughmindedness, suggesting an underestimation of the size of the coefficients of correlation. Furthermore, consider that reliability and validity of the criterion measures are far from being perfect, too. Thus, studies set out to estimate the 3 WD as an instrument for the objective assessment of personality traits should try to use representative samples and multiple operationalizations of the criteria. Given that these precautions are taken, one can estimate from the results of such studies whether the application of the 3 WD humor test as a means for the objective assessment of personality is justified.

Definitely more research should be carried out with the lines of the function of humor tests as a means for establishing a taxonomy of humor and for testing its comprehensiveness and cross-cultural stability. An accepted taxonomy of humor could serve as a frame of reference, allowing the integration of the different findings, and would thus lead to progressive accumulation of knowledge on humor. Experience gathered with the studies done with the 3 WD suggests that the application of translated humor items in other countries is possible. The factor structure and the personality correlates were replicable. Whether the taxonomy underlying the 3 WD humor test is comprehensive or not is open for empirical investigation. Only extremely demeaning and untolerable ethnic jokes and cartoons were intentionally excluded from the original item pools. Thus, the resulting taxonomy should be quite representative for humor printed in the Austrian and German media. Furthermore, many of these jokes and cartoons do not have a German origin. Humor books are translated into different languages, and also international magazines are vehicles for transporting humor from one culture to another, supporting the assumption that universal humor factors are stable across different cultures. Furthermore, the strong association with personality traits and their cross-cultural replicability supports such an assumption. Nevertheless, it cannot be excluded that additional factors will appear in different nations. One has to be careful, however, to have representatives of the discussed taxonomy into the factored item pool in order to be able to estimate whether a factor is new or not. Explicit consideration of pure representatives of the two structural factors is especially important when attempting to verify new content factors. When attempting to test the exhaustiveness of the derived taxonomy, it turned out that the content categories of aggressive, black, and scatological humor based on either incongruity–resolution or nonsense correlated so highly with the "innocent" representatives of the respective structure factor that it did not make sense to separate them (unpublished study). Whereas the item pool of the 3 WD can serve as a basis for replicating the factors in different cultures, it might be necessary to replace some items by ones of the respective countries because of unfamiliar physical characteristics of the persons portrayed.

The utility of the 3 WD with respect to the other functions of humor tests depends on the degree of exhaustiveness of the underlying taxonomy. In this context the present inventory would be applied to test the effects of personality, mood, or of other factors on the appreciation of humor. Prior attempts to validate personality factors in humor were predisposed to fail, because very frequently humor categories with unproven empirical homogeneity were used or the hypotheses related to postulated aspects of jokes or cartoons, which in humor research were not proven to have effects on the perceived funniness. Consequently, the interest of personality theorists in humor ceased. Because humor research is much more advanced now and humor tests exist that are based on theory, the field will become attractive to personality research again.

The use of the 3 WD can be recommended for testing hypotheses relating to the functions and effects of humor as stated in different humor theories. For example, over the last decade there exists an increasing number of articles speculating about the health benefits of humor and laughter (e.g., humor is seen as a stress and pain reducer, a coping device, or a means to enhance immune functioning). Studies testing such hypotheses employed a unidimensional concept of humor (i.e., the subjects were divided into subgroups of "high" or "low" in sense of humor according to their score on *one* scale only). Application of the 3 WD would lead to a refinement of these global hypotheses by specifying which of the humor categories are involved in the effects and which ones are not. Pilot studies relating the 3 WD to health variables suggest that nonsense is better than incongruity–resolution, whereas aversiveness of all categories is related to many self-reported disturbances.

Finally, the items of the 3 WD might also be used in emotion research as a standardized method for the induction of positive affect. When serving this purpose, the items are presented to subjects in the form of a series of slides, and an explicit state instruction is used. Furthermore, besides the verbal ratings, behavioral responses are also assessed.

Because humor is related to many psychic phenomena, there is a need for a standardized humor test in several fields within psychology. One aim of this chapter is to draw the attention of personality research to this field again; decades ago, humor was an integrated field of inquiry for personality psychology. The picture that psychology draws of man will remain particularly incomplete, if such a genuine human ability like the appreciation of humor remains a missing element.

SUMMARY

Research relating to the construction and validation of the 3 WD Humor Test (Ruch, 1983) is reviewed. A two-modal taxonomy of humor is proposed covering three stimulus factors of incongruity–resolution humor, nonsense humor, and sexual humor, and two response dimensions of funniness and aversiveness. This chapter presents: (a) a review of studies aimed at developing the taxonomy and testing its cross-national stability; (b) psychometric properties of the scales; and (c) an evaluation of the hypotheses regarding the existence and nature of two different humor structures, the significance of the humor content, and the validity of the separation of the funniness and aversiveness aspects in the appreciation of humor based on a review of studies conducted in four nations. In validity estimates, special attention is given to the correlations of the 3 WD scales with measures of conservatism, toughmindedness, sensation seeking, and intolerance of ambiguity. The results demonstrate a close interlocking between appreciation of humor and personality. A potential use of the humor test as a means for the objective assessment of personality traits is discussed. The review of the studies also demonstrates several unresolved issues in the assessment of the appreciation of humor.

ACKNOWLEDGMENT

The author thanks Lambert Deckers for helpful comments on an earlier version of this chapter.

REFERENCES

Accoce, J. (1986). *Humor and personality.* Unpublished masters thesis, Universite Rene Descartes, Paris.

Adorno, T. W., Frenkel-Brunswik, E., Levinson, D. J., & Sanford, R. N. (1950). *The authoritarian personality.* New York: Harper & Row.

Andrews, T. G. (1943). A factorial analysis of responses to the comic as a study in personality. *Journal of General Psychology, 28,* 209–224.

Bariaud, F. (1983). *La genese de l'humour chez l'enfant.* Paris: Presses Universitaires de France.

Breme, F. J. (1976). Humor and its relationship to needs (doctoral dissertation, University of Missouri, 1975). *Dissertation Abstracts International, 37* (4-A), 77, 1981-A.

Brengelmann, J. C., & Brengelmann, L. (1960). German validation of questionnaires assessing dogmatic and intolerant attitudes. *Zeitschrift für experimentelle und angewandte Psychologie, 7,* 451–471.

Busse, P. (1987). *The effects of humor preference and degree of information on behavior in tasks relating to aesthetics, learning, and perception.* Unpublished masters thesis, University of Düsseldorf, FRG.

Carroll, J. L. (1989). Changes in humor appreciation of college students in the last 25 years. *Psychological Reports, 65,* 863–866.

Cattell, R. B., & Luborsky, L. B. (1947). Personality factors in response to humor. *Journal of Abnormal and Social Psychology, 42,* 402–421.

Cattell, R. B., & Tollefson, D. L. (1966). *The handbook for the IPAT humor test of personality.* Champaign, IL: IPAT.

Ciftci, H. (1990). *Empirical study on the effects of migration on attitudes and some selected personality dimensions of Turkish citizens.* Unpublished masters thesis, University of Düsseldorf, FRG.

Cloetta, B. (1983). Questionnaire MK for the assessment of machiavellianism and conservatism. *Schweizerische Zeitschrift für Psychologie und ihre Anwendungen, 42,* 127–159.

Diener, E., & Emmons, R. A. (1984). The independence of positive and negative affect. *Journal of Personality and Social Psychology, 217,* 1103–1117.

Ehrenstein, W. H., & Ertel, S. (1978). On the genesis of the funniness judgment. *Psychologische Beiträge, 20,* 360–374.

Eysenck, H. J. (1942). The appreciation of humour: An experimental and theoretical study. *British Journal of Psychology, 32,* 295–309.

Eysenck, H. J. (1943). An experimental analysis of five tests of "appreciation of humor." *Educational and Psychological Measurement, 3,* 191–214.

Eysenck, H. J. (1954). *The psychology of politics.* London: Routledge & Kegan.

Eysenck, H. J. (1976). *Sex and personality.* London: Open Books.

Eysenck, H. J., & Wilson, G. D. (1978). *The psychological basis of ideology.* College Park: University of Maryland Press.

Frenkel-Brunswik, E. (1949). Intolerance of ambiguity as an emotional and perceptual personality variable. *Journal of Personality, 18,* 108–143.

Freud, S. (1905). *Der Witz und seine beziehung zum unbewußten* [Jokes and its relationship to the unconscious.] Wien: Deuticke.

Furnham, A., & Bunyan, M. (1988). Personality and art preferences. *European Journal of Personality, 2,* 67–74.

Gillies, J., & Campbell, S. (1985). Conservatism and poetry preference. *British Journal of Social Psychology, 24,* 223–227.

Glasgow, M. R., Cartier, A. M., & Wilson, G. D. (1985). Conservatism, sensation-seeking and music preferences. *Personality and Individual Differences, 6,* 395–396.

Hehl, F. J., & Ruch, W. (1985). The location of sense of humor within comprehensive personality spaces: An exploratory study. *Personality and Individual Differences, 6,* 703–715.

Hehl, F. J., & Ruch, W. (1990). Conservatism as a predictor of responses to humour-III. The prediction of appreciation of incongruity–resolution based humour by content saturated attitude scales in five samples. *Personality and Individual Differences, 11,* 439–445.

Herzog, T. R., & Larwin, D. A. (1988). The appreciation of humor in captioned cartoons. *Journal of Psychology, 122,* 597–607.

Jansa, E. (1990). *Stimulus uncertainty and hedonic value: Effects of personality, humor preference, and time pressure on the optimal level of information in abstract patterns.* Unpublished masters thesis, University of Düsseldorf, FRG.

Joachim, U. (1986). *Humor: Investigation of a phenomenon from a personality psychology perspective.* Unpublished masters thesis, University of Bielefeld.

Kischkel, K. H. (1984). A scale to assess tolerance of ambiguity. *Diagnostica, 30,* 144–154.

Korioth, I. (1985). *Analysis of incongruity–resolution humor: Variation of content in dependence of identification classes and sets of attitudes.* Unpublished masters thesis, University of Düsseldorf, FRG.

Litle, P., & Zuckerman, M. (1986). Sensation seeking and music preferences. *Personality and Individual Differences, 7,* 575–577.

McGhee, P. E. (1979). *Humor: Its origin and development.* New York: W. H. Freeman.
McGhee, P. E., Ruch, W., & Hehl, F. J. (1990). A personality-based model of humor development during adulthood. *Humor, 3,* 119–146.
Mones, G. A. (1974). Humor and its relationship to field dependence–independence and open mindedness and closed mindedness. *Dissertation Abstracts International, 35*(9-B), 4657–4658.
Nias, D. K. P. (1981). Humour and personality. In R. Lynn (Ed.), *Dimensions of personality: Papers in honour of H. J. Eysenck* (pp. 287–313). Oxford: Pergamon Press.
Rath, S. (1983). *Similarities and differences in appreciation of humor and the relationships to personality.* Unpublished doctoral dissertation, University of Graz, Austria.
Regul, R. (1987). *Differences in conservatism and humor among psychiatric patients.* Unpublished masters thesis, University of Düsseldorf, FRG.
Rokeach, M. (1982). *Value survey. Form G.* Sunnyvale, CA: Halgren Tests.
Rothbart, M. K., & Pien, D. (1977). Elephants and marshmallows: A theoretical synthesis of incongruity–resolution and arousal theories of humour. In A. J. Chapman & H. C. Foot (Eds.), *It's a funny thing, humour* (pp. 37–40). Oxford: Pergamon Press.
Ruch, W. (1980). *Common structures in appreciation of humor and personality.* Unpublished doctoral dissertation, University of Graz, Austria.
Ruch, W. (1981). Humor and personality: A three-modal analysis. *Zeitschrift für Differentielle und Diagnostische Psychologie, 2,* 253–273.
Ruch, W. (1983). *Humor-Test 3 WD (Form A, B and K).* Unpublished manuscript, University of Düsseldorf, Department of Psychology, Düsseldorf, FRG.
Ruch, W. (1984). Conservatism and the appreciation of humor. *Zeitschrift für Differentielle und Diagnostische Psychologie, 5,* 221–245.
Ruch, W. (1986, September). *The validity of a new model of humour.* Paper presented at the third European Conference on Personality Psychology, Gdansk, Poland.
Ruch, W. (1988). Sensation seeking and the enjoyment of structure and content of humour: Stability of findings across four samples. *Personality and Individual Differences, 9,* 861–871.
Ruch, W. (1990). *The emotion of exhilaration.* Unpublished habilitation thesis, University of Düsseldorf, FRG.
Ruch, W., Accoce, J., Ott, C., & Bariaud, F. (1991). Cross national comparison of sense of humor: France and Germany. *Humor, 4,* 397–474.
Ruch, W., Daum, I., Schugens, M., & Leonard, J. (1984, May). *Individual differences in physiological response patterns during experimentally induced humor situations.* Poster presented at the Second European Conference on Personality, Bielefeld, FRG.
Ruch, W., & Hehl, F. J. (1983a). Intolerance of ambiguity as a factor in the appreciation of humour. *Personality and Individual Differences, 4,* 443–449.
Ruch, W., & Hehl, F. J. (1983b). Common structure in humor and attitudes? In G. Lüer (Hrsg.), *Bericht über den 33. Kongreß der DGfPs in Mainz 1982* (pp. 627–630). Göttingen: Hogrefe.
Ruch, W., & Hehl, F. J. (1984, June). *Personality correlates of sense of humor.* Paper presented at The Fourth International Congress on Humor, Tel Aviv, Israel.
Ruch, W., & Hehl, F. J. (1985). Diagnosis of humor – humor as a diagnostic tool. In F. J. Hehl, V. Ebel, & W. Ruch (Eds.), *Diagnostik psychischer und psychophysiologischer Störungen.* (Vol. 2, pp. 253–325). Bonn: DPV.
Ruch, W., & Hehl, F. J. (1986a). Conservatism as a predictor of responses to humour-I. A comparison of four scales. *Personality and Individual Differences, 7,* 1–14.
Ruch, W., & Hehl, F. J. (1986b). Conservatism as a predictor of responses to humour-II. The location of sense of humour in a comprehensive attitude space. *Personality and Individual Differences, 7,* 861–874.

Ruch, W., & Hehl, F. J. (1987). Personal values as facilitating and inhibiting factors in the appreciation of humor content. *Journal of Social Behaviour and Personality, 2,* 453–472.

Ruch, W., & Hehl, F. J. (1988). Attitudes to sex, sexual behaviour and enjoyment of humour. *Personality and Individual Differences, 9,* 983–994.

Ruch, W., McGhee, P. E., & Hehl, F. J. (1990). Age differences in the enjoyment of incongruity–resolution and nonsense humor during adulthood. *Psychology and Aging, 5,* 348–355.

Ruch, W., Rath, S., & Hehl, F. J. (1988, July). *Smiling/laughter, physiological processes, cognitive evaluation and mood: Is there a "humor response" construct?* Paper presented at the 12th International Congress of Anthropological and Ethnological Sciences, Zagreb, Jugoslawien.

Saper, B. (1984, June). *Some correlations of sense of humor with selected physical and psychological variables.* Paper presented at the Fourth International Congress on Humor, Tel Aviv, Israel.

Schiller, P. von (1938). Configurational theory of puzzles and jokes. *Journal of General Psychology, 18,* 217–234.

Schmiedel, J. (1987). *Different aspects of incongruity in jokes and their relevance in the explanation of humor.* Unpublished masters thesis, University of Düsseldorf, FRG.

Shultz, T. R. (1972). The role of incongruity and resolution in children's appreciation of cartoon humor. *Journal of Experimental Child Psychology, 13,* 456–477.

Suls, J. M. (1972). A two-stage model for the appreciation of jokes and cartoons: An information-processing analysis. In J. H. Goldstein & P. E. McGhee (Eds.), *The psychology of humor* (pp. 81–100). New York: Academic Press.

Unterweger, S. (1983). *The judgment of humor from a diagnostical point of view.* Unpublished doctoral dissertation, University of Graz, Austria.

Watson, D., & Tellegen, A. (1985). Toward a consensual structure of mood. *Psychological Bulletin, 98,* 219–235.

Wilson, Ch. P. (1979). *Jokes: Form, content, use and function. European monographs in social psychology* (Vol. 16). London: Academic Press.

Wilson, G. D. (1973). A dynamic theory of conservatism. In G. D. Wilson (Ed.), *The psychology of conservatism* (pp. 257–266). London: Academic Press.

Wilson, G. D., & Patterson, J. R. (1970). *The conservatism scale.* Windsor, England: NFER.

Yarnold, J. K., & Berkeley, M. H. (1954). An analysis of the Cattell–Luborsky Humor Test into homogeneous scales. *Journal of Abnormal and Social Psychology, 49,* 543–546.

Zuckerman, M. (1979). *Sensation seeking: Beyond the optimal level of arousal.* Hillsdale, NJ: Lawrence Erlbaum Associates.

Zuckerman, M. (1984). Sensation seeking: A comparative approach to a human trait. *Behavioral and Brain Sciences, 7,* 413–471.

3

The Construct of Machiavellianism: Twenty Years Later

Beverley Fehr
University of Winnipeg

Deborah Samsom
Delroy L. Paulhus
University of British Columbia

The rationale for this review of the literature on Machiavellianism from 1971 to 1987 was threefold. First, a comprehensive review of this personality construct has not been undertaken since the publication of *Studies in Machiavellianism* by Christie and Geis (1970). Second, because Christie is currently developing a new measure of Machiavellianism, it seems timely to summarize and evaluate the literature that has accumulated on the current Mach scales. Third, the validity of the construct has been questioned recently.

Three broad domains are discussed. The first section explores the relation of Machiavellianism to major personality dimensions. The goal is to evaluate the coherence of Machiavellianism within a larger nomological network. The second section evaluates the utility of the Mach scales in predicting behavior. The last section focuses on controversies surrounding the reliability and construct validity of the Mach scales.

The concept of Machiavellianism derived from the writings of the 16th-century Italian author, Niccolo Machiavelli. In his treatises, *The Prince* and *The Discourses,* Machiavelli presented his view of people as untrustworthy, self-serving, and malevolent, and advocated that a ruler maintain power in an exploitative and deceitful manner. Some four centuries later, during the 1960s, Richard Christie proposed that the tendency to accept Machiavelli's worldview was a measurable individual-difference variable. An extensive program of construct validation culminated in the publication of the definitive monograph by Christie and Geis (1970).

In that monograph, Christie (1970b) described how three themes in

77

Machiavelli's writings were translated into items on a questionnaire. The first theme was the endorsement of such manipulative tactics as the use of flattery and deceit in interpersonal interactions. The second theme was a cynical view of human nature in which others are regarded as weak, untrustworthy, and self-serving. The third theme was a disregard for conventional morality. Christie also detailed the 10 years of scale development, culminating in the final two versions of the questionnaires (the Mach IV and the Mach V) for use in subsequent research.

Judging by the vast quantity of literature, the concept and measurement of Machiavellianism captured considerable attention among researchers. A bibliography by Hanson (1978) listed 183 references and a later one by Hanson and Vleeming (1982) listed 333 references. The research that accumulated in the 1960s was reviewed by Christie and Geis (1970) and by Geis (1978). A later review, published by Vleeming (1979a), provided an overview of 34 articles that appeared in the psychological literature from 1970 to 1979. However, that article is brief and rather narrow in focus. This chapter is a more comprehensive and up-to-date review of over 150 articles.

This chapter was motivated in part by the publication of critiques of the concept and measurement of Machiavellianism by Hunter, Gerbing, and Boster (1982) and by Ray (1983). They concluded that the multidimensionality of the Mach IV and Mach V scales leaves the entire construct of Machiavellianism open to question. A serious response to these critiques requires a thorough review of what is known to date. The first section of our review is concerned with personality correlates of Machiavellianism. The second section deals with behavioral validation of the construct. In the final section, the focus is on recent controversies over the reliability and construct validity of the Mach scales. In all three sections, the emphasis is on what the recent work adds to our understanding of Machiavellianism as originally reviewed by Christie and Geis (1970).[1] The review culminates with an evaluation of the construct of Machiavellianism in light of our current knowledge. It concludes that Machiavellianism remains a valid construct, despite criticisms leveled against it. However, problems with the relation between theory and measurement, particularly when using the Mach V scale, are noted. It is recommended that interested researchers use the Mach IV scale and score the subfactors (Tactics and Cynicism) separately.

PERSONALITY CORRELATES

A number of researchers have investigated the relation between Machiavellianism and other self-report personality measures (e.g., need for achieve-

---

[1]Some topics (e.g., developmental aspects of Machiavellianism, cross-cultural differences) have not been developed since the 1970 monograph and hence are not addressed here.

ment, locus of control, anxiety, etc.).[2] These studies help clarify the construct by examining how Machiavellianism is embedded in a nomological network. A coherent pattern of relations with other measures would reflect favorably on the construct validity of Machiavellianism. Research on the construct's position in interpersonal space, perceived personality correlates of Machiavellians, and simulations of Machiavellianism are discussed first.

Position in Interpersonal Space

The interpersonal circumplex is the well-established circular pattern of interpersonal measures in two-dimensional space (Leary, 1957; Wiggins, 1979). Showing the Cartesian location of an interpersonal measure provides a method of characterizing the measure in terms of relative amounts of dominance and nurturance. Wiggins and Broughton (1985) showed that the Mach IV scale falls in the second quadrant virtually superpositioned on *calculating*. Paulhus and Martin (1987) found the same pattern.[3] The robustness of this finding is important for two reasons: First, it confirms the fundamental interpersonal nature of Machiavellianism. Second, the location in interpersonal space aptly characterizes the Machiavellian's interpersonal qualities: dominance without nurturance, that is, unmitigated dominance.

Perceived Correlates

Cherulnik, Way, Ames, and Hutto (1981) investigated observers' perceptions of the personality attributes displayed by Machiavellians. Subjects rated videotaped interviews with high and low Mach males. High Machs were perceived as clever, bold, ambitious, dominating, persuasive, relaxed, talented, and confident. Low Machs were described as cowardly, indecisive, gullible, insecure, emotional, and unintelligent. Overall, highs were liked more than lows.

Falbo (1977) had subjects engage in a discussion in groups of three to five same-sex persons. Later, they rated one another in terms of considerateness, honesty, friendliness, expressing oneself well, liking, and whether future interaction was desired. Subjects' Mach V scores were largely uncorrelated with the ratings they received from the other group members, except for a small positive correlation between Machiavellianism and friendliness. The inconsistency between Falbo (1977) and Cherulnik et al.

---

[2]To simplify communication, reported correlation coefficients are referred to as low (below .3), moderate (.3 to .5), or high (above .5).

[3]Paulhus and Martin (1987) also positioned Machiavellianism in capability space: High Machs were found to report equal capabilities for negative and positive behaviors.

(1981) concerning the perceived personality traits of Machiavellians may be attributable to methodological differences between the studies. First, different sets of trait descriptors were used. Second, in the Cherulnik et al. study subjects observed a videotaped interview, whereas in the Falbo study they actually interacted with high and low Machs. Finally, the high and low Machs being rated may have behaved differently in the two studies: An interview might elicit more deliberate impression management, for example, than a casual discussion with one's peers.

Simulations

Skinner, Giokas, and Hornstein (1976) asked individuals to complete a variety of questionnaires as if they were high Machs. Simulating highs scored significantly higher than control subjects on the Ascendance–Dominance, Trust–Suspicion, and Impulsiveness factors of the Howarth Personality Questionnaire (Howarth, 1973), and significantly lower on Superego, Cooperativeness–Considerateness, and Inferiority. These characteristics are consistent with the actual personality correlates of high Machs reported by Christie and Geis (1970).

The Skinner et al. study provides important information about the meaningfulness of this construct to the layperson. Apparently, Machiavellianism is a readily available cognitive category, one that matches the self-reports of high Machs. The category seems to be cognitively equivalent to the trait adjective *calculating* (Wiggins & Broughton, 1985).

Need for Achievement

Early work suggested that the relation between achievement motivation and Machiavellianism was ambiguous. Christie (1970c) described a study of Hungarian refugees by Weinstock (1964) in which a low positive correlation was found between scores on a shortened Mach IV scale and a short achievement scale. He also mentioned the Geis, Weinheimer, and Berger's (1966) study of male college students in which no relationship was found between Mach scores and their achievement measure. Studies using Mehrabian's (1969) achievement scales yielded mixed results. Johnson (1980) obtained positive correlations in two groups of male undergraduates, whereas Smith (1976) obtained a moderate *negative* correlation and a near-zero, positive correlation when his own short scale was used. Finally, Vleeming (1984), in a multiple regression analysis, reported a nonsignificant relation ($R = .15$) between scores on the Mach IV and a Dutch achievement scale.

Other research has investigated the relation between need for achievement and Machiavellianism in specific subject populations. Skinner (1981) reasoned that, because high Machs prefer business-oriented occupations (see section titled Occupational Choice), the correlation would be significantly higher between achievement motivation and Mach scores for business students than for nonbusiness students. Scores on the Mach V and Mehta's (1969) measure of achievement were moderately correlated in a sample of male business students and uncorrelated in nonbusiness students. Okanes and Murray (1980) investigated sex differences in the relation between achievement motivation and Machiavellianism in a business setting. They discovered that females in management positions scored significantly higher than males on the Mehrabian Achievement Scales but found no sex differences in Mach IV scores. Contrary to Skinner (1981), they found a low *negative* correlation between achievement motivation and Machiavellianism. When the correlation was computed for each gender separately, the correlation remained low and negative for females; for males, the measures were uncorrelated.

Finally, Okanes and Murray (1982) investigated cultural differences in the relation between Machiavellianism and need for achievement. They predicted that students from the United States and the Philippines would score significantly higher on Mehrabian's achievement and the Mach IV scales than would students from Arab countries like Algeria and Iran. The Taiwanese were expected to score in the middle range for both measures. The hypotheses were based on a number of cultural differences associated with these countries. Predictions were not supported.

To summarize, Christie's (1970c) assessment still seems applicable to the current picture: "Available evidence does not suggest a strong positive relationship between Machiavellianism and the achievement motive" (p. 44).

Hostility and Self-Reported Aggression

Christie (1970c) described only one study in this area: Wrightsman and Cook (1965) found moderate to high positive correlations between Mach scores and various measures of hostility. Guterman (1970) reported that high Machs were more likely to score high on a measure of outward aggression, which assessed hostile feelings, than middles or lows. Conversely, highs had lower scores on a measure of inward aggression than did the other two groups. Touhey (1971) obtained moderate correlations for males between scores on Guterman's Mach scale and single-item measures of self-reported difficulties with aggression and self-control. For females, the correlation with Mach scores was low for the aggression item and high for the difficulties with self-control item. Finally, Jones, Nickel, and Schmidt (1979) reported that high Mach males were more hostile than lows (as measured by the Multiple Affect Adjective Checklist by Zuckerman & Lubin, 1965).

Thus, Machiavellianism and hostility appear to be related. Christie questioned whether high Machs actually are more hostile than lows, or whether they are simply more willing to admit feelings of hostility. He favored the latter interpretation, given that the highest correlation ($r = .60$) in Wrightsman and Cook's study was between two scales that have both been criticized for social desirability problems: the Mach IV and Siegel's (1962) Hostility scale. Christie's suggestion that high Machs may simply be more forthright in admitting feelings of hostility than lows remains viable. There is little evidence that high Machs are behaviorally more hostile or aggressive than low Machs (see section on Antisocial Behavior).

Locus of Control

Many studies have investigated the relation between Machiavellianism and internal versus external locus of control as measured by Rotter's (1966) I–E scale. Although some of the results are contradictory (e.g., Vleeming, 1984, found no relation between these variables using an abbreviated version of a Dutch locus of control scale), the bulk of the research indicates a positive correlation between Machiavellianism and externality. For example, Christie (1970c) reported that Wrightsman and Cook (1965) found a moderate correlation between Machiavellianism and externality. *Moderate* correlations have been found in other studies using diverse subject groups: undergraduate students (Paulhus, 1983), abnormal, personality and educational psychology students (Solar & Bruehl, 1971), Italian university students (Galli & Nigro, 1983), high school principals (Richford & Fortune, 1984), and MBA students (Biberman, 1985). Prociuk and Breen (1976) obtained a moderate positive correlation between externality and Mach V scores only for men, not for women.

Several other studies found *low* positive correlations between Machiavellianism and externality. In a group of sales managers surveyed by mail, Comer (1985) speculated that the correlation was low because his subjects typically held positions of power within large organizations and therefore would be less external than students. However, correlations of similar magnitude have been reported in studies using other subject groups including university students (Zenker & Wolfgang, 1982, although a moderate correlation was obtained when the correlation was computed for female subjects only; Maroldo et al., 1976, although no relation was found when the correlations were computed for males and females separately), and in a study of American and German students (Maroldo & Flachmeier, 1978). The correlation was also low and positive in male hockey players (Russell, 1974).

Relations with Levenson's (1974) measures of locus of control, the Internal, Powerful Others, and Chance scales, have also been examined. Correlations between Mach scores and the Internal scale are generally low and negative across different groups: American students (Hunter, Gerbing, & Boster, 1982), Italian students (Galli, Nigro, & Krampen, 1986), and German students (Galli et al., 1986, although when the data were analyzed for men only, no relation was found; for women, a moderate, negative correlation was obtained).[4] Levenson and Mahler (1975) reported a high negative correlation between Mach IV scores and the Internal scale for women only.

Correlations between the Mach scales and the Powerful Others scale are moderate and positive in most samples: American students (Hunter et al., 1982), Italian students (Galli et al., 1986), and German students (Galli et al., 1986, although the relation was somewhat weaker for men only). Prociuk and Breen (1976) found a moderate correlation between Mach V scores and the Powerful Others scale only for males. Positive correlations also have been obtained between the Chance scales and Mach scales by Hunter et al. (1982), Galli et al. (1986, although only for Italian, not German, students), and for males by Levenson and Mahler (1975).

Overall, high Machs tend to score in an external direction on measures of locus of control. This holds for Levenson's subscales of externality (Powerful Others and Chance) as well as Rotter's general measure of externality. However, in some studies, the relation holds for only one gender and also may vary depending on the subjects' ethnicity.

The rather consistent finding that high Machs have an external locus of control appears conceptually contradictory in light of the Machiavellian's ability to control and manipulate interpersonal situations. A study by Paulhus (1983) helped resolve this paradox. Paulhus conceived locus of control as domain specific and, accordingly, developed three measures associated with three major spheres of behavior: personal achievement, interpersonal control, and sociopolitical control. He correlated the Mach V scale with each of these subscales and found that the positive relation between Machiavellianism and externality is attributable to the sociopolitical dimension of perceived control. In contrast, the interpersonal component exhibited a *positive* relation between internality and Machiavellianism. (Machiavellianism and personal achievement were uncorrelated.) These results are quite consistent with Christie and Geis' (1970) portrayal of the Machiavellian character. This individual is cynical about political control and, hence, scores low on the sociopolitical control measure. However, the

---

[4]Correlations corrected for attenuation were also reported by Hunter et al. (1982). In this chapter, we report the unattenuated correlations because they are most comparable to those given in other studies (i.e., the other studies we reviewed did not correct for attenuation).

high Mach does expect to be in control when dealing with other people and, consequently, scores high on the interpersonal measure.

Dogmatism–Authoritarianism

Christie (1970c) discussed the relation between authoritarianism and Machiavellianism, noting that in 1955 and 1956 no relation had been found, but in a 1964 study, Mach IV scores correlated −.20 with authoritarianism. He suggested that an unflattering view of people is common to authoritarianism and Machiavellianism. Although Christie never tested this prediction, it should be noted that in one of his factor analyses (Christie & Lehmann, 1970) both F scale and Mach items were included. Items from both scales loaded on one of the factors; Interestingly, the Mach items were mainly those that refer to a cynical view of others.

According to Steininger and Eisenberg (1976), Rokeach's dogmatism scale can be taken as a measure of authoritarianism. They investigated the relation between Machiavellianism and dogmatism using the Kiddie Mach and their short dogmatism scale (which correlates .9 with Rokeach's scale). Total scores on the two scales were moderately correlated for females; for males the correlation was low. Based on Christie's speculation that an unflattering view of people is common to both constructs, they expected that the highest correlations would be found with the views component of Machiavellianism and the Derogation and Aloneness factor of their dogmatism scale. Results supported predictions, although for males these correlations were moderate, not high; for females they were moderate to high (depending on whether positively or negatively worded views items were used). Similarly, Hunter et al. (1982) predicted that their cynicism component of Machiavellianism would be more highly correlated with dogmatism (Troldahl & Powell, 1965) than the total Mach score. The correlation between cynicism and dogmatism was moderate; the correlation using the total Mach score was low. Vleeming (1984), in a multiple regression analysis, found a significant relation between Mach IV scores and a Dutch authoritarianism scale, which was attributable largely to two of his four Mach clusters: flattery and cynicism.

Finally, in a series of factor analytic studies, Kline and Cooper (1983, 1984a) and Cooper, Kline, and May (1986) failed to find significant relationships between any Mach components and scores on Kohn's (1972) authoritarianism measure. The findings using Ray's (1974) dogmatism scale were inconsistent: Negative relations with the Mach components were found in some analyses; other analyses showed no relation. Ray (1979) also found no relation between Mach IV scores and his authoritarianism scale.

Overall, the pattern of findings with regard to both dogmatism and authoritarianism tends to support Christie's original authoritarianism predictions. Total Mach scores are not very highly correlated with these measures. However, there is a significant association between the views component of Machiavellianism and dogmatism/authoritarianism.

Cognitive Style

Christie and Geis (1970) concluded that low Machs are more interpersonally involved and more sensitive to the emotions, needs, and intentions of others than are highs. Therefore, Delia and O'Keefe (1976) hypothesized that low Machs would score higher on interpersonal cognitive complexity (measured with the Role Category Questionnaire; Crockett, 1965) than would highs, given that individuals who are very involved with others develop more complex systems of interpersonal constructs to represent and interpret the actions of others. Subjects described a liked and a disliked peer. The total number of constructs produced in the descriptions constituted the measure of cognitive complexity. They found moderate to high negative correlations between Mach IV scores and number of constructs generated. In a second study, the constructs were classified as psychological or not psychological. There was a moderate negative correlation between Mach scores and the tendency to discriminate among others along psychological dimensions. Thus, low Machs seem to have a more elaborated, more extensive, system of interpersonal constructs than do highs. Unfortunately, when Sypher, Nightingale, Vielhaber, and Sypher (1981) replicated Delia and O'Keefe's first study, they found no relation between Mach IV scores and Crockett's RCQ in two groups of students.

Maroldo et al. (1976) found no relation between a modified Mach IV and cognitive style as measured by the Object Sorting Test Form (Clayton & Jackson, 1961). Maroldo and Flachmaier (1978) replicated the study. They obtained a low *positive* correlation in an American sample, and a low *negative* correlation in a German sample. In sum, the research on the cognitive style of Machiavellians is unimpressive. The few existing studies report generally weak results and tend not to be replicable.

Self-Monitoring

According to Ickes, Reidhead, and Patterson (1986), one would expect a positive correlation between self-monitoring and Machiavellianism because both involve the use of impression management. However, both Snyder (1974) and Barnes and Ickes (1979) failed to find a relation between these constructs, and Ickes et al. (1986) obtained only a low positive correlation between the Mach V and Snyder's (1974) Self-Monitoring scale. Bell, McGhee, and Duffey (1986) also found low positive correlations between self-monitoring and Kiddie Mach scores. In explaining the lack of strong association between these variables, Ickes et al. posited that although high Machs and high self-monitors use impression management strategies they use these strategies in different ways and for different reasons. They predicted and found that Machiavellianism was associated with a focus on self during social interactions, whereas self-monitoring was associated with a focus on the interaction partner.

Psychopathology

According to Christie (1970a), one of the characteristics of high Machs is a "gross lack of psychopathology" (p. 3). Nevertheless, researchers have continued to explore whether any relation between Machiavellianism and various forms of psychopathology might exist. With regard to the global categories of neuroticism and psychoticism, Kline and Cooper (1983, 1984a) and Cooper, Kline, and May (1986) consistently found that the components of Machiavellianism and Psychoticism as measured by the Eysenck Personality Inventory were positively associated, whereas Machiavellianism and Neuroticism were unrelated. Skinner (1982b) administered the EPI to 346 male subjects. The 32 subjects classified as high Machs did not differ significantly from the remaining 314 subjects in terms of Psychoticism or Neuroticism. The lack of relationship with Psychoticism may have been due to the high criterion for designating high Machs. At any rate, the meaning of such correlations awaits clarification of the Psychoticism scale (Howarth, 1986).

Psychopathy. Of all forms of psychopathology, the concept of psychopathy bears the strongest resemblance to Machiavellianism: Both portray a character low in emotionality and prone to underhanded behavior. This resemblance is supported empirically, at least for males. Ray and Ray (1982) found a moderate correlation between scores on the Mach IV and the MMPI Psychopathic Deviant scale in a group of Australian voters (most of whom were male). Smith and Griffith (1978) reported a low correlation between these measures in a group of students, most of whom were male. In Skinner's (1982b) study, high Mach males scored significantly higher than low Mach males on the Psychopathic Deviate scale.

The most exciting development has been a clarification at the factor level. Harpur and his associates (Harpur, Hakstian, & Hare, 1988; Harpur, Hare, & Hakstian, 1989) have factored the Psychopathy Checklist (PCL) and its revision (PCL-R; Hare, 1991) to yield two factors: The first involves a callous lack of empathy in one's view and treatment of others; the second describes a widespread pattern of antisocial behavior. Factor 1 is clearly the Machiavellian syndrome including both views and tactics. To examine this link directly, the Mach IV and the PCL were administered to a sample of

100 prison inmates. The correlations of Mach IV with PCL Factors 1 and 2 were significantly different, .29 and .15, respectively (Hare, 1991). This differential linkage has important implications: It appears that psychopaths simply may be high Machs who have run up against the law.

Anxiety.   Christie (1970c) reported a study (Christie & Budnitsky, 1957) of four classes of medical school students in which moderate positive correlations were found between the Mach IV and Heineman's (1953) version of the Taylor Anxiety Scale. Later, when the same classes were tested with the Mach V (which does not correlate with external measures of social desirability), the correlations were considerably lower, ranging from − .01 to .21. Christie concluded that the original correlations between Machiavellianism and anxiety were attributable to social desirability problems with the Mach IV. However, Jones, Nickel, and Schmidt (1979) administered the Mach V and the Multiple Affect Adjective Checklist to a group of male students and found that high Machs scored significantly higher on anxiety than did lows.

Similarly, when Nigro and Galli (1985) had Italian undergraduates complete the Mach IV and the Spielberger, Gorsuch, and Lushene (1970) State–Trait Anxiety Inventory, they found positive correlations between Machiavellianism and both state and trait anxiety. Poderico (1987) replicated the Nigro and Galli study with children, using an Italian translation of the Kiddie Mach Scale and an Italian Children's Anxiety Scale that measured school and environmental anxiety. Low positive correlations were obtained between Machiavellianism and both kinds of anxiety. Overall, the relation between Machiavellianism and anxiety is quite replicable.

Depression.   LaTorre and McLeoad (1978) examined the relation between scores on Guterman's Machiavellianism scale and clinical depression in a geriatric sample and found that suicidally depressed males were significantly less Machiavellian than nondepressed males. Depressed and nondepressed females did not differ statistically in Machiavellianism, although depressed females tended to be *more* Machiavellian. The authors interpret this trend in light of the finding that attempted suicides by females are often for manipulative, rather than for destructive, purposes. Skinner (1982b) found no difference between the scores of high and low Mach males on the IPAT Depression Scale. Thus, Machiavellianism and depression seem to be largely unrelated.

To summarize, the clearest finding concerning the relation between psychopathology and Machiavellianism is the positive association between Machiavellianism and psychopathy. In fact, very recent work suggests that a convergence between the bodies of research on Machiavellianism and psychopathy may not be far off. There is evidence of some relation between anxiety and Machiavellianism. This combination of correlates represents an ostensible paradox—how can high Machs be both psychopathic and anxious? After all, aren't psychopaths free of anxiety? Recent research by Hare and his colleagues among others refutes this stereotype: Although psychopaths may not experience anxiety while exploiting others, their trait levels of anxiety are high. Thus, it is not surprising that high Machs, in turn, suffer from anxiety. Perhaps, as Nigro and Galli (1985) suggested, the anxiety of the high Mach reflects not psychopathology as much as the high Mach's vigilance in seeking out opportunities to be manipulative. As noted earlier, the high Mach's interpersonal motive is pure dominance unmitigated by nurturance. This tendency to see social interactions as a struggle for supremacy may put the high Mach in a perpetual state of unease.

Overview of Personality Correlates

The accumulated body of research on personality correlates has fleshed out a nomological network that is generally consistent with that presented by Christie and Geis (1970). At the same time, some clarifications have emerged. Rather than actively hostile, the high Mach strives for dominance unmitigated by nurturance. The high Mach has a strong perception of control in the interpersonal (but not sociopolitical) realm. Although total Mach scores are not strongly correlated with authoritarianism–dogmatism, there is a positive relation with the cynicism component of Machiavellianism. Machiavellianism also emerges as a central component in the Psychopath Checklist. On the other hand, high Machs seem not to differ from lows in terms of achievement motivation, self-monitoring, cognitive style, or depression.

BEHAVIORAL VALIDATION

Behavioral differences between high and low Machs are most likely to be observed in situations where there is latitude for improvisation, face-to-face contact, and when the affect evoked in the situation (e.g., becoming interpersonally involved with one's interaction partner) is irrelevant to performance. After reviewing the research conducted from 1959 to 1969, Geis and Christie (1970) concluded that, when these situational factors are present, "high Machs manipulate more, win more, are persuaded less, persuade others more and otherwise differ significantly from low Machs" (p. 312). These three situational factors continue to be important determinants of behavioral differences between high and low Machs (see following sections). Comparisons across these situational factors assume that subjects are equally motivated to reach the particular goal: garnering money, scoring high on a test, or impressing people. The research reported in this section includes laboratory studies as well as real-world studies.

Unethical Behavior

Unethical decision behavior was studied by Hegarty and Sims (1978) in a role-play business context. Business graduate students were required to make a series of decisions on whether to stop the payment of kickbacks to purchasing agents and run the risk of losing profits (vs. condoning this unethical practice). As predicted, Machiavellianism was associated with advocating the payment of kickbacks. In follow-up studies, they varied factors such as the size of the kickback and the ethics policy held by the corporation (Hegarty & Sims, 1979). Again, Machiavellianism was positively associated with unethical behavior.

Other studies have examined the extent to which Machiavellians engage in unethical practices such as cheating, stealing, and lying.

Cheating.   Overall, high Machs do not seem to cheat more than low Machs. For example, Dien and Fujisawa (1979) found that scores of 11-year-olds on a Japanese version of the Kiddie Mach did not predict whether the children had cheated in an earlier experiment (when the children were 4 years of age). Instead, situational factors seem to determine whether high and low Machs will cheat. Bogart, Geis, Levy, and Zimbardo (1970) found that high Machs were more likely to cheat in situations where there was a low probability of getting caught; lows were more likely to cheat if the situation was interpersonally involving (e.g., cheating in order to comply with a partner). Similarly, Cooper and Peterson (1980) found that high Machs were more likely to cheat when working alone on a task (where the chance of detection was minimal); lows were more likely to cheat when in competition with another person, presumably because they became emotionally involved in this interpersonal situation.

Stealing.   Similar situational factors seemed to operate in Harrell and Hartnagel's (1976) study of Machiavellianism and stealing. They found that low Machs' behavior depended on affective interpersonal factors like whether or not their supervisor trusted them — they stole from a distrustful, but not a trusting, supervisor. High Machs stole from both kinds of supervisors.

Lying.   An early study (Exline, Thibaut, Hickey, & Gumbert, 1970) indicated that, of the subjects who chose to lie, high Machs were more successful at doing so than lows. However, this was not the case in five of seven studies summarized by Geis and Christie (1970). Subsequent research has tried to elucidate whether high Machs lie more convincingly than lows. Geis and Moon (1981) videotaped subjects who denied knowledge of a theft. Half the subjects had been directly implicated in the theft; the other half made a truthful denial. As predicted, high Machs who were lying were believed more often by naive viewers than low Machs. In fact, the viewers were unable to discriminate between lying and truthful high Machs. (High and low Machs did not differ in their ability to convince others when they were telling the truth.) In a similar study, DePaulo and Rosenthal (1979) videotaped high and low Machs who described someone they disliked, whereas pretending to like that person, and vice versa. The main effect for Machiavellianism only approached significance, but there was a significant interaction: High Machs were particularly successful deceivers in the condition where they feigned disliking someone whom they actually liked.

Thus, high Machs seem to be more believable liars than low Machs. Janisse and Bradley (1980) predicted that the ability of high Machs to lie might extend to control over autonomic reactivity, namely pupillary responses. However, high and low Machs experienced a similar change in pupil size during deception. Bradley and Klohn (1987) further explored whether highs and lows differed in their physiological responses in a study where subjects did or did not commit a mock crime. Galvanic skin response and pulse rate were recorded during a subsequent interrogation concerning the crime. Contrary to expectations, guilty high Machs scored higher than guilty lows on the physiological measures while lying.

In summary, whereas there is some evidence that high Machs are more unethical than lows, generally, situational factors such as the degree of affective involvement in the situation determine whether high or low Machs are more likely to engage in unethical behavior. A recent correlational study by Leary, Knight, and Barnes (1986) is relevant to the issue of the situational specificity of Machiavellian unethical behavior. Scores on the Mach V scale and the Ethics Position Questionnaire (Forsyth, 1980) were correlated. They found a low positive correlation between Machiavellianism and Relativism, suggesting that "high Machs disavow the possibility of formulating absolute, cross-situational moral rules" (p. 78). The correlation with Idealism was moderate and negative, leading to the conclusion that "a pragmatic, nonidealistic ethical orientation is more fundamental to Machiavellianism than the degree to which one's ethical views are relative or absolute" (p. 78).

Other Forms of Manipulation

Falbo (1977) found that high Machs reported using strategies such as conscious manipulation of one's facial expressions, manipulation of others' emotions, making others think that what you want them to do is their own idea, deceit, and hinting when trying to convince others. Middle Machs were more likely to report using persuasion and threat, whereas low Machs reported using simple statements, persistence, and assertion. Falbo concluded that Machiavellians spontaneously report using the kinds of strategies that Christie and Geis (1970) claim are effective for them. Apart from the *unethical* tactics (covered in the previous section), behavioral evidence is available on ethical strategies commonly employed by high Machs: persuasion, self-disclosure, and ingratiation.

Persuasion. The high Mach's persuasive ability was explored by Sheppard and Vidmar (1980) in a mock courtroom situation. High and low Mach subjects acted as lawyers. When subjects who had witnessed a videotaped crime scene were interviewed by the high Mach lawyers, their testimony was biased in the direction desired by the lawyer. Moreover, subjects acting as judges allocated a smaller percentage of the blame to the high Mach's client than to the low Mach's client, based on the testimony of the witnesses.

Several studies have found that high Machs are particularly adept at persuading others in bargaining situations. Huber and Neale (1986) assigned business students the role of buyer or seller. Buyers and sellers negotiated with one another until they reached an agreement. Mach V scores correlated .28 with profits. In Geis' (1970a, 1970b) Con Game study, where players could make and break coalitions with other players to maximize their own winnings, Mach scores correlated .71 with total number of points won. Highs were particularly successful in the ambiguous bargaining condition that provided them with greater latitude for improvisation.

The role of a different situational factor, emotional involvement, was explored in the legislature game study (Geis, Weinheimer, & Berger, 1970). Male students acted as congressmen who had to convince each other to vote for or against various issues. When the issues were trivial, there was no difference between the number of points won (votes obtained in one's favor) by high and low Machs. However, when emotionally involving issues were used, highs won significantly more points. (Rosenthal, 1978, failed to replicate these results when he had female subjects play this game.)

Fry (1985) was struck by Christie and Geis' repeated demonstrations that low Machs typically fare poorly when negotiating face to face with highs, presumably because of lows' greater susceptibility to emotional arousal. He reasoned that a visual barrier between bargainers might reduce arousal in lows, thereby enabling them to bargain more effectively. Consistent with predictions, when a visual barrier was present, high–low, high–high and low–low Mach pairs of male subjects were equally effective bargainers. However, in a face-to-face bargaining condition, the joint outcomes of high–low Mach pairs were significantly lower than those of the other pairs, due to the ineffective performance of the low Mach partner. (Interestingly, the performance of low Machs was not hampered when bargaining face to face with another low Mach.)

Finally, Burgoon, Lombardi, Burch, and Shelby (1979) were interested in the kind of information that Machiavellians would find most persuasive. They hypothesized that high Machs would be susceptible to authority-based influence attempts because such sources could supply them with valid and persuasive information that could be used later to persuade someone else. Subjects read a message advocating tuition increases attributed to either a fellow student or an economics expert on the university's Board of Regents. Low Machs were more influenced by appeals from a peer, whereas high Machs shifted their attitudes to conform with those of the authority figure. (Falbo, 1977, however, did not find that low Machs conformed more than highs to peers' opinions in an Asch-type paradigm. However, his conformity task entailed rating funniness of cartoons, which may not have been as emotionally involving to university students as raising tuition fees.)

Self-Disclosure.   Strategic self-disclosure is another manipulative tactic that high Machs may have at their disposal. In a series of studies, Jones, Nickel, and Schmidt (1979) found that high Mach males were less disclosing to a hypothetical partner than lows when expecting to engage in a competitive task with him.

Gender differences were explored by Domelsmith and Dietch (1978), who administered the Mach V and the Dietch Self-Disclosure Inventory (Dietch & House, 1975) to undergraduates. For males, Machiavellianism was moderately correlated with *unwillingness* to disclose, whereas for females, Machiavellianism was moderately correlated with *willingness* to disclose. The authors speculate that given the constraints of sex-role stereotyping, self-disclosure may be a socially appropriate channel of manipulation for women, but not for men. Similar results were obtained by Brown and Guy (1983) when they replicated this study with different measures.

Both of these studies were criticized by Dingler-Duhon and Brown (1987) for using trait, rather than behavioral, measures of self-disclosure. They had subjects write a dialogue in which they solicited donations for the Cancer Society (influence strategy condition). In the affiliative condition, subjects wrote a description of themselves that they believed would be shown to their partner in the next part of the experiment. The descriptions were scored according to degree of self-disclosure. In the influence condition, high Mach males were more self-disclosing than low Mach males, whereas both high and low Mach females used intermediate levels of disclosure. In the affiliative condition, there was a trend for low Mach males to be more self-disclosing than highs; for females, the trend was in the opposite direction. The authors comment that, although it may not be socially appropriate for males to admit using self-disclosure as an influence strategy, high Mach males nevertheless are quite willing to use it.

Ingratiation. Pandey and Rastogi (1979) predicted that high Machs would be more ingratiating in a competitive situation than would lows. Male students at the Indian Institute of Technology read a scenario in which they were being interviewed for a job. High Machs endorsed the use of ingratiation tactics more than lows in both the competitive (more applicants than jobs) and noncompetitive (more jobs than applicants) conditions.

In a related study, Pandey (1981) conjectured that established organizations would present fewer opportunities for ingratiation than would recently established organizations, because new organizations tend to lack structure. High Machs were expected to capitalize on the latitude for improvisation provided by the lack of structure. Subjects imagined working in either type of organization. The results were largely nonsignificant, although there was a tendency for high Machs to endorse the use of ingratiation regardless of type of organization.

To summarize, high Machs endorse the use of certain manipulative tactics that are not blatantly unethical. Moreover, they appear to be better at some of these forms of manipulation, such as persuasion. However, whether or not they choose to utilize these abilities depends to some extent on the situation. For example, high Machs disclose more than lows only if it is to their advantage to do so. In a competitive situation, for instance, high Mach males reveal little about themselves. Surprisingly, the degree of competitiveness seems to have little impact on whether Machiavellians favor the use of ingratiation tactics: There is a tendency for highs to endorse the use of ingratiation regardless of the situation.

Leadership

All the research on leadership has postdated Christie and Geis (1970). The leadership capabilities of high Machs typically have been examined in an unstructured situation where the dependent measure is who emerges as leader and takes the initiative in controlling and structuring group interaction. Gleason, Seaman, and Hollander (1978) predicted that in a situation of high task structure where there was little ambiguity and little opportunity for manipulation, low Machs would exhibit more leadership behaviors than high Machs and would be perceived as leaders by group members. Male subjects participated in either a structured or unstructured model-building task. Contrary to expectations, middle Machs emerged as the preferred leaders in both conditions.

Rather than study emergent leadership, Drory and Gluskinos (1980) examined differences in behavior and performance of all male, task-oriented groups led by either high or low Machs. They were surprised to discover that the Machiavellianism of the leader had no effect on group productivity nor on group members' perceptions of their leader. Data from observers revealed that high Mach leaders gave more orders and initiated more of the group interaction than did lows. They also engaged in significantly less tension-reducing behavior in the group and were less caught up in arguments and suggestions. Finally, high Mach leaders demonstrated remarkable flexibility in responding to the situational demands of the task, whereas the behavior of low Mach leaders remained relatively invariant.

These studies suggest that, in general, Machiavellianism does not predict the emergence of group leadership, nor the effectiveness of a leader. However, a couple of points are worth noting. First, in both of these studies, leadership ratings were made exclusively (Drory & Gluskinos) or predominantly (Gleason et al.) by middle Machs. Perhaps middle Machs prefer a leader who is similar to themselves (and therefore did not favor either the high or the low Mach leader in the Drory and Gluskinos study and chose a middle Mach in the Gleason et al. study). Future research should examine the interaction between the Machiavellianism of the group members and the Machiavellianism of the leader in predicting who is preferred and most effective as group leader.

Prosocial and Antisocial Behavior

With regard to antisocial behavior, Geis and Christie (1970) commented that "In no instance that we can recall have high Machs appeared behaviorally hostile, vicious, or punitive toward others" (p. 306). They explained that high Machs "are adept at getting what they want from others without overt hostility" (p. 307). Research conducted since then provides a more detailed picture.

Russell (1974) correlated Mach V scores of ice-hockey players with various naturalistic measures of aggression. He obtained low positive correlations between Mach scores and total penalty time, penalties for physical aggression against other players, and penalties for challenging game officials. Machiavellianism and performance (number of goals, assists) were uncorrelated.

Harrell (1980) had subjects work on a task with a confederate who began stealing money from them. When confronted by the experimenter, the confederate was either remorseful or not. In the next phase, subjects delivered a burst of noise to the confederate whenever she made an error on a problem-solving task. Low Machs were much more aggressive (gave significantly longer bursts of noise) to the nonremorseful confederate than to the remorseful confederate. High Machs were equally aggressive in both conditions. Thus, again, an emotional–interpersonal issue, like the remorsefulness of the confederate, dramatically affected the behavior of low Machs, but not highs.

Finally, Kerr and Gross (1978) hypothesized that because high Machs expect exploitation and selfish behavior to occur in social interactions, they might be prone to identifying with an aggressor. However, their hypothesis that high Machs would identify with a confederate who tormented them was not supported. Although high Machs may admire an exploitive leader in the abstract, they do not enjoy being victims.

Looking at prosocial behavior, Wolfson (1981) examined differences between high and low Machs in three conditions: working on a task with two other same-Mach subjects (face-to-face condition), working on the task individually but in the presence of two other same-Mach subjects (back-to-back condition), and working alone. An accident was staged in the hallway. When working alone, 92% of the highs and 92% of the lows responded to the accident. In the back-to-back condition, more lows than highs helped (100% vs. 75%). In the face-to-face condition, only 33% of the high Machs helped compared to 75% of the lows. In explaining this result, Wolfson suggests that "the high Machs' more aloof interpersonal responses possibly led to a state of mutual inhibition in which each subject's apparent calm decreased the others' helping behavior" (p. 193).

The results of the studies on aggression and helping are consistent with other research findings, suggesting that high Machs are emotionally detached and task oriented, whereas lows attend more to people than to the task at hand. Thus, it is the latter who respond with pro or antisocial behavior commensurate with the situationally induced affect. The one study showing more aggression among high Machs (Russell, 1974) occurred in a team sport where aggression is an *instrumental* activity.

Occupational Choice, Success, and Satisfaction

A large number of studies have examined the relation between Machiavellianism and occupational preferences, success, and satisfaction with one's occupation.

Occupational Choice.   A stereotyped view of the high Mach suggests that he or she would prefer a business career. Consistent with the stereotype, subjects faking Machiavellianism prefer business-related occupations whereas helping professions are least preferred (Skinner et al., 1976). Research on actual career choices points to the same conclusion. For example, Wertheim, Widom, and Wortzel (1978) found that law and management students had the highest Mach scores, followed by education students. Social work students had the lowest scores. Steininger and Eisenberg (1976) found that business students scored higher on Machiavellianism than did English and Sociology students. Chonko (1982) also reported that purchasing managers were more Machiavellian than other groups in the literature.

However, in a subsequent study in which over 1,000 members of the American Marketing Association were surveyed, Hunt and Chonko (1984) found that those who majored in business administration were *not* more Machiavellian than those who majored in other areas (e.g., social sciences). Moreover, contrary to predictions, marketers in sales and advertising positions were not more Machiavellian than marketers in staff and research positions. They concluded that marketers are no more Machiavellian than the rest of North American society.

Skinner et al.'s subjects assumed that high Machs would shy away from helping professions. However, Christie and Geis (1970) reported that medical students who declared psychiatry as their speciality were *more* Machiavellian than those who declared other specialties. This finding prompted Abramson (1973) to administer the Mach V to counseling graduate students ($N = 18$) and graduate students in educational or experimental psychology ($N = 12$). The groups did not differ in their total Mach scores. However, counseling students scored higher when the comparison was made using five tactics items. Videotaped counseling sessions (available for 10 of the counseling students) were rated in terms of counselor effectiveness (e.g., empathy, respect). All correlations between the indices of counselor effectiveness and Mach V scores were negative and remained so when only five tactics items were used. Abramson concluded that, although high Machs may be drawn to counseling because face-to-face interaction and latitude for improvisation are involved, they are not likely to be effective.

Abramson's study was criticized by Zook and Sipps (1987) on methodological grounds. They replicated the study using subjects from a variety of universities, larger sample sizes, and the Mach IV. Contrary to Abramson, they found that counseling students were significantly *less* Machiavellian than experimental psychology graduate students.

To summarize, the research on the occupational choices of Machiavellians is largely consistent with what Skinner et al.'s simulating subjects surmised. Individuals with a Machiavellian orientation seem to prefer business-related careers. (Whereas the Hunt and Chonko study does not support this conclusion, remember that the subjects who had not majored in business nevertheless were working in a business setting, which could account for why they were as Machiavellian as the business majors.) High Machs tend not to choose helping professions, although as Zook and Sipps pointed out, the *kind* of helping profession studied may make a difference: Psychiatrists may be more Machiavellian than counselors or social workers.

Occupational Success. Are Machiavellians successful in their chosen professions? Christie (1970c) was surprised when a national survey revealed that high Machs did not have more prestigious jobs or higher incomes than low Machs. Similarly, Turnbull (1976) found no relation between Machiavellianism and success measured by sales productivity. Touhey (1973) also failed to find an overall relation between Machiavellianism and social mobility (assessed as the discrepancy between one's father's and one's own socioeconomic status) in a sample of men from a variety of occupational settings. However, when subjects' IQ scores were taken into account, greatest social mobility was found for the high Mach–high IQ group; lowest mobility was found in the high Mach–low IQ group. Based on this finding, Turner and Martinez (1977) reexamined Christie's survey data and found that education had a similar moderating effect. For men with above-average education, there was a significant positive relation between Machiavellianism and occupational attainment (salary, job prestige); for men with below-average education, a significant negative relation was found. For women, Machiavellianism and occupational status were positively correlated. (Note, however, that only 26% of the female subjects held positions that were classifiable in terms of occupational status.)

Hunt and Chonko (1984) expected to replicate the Turner and Martinez positive relation between Machiavellianism and occupational success in a highly educated group of marketers. They obtained a correlation of −.15 between Mach scores and income, which was spurious because Machiavellianism no longer predicted income when age, gender, and education level were entered into a regression analysis as control variables. The same pattern of findings was obtained when job title, rather than income, was used as the measure of occupational success.

Similarly, Gemmill and Heisler (1972) found no relation between Machiavellianism and two indices of social mobility (management level, number of positions held) in a group of managers. These relations remained nonsignificant when partial correlations were computed holding education and number of years in career constant. In a related study, Heisler and Gemmill (1977) reported small negative and positive correlations between Mach scores and social mobility (number of positions held) in two groups of managers. Correlations between salary and Mach scores were small to moderate and negative.

One of the earliest papers on Machiavellianism examined the relation between Mach scores and academic success. Singer (1964) conducted a number of studies and found low to moderate correlations between Mach V scores and GPA. The correlations were lower for women than for men, leading Singer to speculate that it may be not be socially acceptable for women to use direct manipulation to obtain good grades; instead, women might use "strategies of attractiveness and appearance rather than deceit and management" (p. 140). Ames and Kidd (1979) suggested that the weak relation between women's GPA and Mach V scores in Singer's studies might best be accounted for in terms of gender-role orientation rather than gender per se. Based on the fear of success literature, they suggested that feminine-typed women might "manipulate to prevent themselves from appearing overly successful academically" (p. 224). They expected and found no overall relation between Mach scores and GPA. For feminine-typed women (as measured by the Bem Sex Role Inventory), the correlation was −.64; for masculine-typed women, the correlation was .61. The authors acknowledge that there are many possible interpretations for these findings. For example, it is unclear whether feminine Machiavellian women are using manipulation to reduce their grades or are simply rejecting the use of manipulative tactics. The data do suggest that masculine-typed Machiavellian women may be willing to use manipulation to get good grades.

Obtaining good grades may be a primary goal for high Machs in academic settings. Kauffman, Chupp, Hershberger, Martin, and Eastman (1987) correlated Mach scores with Eison's LOGO. They obtained a correlation of .43 with GO (Grade Orientation—being primarily interested in obtaining a good grade) and .13 with LO (Learning Orientation—viewing education as an opportunity to acquire knowledge and enlightenment).

Finally, in a study of athletic success, Paulhus, Molin, and Schuchts (1979) found that, for university tennis and football players, success in their sport was moderately correlated with the tactics component of Machiavellianism.

Overall, Machiavellianism and occupational success appear to be unrelated. Early studies suggested that these variables were positively associated in highly educated or intelligent groups. However, more recent studies have tended not to support this conclusion. There is evidence of some relation between Machiavellianism and success in academic settings. However, this relation seems to hold only for men or masculine-typed women.

Job Satisfaction. The relation between job satisfaction and Machiavellianism has also been investigated. Three studies of business managers have been published (Gemmill & Heisler, 1972; Heisler & Gemmill, 1977; Hollon, 1983), all of which indicate that Machiavellianism is negatively related to job satisfaction and positively correlated with job tension. Biberman (1985) found no relation between Mach scores and satisfaction in a sample of MBA students, many of whom held management positions. However, satisfaction was assessed by only a single self-report item.

Richford and Fortune (1984) reported a low negative correlation between Mach scores and job satisfaction in a group of high school principals.

In a sample of marketers, Hunt and Chonko (1984) found negative associations between Mach scores and each of their seven measures of job satisfaction, even when income, age, gender, and education were entered into the regression as control variables. In fact, Machiavellianism was the best predictor of satisfaction in marketing. Gable and Topol (1987) replicated the Hunt and Chonko study using department store executives as subjects. They found moderate negative correlations between Mach scores and satisfaction for both men and women.

The reasons why Machiavellianism and job satisfaction are negatively correlated remain unclear. In the Hollon (1983) study, Machiavellianism was negatively related not only to job satisfaction but also to perceived participation in decision making, job involvement, and positively related to role ambiguity. Hollon commented: "whether dissatisfied, non-job-involved, stressed, managers, who have perceived ambiguity in their roles and low participation in decision making become Machiavellian or managerial Machiavellianism leads to such work attitudes and perceptions constitutes an unresolved issue" (p. 434).

In the Gemmill and Heisler (1972) study, a number of other measures was included (e.g., perceived opportunity for formal control, social mobility, etc.). Because the variables were interrelated, they did partial correlations between pairs of variables, holding the others constant. Only the relation between Mach scores and perceived opportunity for control remained significant, $r = -.31$. They suggest that the relation between Machiavellianism and job satisfaction and job strain may be due to their relation with perceived control, or from their mutual association with some other variable.

The finding that only the negative relation between Mach scores and perceived control remained significant may be understood in light of Paulhus' (1983) work differentiating the personal, interpersonal, and sociopolitical spheres of control. In most of the studies on job satisfaction, subjects have been managers in a business setting and thus may be operating largely in the sociopolitical, rather than the interpersonal, sphere of control.[5] As mentioned earlier, Machiavellianism is negatively correlated with sociopolitical control, which means that high Machs tend to agree with items like "When I look at it carefully, I realize it is impossible to have any really important influence over what big businesses do." Thus, it is possible that when high Machs become managers they find themselves operating in

---

[5]Even in the Hunt and Chonko study of marketers, the majority held management positions. In Richford and Fortune's study, subjects were high school principals, which could be considered a management position.

an arena in which they expect little control. The result could well be dissatisfaction.[6] Alternatively, the dissatisfaction might simply ensue from the elevated anxiety of high Machs (reviewed in the previous section).

Overview of Behavioral Validation

The construct validity of the Mach scales is strongly supported by the laboratory and real-world evidence. Christie and Geis' (1970) claim that high scores on the Mach scales predict duplicitous behavior has been sustained by the more recent evidence. None of the findings conflict with the original conceptualization of the construct. As noted earlier, however, complex research results have necessitated certain qualifications to this general rule. Real-world evidence indicates that the impact of Machiavellian tendencies on occupational success is rather limited.

PSYCHOMETRIC ISSUES

A number of articles have focused on the instruments for measuring Machiavellianism. The Mach scales have been scrutinized with regard to social desirability, reliability, and construct validity. The Mach V has been the main target of criticism, although the Mach IV has not been exempt.

Social Desirability

In most of the published research, either the Mach IV or the Mach V was used to measure Machiavellianism. The Mach IV scale consists of 20 statements to which the individual responds on a 7-point Likert scale ranging from strong disagreement to strong agreement. Half the items are reversed. Christie (1970b) suggested that a constant of 20 be added to the total score to create a neutral score of 100. After adding the constant, the lowest possible score is 40 and the highest is 160.

Even in the early years of scale development, there was concern about possible confounding with socially desirable responding. Because high scores on the Mach IV require socially undesirable responses, the scale may in fact be measuring differential tendencies to respond in an undesirable manner. Christie (1970b) reported significant negative correlations between

---

[6]Interestingly, Richford and Fortune begin their article with the following statement: "In order to meet the increasing demands of their jobs when their perceived opportunity for formal organization control is diminishing, secondary school principals resort to interpersonal manipulation in an effort to augment their effectiveness" (p. 17). They go on to comment that principals are currently in a position where they are given little autonomy and little control within the education system.

desirable responding and the Mach IV scale: $-.17$ for the Marlowe-Crowne Social Desirability scale and $-.35$ to $-.45$ for the Edwards Social Desirability scale. Although these correlations do not seem overly threatening, he expressed particular concern about one sample where the correlation for female subjects was $-.75$ (Budner, 1962).

To minimize the influence of social desirability, Christie developed the Mach V. This inventory utilizes a forced-choice format with paired unrelated items (a "Mach statement" and a "non-Mach statement") matched in social desirability. A third item with negatively correlated social desirability is added to the matched pair (the "buffer statement"). To complete the Mach V, respondents must indicate which of the three items they agree with most, which they agree with least, and leave the other blank. Scores are assigned to each of the six possible combinations. The highest score is obtained when the Mach item is agreed with most, the item matched on social desirability is agreed with least, and the buffer item is left blank. The assumption is that the Mach statement and the matched (non-Mach) statement will be more salient than the buffer statement to those persons with the highest and lowest Machiavellian orientations. After adding a 20-point constant, scores can range from 40 to 160, with 100 as the middle point. Although Mach scores correlate negatively with the "internal" measure of social desirability (i.e., responses to the buffer items), Christie (1970b) reported that no significant correlations had been found between the Mach V and external measures of social desirability.

There has been much debate surrounding the relation between socially desirable responding and the Mach V scale. Rogers and Semin (1973) noted that, whereas Christie may have removed effects of social desirability with the triadic forced-choice format, he reintroduced them through the scoring system. They pointed out that, if the social desirability matching was invalid (e.g., a different subject population), Christie's scoring distinction in terms of the matched item would not make sense. In fact, Vleeming (1979b) wondered whether the low reliabilities and significant correlations with social desirability obtained with his Dutch Mach V scale might be attributable to invalid social desirability matching. Ray (1982) similarly argued that it is virtually impossible to equate alternative items in terms of social desirability because of differences across groups and individuals in what is seen as socially desirable. Although he acknowledged that Likert scales do not alleviate social desirability problems, Ray (1979) recommended the Mach IV because social desirability scores derived from a separate social desirability measure could at least be partialed out.

Bloom (1980) disagreed with Ray's view that the Mach V is plagued with social desirability problems, quoting Christie's (1970b) statement that the "hidden nature of the forced choice makes it difficult for the average respondent to decide what the 'right' answer is" (p. 21). Christie based this statement on several pieces of evidence. First, subjects consistently score higher on the Mach V than on the Mach IV. Second, subjects cannot identify the items keyed for Machiavellianism on the Mach V even when told the principle that underlies the scoring method. Third, various manipulations of the Mach V instructions, including requests to score high, to make a good impression on an employer, and to fake low, do not yield scores that differ significantly from those obtained with the standard instructions. Fourth, the Mach V shows no significant correlation with the Edwards and Marlowe–Crowne Social Desirability scales. Bloom conceded that there is a negative correlation between the Mach V and the internal measure of social desirability that is built into the Mach V scoring system. However, he maintained that this correlation should not be considered a weakness of the Mach V because Christie and Geis have not found this measure of social desirability useful as a measure of individual differences. Bloom's final defense of the Mach V was that the scale has had considerable success in predicting Machiavellian behavior.

The third point requires comment. Two studies published since Christie and Geis (1970) suggest that subjects *can* fake scores on the Mach V scale (Skinner, 1982a; Skinner et al., 1976). Subjects were asked to complete the Mach V as a Machiavellian would. The faked Mach responses were significantly higher than honest scores of low Machs and congruent with those of true high Machs. Studies by Alexander and Rudd (1984) and Alexander and Beggs (1986) similarly pointed to the conclusion that Mach V scores can be simulated, although the results of these studies have not been entirely consistent.[7]

With regard to the fourth point, note that whereas Mach V scores typically do not correlate with external measures of social desirability, Vleeming (1979b) obtained correlations of − .35 and − .40 between the short version of the Crowne and Marlowe Social Desirability scale and two versions of his Dutch translation of the Mach V.

In conclusion, the Mach IV has been criticized on grounds that scores on this scale correlate too highly with measures of social desirability, which is why Christie developed the Mach V. Our response to this criticism is two-fold. First, the Mach V may not be as immune from socially desirable responding as Christie had hoped. Research by Skinner and his colleagues and others shows that subjects *can* fake Machiavellian responses to the Mach V. Moreover, Vleeming (1979b) reported substantial correlations between an external measure of social desirability and his Dutch Mach V scale.

Second, studies published since Christie and Geis' (1970) monograph

---

[7]The results from Alexander and Rudd's (1984) studies are not as clear-cut. It appears that subjects had some difficulty faking Mach responses to the Mach V if the buffer items were removed.

have not consistently found high correlations between the Mach IV and measures of socially desirable responding. Vleeming (1984) in a multiple regression analysis did report a multiple correlation of .49 between scores on these two scales. This relation was mainly due to association between social desirability and one of his four clusters, honesty (the others were flattery, Mach views, and cynicism). Biberman (1985) reported a correlation of only −.10 between scores on the Mach IV and the Crowne and Marlowe scale. Zook and Sipps (1986) obtained correlations of −.10 and −.05 between scores on these scales for male subjects; −.25 and −.19 for female subjects. Even Geis, Christie, and Nelson (1970) found a correlation of only −.17 between these measures. These correlations suggest that the Mach IV is not as plagued with social desirability problems as was originally thought.

Reliability

Williams, Hazelton, and Renshaw (1975) noted that the correlation between scores on the Mach IV and V can be taken as an index of reliability. These correlations are not always as high as one might expect. They obtained a correlation of .58 between total scores on the two scales; correlations between corresponding items ranged from .11 to .50. Geis (1970a) reported a correlation of .73 between scores on the two scales in one study, but only .37 in another (Geis, Christie, & Nelson, 1970). Geis and Moon (1981) obtained correlations of .52, .59, and .69 in three groups of students. Finally, Durkin (1970) reported a correlation of .66 between scores on the Mach IV and V.

Both the Mach IV and the Mach V have been criticized for poor internal consistency. Alpha coefficients above .70 are typically found for the full Mach IV scale, although recently White (1984) reported an alpha of only .46. Ray (1979) reported a coefficient alpha of .54 for a shortened 10-item Mach IV scale. In a later study, Ray (1983) stated that the shortened scale actually comprised only 8 items (2 of the original 10 were dropped because they did not correlate significantly with the total score). When all 10 items were reanalyzed, the reliability alpha was reduced to .49. When the reliability of the full Mach IV scale was assessed, alpha coefficients of .70 and .65 were obtained (Ray, 1983; Ray & Ray, 1982). Zook and Sipps (1986) reported an alpha of .68 for their revised version of the Mach IV (3 items were reworded to make them gender neutral). Alpha coefficients of .70 to .76 have been reported by many researchers (e.g., Comer, 1985; Gable & Topol, 1987; Hollon, 1983; Hunt & Chonko, 1984; Ray & Ray, 1982; Vleeming, 1984; Zook and Sipps, 1986). These results suggest that the full Mach IV has acceptable internal reliability. Note that even the shortened version of this scale described by Ray (1983) appears reasonably consistent ($\alpha = .68$), when corrected by the Spearman-Brown formula.

Split-half reliabilities for the Mach IV ranged from .69 to .88 in studies reported in Christie and Geis. More recently, Geis and Moon (1981) obtained coefficients of .69, .59, and .52 in three samples. Pandey and Singh (1987) reported a split-half reliability coefficient of .76 in a group of Indian women. Zook and Sipps (1986) obtained a .67 test–retest correlation in a sample of undergraduate students over a 6-week period.

With respect to the Mach V scale, Christie (1970b) stated that "In most samples the reliability . . . hovers in the .60s" (p. 27). Martinez (1981) reported an alpha of .65 when using the Mach V along with some other items, and .68 when using a 10-item Mach V (Turner & Martinez, 1977). Leary et al. (1986) obtained an alpha of .55 in their study. Vleeming (1979b) reported alphas ranging from .14 to .41 for two versions of his Dutch Mach V scale, scored in different ways.

Rogers and Semin (1973) examined the part–whole correlations of the 20 Mach V triads in a British sample and found that a number of correlations were low. The magnitude of the correlation appeared to be linked to the forced-choice triad format of the scale. They therefore proposed an alternative scoring system that ignored item matching. (Points were given based on whether the Mach item in the triad was chosen first, second, or last.) An increase in the standard deviation and in part–whole correlations was obtained with this new scoring system: Part–whole correlations improved from .08 to .44 (using Christie and Geis' scoring system) to .11 to .50. (Median part–whole correlations increased from .25 for the old scoring system to .295 for the new system.)

Since the publication of the Rogers and Semin article, a number of researchers have adopted their scoring system (e.g., Dingler-Duhon & Brown, 1987; Domelsmith & Dietch, 1978; Gleason et al., 1978; Martinez, 1981; Turner & Martinez, 1977). However, Shea and Beatty (1983) found that alpha increased only from .44 to .55 when the Rogers and Semin scoring system was used.

The Mach V has not fared much better in terms of split-half reliability. In the studies reported in Christie and Geis (1970), coefficients range from .56 to .64. Shea and Beatty (1983) obtained coefficients of .29 and .36 (using Christie & Geis' and Rogers & Semin's scoring systems, respectively). These figures rose to .45 and .53, respectively, when adjusted with the Spearman-Brown prophecy formula. Geis and Moon (1981) reported coefficients of .33, .35, and .06 in three samples. Finally, Geis, Christie, and Nelson (1970) reported a Kuder–Richardson reliability of .22 for the Mach V.

Thus, the Mach V does not measure up in terms of internal consistency. Shea and Beatty (1983) caution against the use of Rogers and Semin's scoring system as a way of improving reliability. Even though they found that alpha and split-half reliabilities improved when Rogers and Semin's method was used, neither coefficient approached the conventionally accepted criterion of .80. Therefore, they recommend using Likert scales and abandoning the "cumbersome and biased triadic-choice model adopted by Christie" (p. 512).

Bloom (1984) replied to the Shea and Beatty article, arguing that .80 is only a convention and that lower reliabilities can be acceptable. Contrary to Shea and Beatty, he maintains that classical test theory does not state that reliability is necessarily the lower limit of a test's validity. In his view, this point is crucial in light of all the research supporting the predictive validity of the Mach V. Utilizing such research, the squared estimate of the Mach V's predictive validity can be taken as a lower limit on reliability. This lower limit is frequently higher than the internal consistency directly measured. Bloom concludes by stating that Shea and Beatty's arguments about the reliability of the Mach V are not in themselves damaging to the status of the scale. However, should the Mach V be shown to lack construct validity, then Bloom would agree that a new measure of Machiavellianism is in order. It is to this issue that we turn next.

Dimensionality

When Christie and his colleagues were constructing the Mach IV, they classified the items into three categories: duplicitous tactics, a cynical view of human nature, and a disregard for conventional morality. The fewest items fell into the last category because, as Christie (1970b) explained, "the construction of items tended to follow Machiavelli's writings rather closely and Machiavelli was less concerned with abstractions and ethical judgments than with pragmatic advice" (p. 14). Not surprisingly, the morality component of Machiavellianism has been least robust. (In fact, only two morality items were retained when the Mach IV was constructed, and one of these items, #19, has been dropped by researchers because of low correlations with other items and other psychometric failings; e.g., Ahmed & Stewart, 1981; Hunter et al., 1982.) Factor analyses by Christie and Lehmann (1970), in which Mach items have been analyzed along with Anomie and F Scale items, have yielded factors labeled Anomic Disenchantment, Machiavellian Tactics, Pollyanna Syndrome, Honesty, and Machiavellian Orientation. As a whole, these analyses have provided support for the tactics–views distinction.

Because none of the Christie and Lehmann factor analyses used only Mach items, Williams, Hazelton, and Renshaw (1975) factored both the Mach IV and Mach V. The separation between tactics and views was generally supported with the Mach IV. They concluded that in terms of face validity, the Mach IV seems to tap the constructs suggested by Christie, although it has several weaknesses (e.g., only 13 of 20 items had acceptable factor loadings). The factor structure of the Mach V was less clear. In fact, they declared the factors uninterpretable (which they attributed, in part, to the Mach V scoring system). We tabulated whether the items loading on each factor were views, tactics, or morality items and found some evidence of a tactics–views distinction, although it was by no means crystal clear. Williams et al. found little correspondence between the Mach IV and Mach V factors.

Martinez (1980) was puzzled by Williams et al.'s failure to find a clear robust factor structure for the Mach V. He speculated that the ethnicity of the subjects might be important and therefore administered the Mach V to an American and a Mexican-American sample. The factors obtained for each group were quite different, leading Martinez to question the consistency of the internal structure of the Mach V scale across different ethnic groups. In each group, there is a tendency for views and tactics items to load on separate factors, although both kinds of items appear on the same factors as well.

In another study of ethnic groups, Kuo and Marsella (1977) compared the factorial structure of the Mach IV scale in matched samples of Chinese and American students. Even though some of the factors were given similar labels, the items loading on the factors were quite different for the two groups. As with the Martinez study, the factor structure is not particularly clear for either group. There is support for a tactics–views distinction. However, as in the previous study, it was not uncommon for tactics and views items to load on the same factor.

Ahmed and Stewart (1981) also were prompted to factor analyze the Mach IV because Christie and Lehmann (1970) did not factor only the Mach scales. The results of their factor analysis support the tactics–views distinction, although positively and negatively worded items tended to load on separate factors. The tactics–views distinction is also supported in Hunter, Gerbing, and Boster's (1982) factor analysis of the Mach IV scale. Similar to Ahmed and Stewart's results, positively worded items tended to load on a different factor than negatively worded items. (Where views and tactics items loaded on a single factor, the items were worded in the same direction.) O'Hair and Cody's (1987) factor analysis of the Mach IV scale yielded a clear views and a clear tactics factor, although each consisted of only negatively worded items. Positively worded tactics and views items loaded on the same factor. The direction in which items are keyed also seemed to influence the results obtained in Vleeming's (1984) cluster analysis of the Mach IV. Whereas views and tactics items tended to cluster separately, there was also a strong tendency for items simply keyed in the same way to cluster.

Finally, Kline and Cooper (1984b) did a factor analysis of an early 50-item Mach scale (Mach II, Christie, 1970b). Based on their analyses, they concluded that "In Great Britain, two Machiavellian scales of views and tactics can be used . . . but the morality scale is not viable" (p. 252).

The factor analytic studies of the Mach scales are difficult to integrate because of variations in factor analytic techniques, in the labels chosen for factors, and in the populations examined. Nevertheless, when the items loading on factors are classified as to whether they are tactics or views items, analyses of the Mach scales (especially the Mach IV) consistently support a distinction between the tactics and views factors. With both scales, however, there is a tendency for the tactics–views distinction to be confounded with the direction in which the items are keyed.[8] In our own factor analyses of the Mach IV scale, we found the original two-factor solution to be still viable (Paulhus, 1982). In analyses of four diverse data sets, the four factors cited by Christie and Lehmann (1970) reappeared but the last two eigenvalues were usually small. When two factors were rotated, the original labels of Tactics (including dishonesty) and Cynicism (Views) seemed appropriate. Thus, like Christie and Lehmann, we conclude that the structure simplifies to the two robust factors—tactics and views.

Dimensionality and Construct Validity

Hunter et al. (1982) considered the implications of the multidimensionality of Machiavellianism. They found a mixed pattern of correlations between certain traits and their four Mach IV components. For example, dogmatism correlated .50 with cynicism, .16 with flattery, and it was virtually uncorrelated with deceit or immorality. A mixed pattern of relations was also found with Levenson's Powerful Others scale: Scores were moderately correlated with cynicism and flattery, showed a low correlation with deceit, and were virtually uncorrelated with immorality.

Hunter and colleagues also performed a path analysis and again concluded that the components of Machiavellianism differed radically from one another in their relation to other personality traits. For example,

---

[8]Christie and Lehmann (1970) also found that negatively and positively worded items tended to load on separate factors. They cautioned that "It would therefore seem prudent in interpreting the meaning of these factors to be cognizant of the fact that the way in which the item was presented made a difference in the way respondents reacted to it" (p. 370).

This warning seems to have been forgotten or ignored. Yet, this remains a problem for the Mach scales, particularly in light of the fact that the positive and negative Mach items are not highly correlated; Ray (1983) reported that correlations of .11 and .12 had been found in his studies. Steininger and Eisenberg found very different correlations between their components of dogmatism and positive versus negative Mach items. For male subjects, total dogmatism score correlated − .26 with positive Mach items and − .08 with negative Mach items. For females, these correlations were .58 and .05, respectively.

Machiavellian cynicism was found to be causally antecedent to dogmatism, competitiveness, fatalism, and indirectly antecedent to self-concept. They argued that the entire Mach scale cannot enter into the causal model in a logically consistent manner. Because each of the four components was found to have a different set of causal links to other traits, they maintained that there can be no meaning to a score that is created by summing across them. In short, Hunter et al. concluded that Machiavellianism is not a coherent construct.

In our view, the multidimensional nature of Machiavellianism is not necessarily a threat to its construct validity. What is often overlooked is that Christie intended Machiavellianism to be a multidimensional construct. The Mach scales were constructed expressly with the components of tactics, views, and morality in mind. This fact does not jeopardize the status of the construct, as long as the conceptual link between the components and behavior is coherent. A negative correlation between the components would be disturbing. In fact, the tactics, views, and morality factors have consistently shown positive correlations (e.g., Martinez, 1981; Paulhus, 1982). Even Hunter et al. (1982) and Vleeming (1984) reported that scores on their four factors (clusters) were positively intercorrelated.[9]

The multidimensional nature of Machiavellianism does imply that one should obtain separate scores for each of the components when using the Mach scales in research. Some research taking this approach has already been described (e.g., Cooper et al., 1986; Hunter et al., 1982; Kline & Cooper, 1983, 1984a; Steininger & Eisenberg, 1976; Vleeming, 1984; see also O'Hair & Cody, 1987, and Tamborini, Stiff, & Zillmann, 1987).

The most popular approach has been to distinguish tactics and views. In a series of studies on the political activism of students in the 1960s, Gold, Friedman, and Christie (1971) found that cynicism was positively correlated with endorsement of New Left Philosophy and the use of revolutionary tactics, whereas correlations with Mach tactics were negative.

Pinaire-Reid (1979) predicted that women with a high predisposition to fashion would be higher in Mach tactics and lower in cynicism than individuals with a low predisposition. Her rationale was that some Machs might use an attractive appearance as a manipulative tactic, whereas others might resist high fashion because of their cynicism with regard to the social structure in general. Results supported hypotheses.

Finally, Martinez (1981) hypothesized that tactics scores would be more predictive of bargaining success in the Con Game (see Geis, 1970a) than would cynicism (views) scores, because the former is concerned with methods of dealing with people whereas the latter refers to one's philosophy

---

[9]Further clarity might result from a positioning of tactics, views, and morality in interpersonal space.

of human nature. He found that *total* Mach scores were more highly correlated with bargaining success than scores on either tactics or cynicism. Martinez's study highlights the fact that, although it may sometimes be beneficial to distinguish between tactics and views, the total score may be more useful in predicting certain behaviors. Indeed, the utility of a total Machiavellian score was amply demonstrated in the behavioral validation section of this chapter.

Is the Construct Additive or Emergent?

There are at least two ways the subfactors could combine to predict behavior so successfully. The two may tap an underlying common factor of Machiavellianism. Adding them then provides a total score that is more reliable as well as having a wider band for predicting behavior.

The other possibility is that the combination of the two factors yields an emergent construct. In other words, high scores on both factors are required to generate Machiavellian behavior. An individual needs to believe that duplicitous tactics work *and* be cynical enough to use them. This model is testable by examining the interaction between tactics and cynicism when predicting behavior. We recommend that future work with the Mach IV utilize stepwise regression methods wherein the product of the factors is entered after the main effects. A significant interaction term would indicate that Machiavellianism is an emergent property. As recommended by Ray (1979), a measure of socially desirable responding should also be included in the regression equation.

Conclusions

Despite the criticisms leveled against it, the last 17 years of research on Machiavellianism has been largely supportive of the original formulation by Christie and Geis (1970). The construct is a natural trait category in that its position in judges' implicit personality theories matches its position in the empirically observed nomological network. The efficacy of the Mach scales in predicting Machiavellian behavior is very impressive. There are, however, some psychometric problems with these scales. There is evidence that the Mach IV and Mach V are not parallel forms and therefore should not be treated as such. Indeed, the few inconsistent empirical findings may well be due to use of different Mach scales. Despite some high correlations with social desirability, a number of writers have recommended the Mach IV for use in research. This appears to be sound advice despite Bloom's admirable defense of the Mach V. The Mach V suffers from scoring problems, low internal consistency, and the underlying factor structure is not as clear as that of the Mach IV.

We must conclude that Machiavellianism remains a valid personality construct. It has permitted researchers to make theoretically based predictions, and these predictions have been substantiated by operationalizing the construct with the Mach IV and Mach V scales. We recommend that, in the future, researchers use the Mach IV to separate Tactics and Cynicism, as well as using the combined score. Such information should help clarify the conceptual significance of multiple factors. This clarification remains critical for a full understanding of the impressive ability of the Mach scales to predict behavior.

ACKNOWLEDGMENTS

This chapter was supported in part by a University of Winnipeg Summer Research Furlough Grant awarded to the first author and by a Social Sciences Research Council of Canada grant awarded to the third author.

We thank Ross Broughton for his helpful comments on an earlier draft of this chapter.

REFERENCES

Abramson, E. E. (1973). The counselor as a Machiavellian. *Journal of Clinical Psychology, 29,* 348–349.

Ahmed, S. M. S., & Stewart, R. A. C. (1981). Factor analysis of the Machiavellian scales. *Social Behavior and Personality, 9,* 113–115.

Alexander, C. N., Jr., & Beggs, J. J. (1986). Disguising personal inventories: A situated identity strategy. *Social Psychology Quarterly, 49,* 192–200.

Alexander, C. N., Jr., & Rudd, J. (1984). Predicting behaviors from situated identities. *Social Psychology Quarterly, 47,* 172–177.

Ames, M., & Kidd, A. H. (1979). Machiavellianism and women's grade point averages. *Psychological Reports, 44,* 223–228.

Barnes, R. D., & Ickes, W. (1979). *Styles of self-monitoring: Assimilative versus accommodative.* Unpublished manuscript, University of Wisconsin.

Bell, N. J., McGhee, P. E., & Duffey, N. S. (1986). Interpersonal competence, social assertiveness and the development of humour. *British Journal of Developmental Psychology, 4,* 51–55.

Biberman, G. (1985). Personality and characteristic work attitudes of persons with high, moderate, and low political tendencies. *Psychological Reports, 57,* 1303–1310.

Bloom, R. W. (1980). Comment on "The authoritarian as measured by a personality scale: Solid citizen or misfit?" *Journal of Clinical Psychology, 36,* 918–920.

Bloom, R. W. (1984). Comment on "Measuring Machiavellianism with Mach V: A psychometric investigation." *Journal of Personality Assessment, 48,* 26–27.

Bogart, K., Geis, F., Levy, M., & Zimbardo, P. (1970). No dissonance for Machiavellians. In R. Christie & F. L. Geis (Eds.), *Studies in Machiavellianism* (pp. 236–259). New York: Academic Press.

Bradley, M. T., & Klohn, K. I. (1987). Machiavellianism, the Control Question Test and the detection of deception. *Perceptual and Motor Skills, 64,* 747–757.

Brown, E. C., & Guy, R. F. (1983). The effects of sex and Machiavellianism on self-disclosure patterns. *Social Behavior and Personality, 11,* 93–96.

Budner, S. (1962). Intolerance of ambiguity as a personality variable. *Journal of Personality, 30,* 29–50.

Burgoon, M., Lombardi, D., Burch, S., & Shelby, J. (1979). Machiavellianism and type of persuasive message as predictors of attitude change. *Journal of Psychology, 101,* 123–127.

Cherulnik, P. D., Way, J. H., Ames, S., & Hutto, D. B. (1981). Impressions of high and low Machiavellian men. *Journal of Personality, 49,* 388–400.

Chonko, L. B. (1982). Machiavellianism: Sex differences in the profession of purchasing management. *Psychological Reports, 51,* 645–646.

Christie, R. (1970a). Why Machiavelli? In R. Christie & F. L. Geis (Eds.), *Studies in Machiavellianism* (pp. 1–9). New York: Academic Press.

Christie, R. (1970b). Scale construction. In R. Christie & F. L. Geis (Eds.), *Studies in Machiavellianism* (pp. 10–34). New York: Academic Press.

Christie, R. (1970c). Relationships between Machiavellianism and measures of ability, opinion, and personality. In R. Christie & F. L. Geis (Eds.), *Studies in Machiavellianism* (pp. 35–52). New York: Academic Press.

Christie, R., & Budnitzky, S. (1957). A short forced-choice anxiety scale. *Journal of Consulting Psychology, 21,* 501.

Christie, R., & Geis, F. L. (1970). *Studies in Machiavellianism.* New York: Academic Press.

Christie, R., & Lehmann, S. (1970). The structure of Machiavellian orientations. In R. Christie & F. L. Geis (Eds.), *Studies in Machiavellianism* (pp. 359–387). New York: Academic Press.

Clayton, M. B., & Jackson, D. N. (1961). Equivalence range, acquiescence, and overgeneralization. *Educational and Psychological Measurement, 31,* 371–382.

Comer, J. M. (1985). Machiavellianism and inner versus outer directedness: A study of sales managers. *Psychological Reports, 56,* 81–82.

Cooper, C., Kline, P., & May, J. (1986). The measurement of authoritarianism, psychoticism, and other traits by objective tests: A cross-validation. *Personality and Individual Differences, 7,* 15–21.

Cooper, S., & Peterson, C. (1980). Machiavellianism and spontaneous cheating in competition. *Journal of Research in Personality, 14,* 70–75.

Crockett, W. H. (1965). Cognitive complexity and impression formation. In B. A. Maher (Ed.), *Progress in experimental personality research* (Vol. 2, pp. 47–90). New York: Academic Press.

Delia, J. G., & O'Keefe, B. J. (1976). The interpersonal constructs of Machiavellians. *British Journal of Social and Clinical Psychology, 15,* 435–436.

DePaulo, B. M., & Rosenthal, R. (1979). Telling lies. *Journal of Personality and Social Psychology, 37,* 1713–1722.

Dien, D. S., & Fujisawa, H. (1979). Machiavellianism in Japan: A longitudinal study. *Journal of Cross-Cultural Psychology, 10,* 508–516.

Dietch, J., & House, J. (1975). Affiliative conflict and individual differences in self-disclosure. *Representative Research in Social Psychology, 6,* 69–75.

Dingler-Duhon, M., & Brown, B. B. (1987). Self-disclosure as an influence strategy: Effects of Machiavellianism, androgyny, and sex. *Sex Roles, 16,* 109–123.

Domelsmith, D. E., & Dietch, J. T. (1978). Sex differences in the relationship between Machiavellianism and self-disclosure. *Psychological Reports, 42,* 715–721.

Drory, A., & Gluskinos, U. M. (1980). Machiavellianism and leadership. *Journal of Applied Psychology, 65,* 81–86.

Durkin, J. E. (1970). Encountering: What low Machs do. In R. Christie & F. L. Geis (Eds.), *Studies in Machiavellianism* (pp. 260–284). New York: Academic Press.

Exline, R. V., Thibaut, J., Hickey, C. B., & Gumpert, P. (1970). Visual interaction in relation to Machiavellianism and an unethical act. In R. Christie & F. L. Geis (Eds.), *Studies in Machiavellianism* (pp. 53–75). New York: Academic Press.

Falbo, T. (1977). Multidimensional scaling of power strategies. *Journal of Personality and Social Psychology, 35,* 537–547.

Forsyth, D. R. (1980). A taxonomy of ethical ideologies. *Journal of Personality and Social Psychology, 39,* 175–184.

Fry, W. R. (1985). The effect of dyad Machiavellianism and visual access on integrative bargaining outcomes. *Personality and Social Psychology Bulletin, 11,* 51–62.

Gable, M., & Topol, M. T. (1987). Job satisfaction and Machiavellian orientation among department store executives. *Psychological Reports, 60,* 211–216.

Galli, I., & Nigro, G. (1983). Relationship between Machiavellianism and external control among Italian undergraduates. *Psychological Reports, 53,* 1081–1082.

Galli, I., Nigro, G., & Krampen, G. (1986). Multidimensional locus of control and Machiavellianism in Italian and West German students: Similarities and differences. *International Review of Applied Psychology, 35,* 453–461.

Geis, F. (1970a). The con game. In R. Christie & F. L. Geis (Eds.), *Studies in Machiavellianism* (pp. 106–129). New York: Academic Press.

Geis, F. (1970b). Bargaining tactics in the con game. In R. Christie & F. L. Geis (Eds.), *Studies in Machiavellianism* (pp. 130–160). New York: Academic Press.

Geis, F., & Christie, R. (1970). Overview of experimental research. In R. Christie & F. L. Geis (Eds.), *Studies in Machiavellianism* (pp. 285–313). New York: Academic Press.

Geis, F., Christie, R., & Nelson, C. (1970). In search of the Machiavel. In R. Christie & F. L. Geis (Eds.), *Studies in Machiavellianism* (pp. 76–95). New York: Academic Press.

Geis, F., Weinheimer, S., & Berger, D. (1970). Playing legislature: Cool heads and hot issues. In R. Christie & F. L. Geis (Eds.), *Studies in Machiavellianism* (pp. 190–209). New York: Academic Press.

Geis, F. L. (1978). Machiavellianism. In H. London & J. E. Exner, Jr. (Eds.), *Dimensions of personality* (pp. 305–363). New York: Wiley.

Geis, F. L., & Moon, T. H. (1981). Machiavellianism and deception. *Journal of Personality and Social Psychology, 41,* 766–775.

Geis, F. L., Weinheimer, S., & Berger, D. (1966, September). *Playing legislature: Machiavellianism and log-rolling.* Paper presented at the American Psychological Association Conference, New York.

Gemmill, G. R., & Heisler, W. J. (1972). Machiavellianism as a factor in managerial job strain, job satisfaction, and upward mobility. *Academy of Management Journal, 15,* 51–62.

Gleason, J. M., Seaman, F. J., & Hollander, E. P. (1978). Emergent leadership processes as a function of task structure and Machiavellianism. *Social Behavior and Personality, 6,* 33–36.

Gold, A. R., Friedman, L. N., & Christie, R. (1971). The anatomy of revolutionists. *Journal of Applied Social Psychology, 1,* 26–43.

Guterman, S. S. (1970). *The Machiavellians: A social psychological study of moral character and organizational milieu.* Lincoln: University of Nebraska Press.

Hanson, D. J. (1978). Machiavellianism as a variable in research: A bibliography. *JSAS Catalog of Selected Documents in Psychology, 8*(1), 1–17.

Hanson, D. J., & Vleeming, R. G. (1982). Machiavellianism: A bibliography. *JSAS Catalog of Selected Documents in Psychology, 12*(1), 1–32.

Hare, R. D. (1991). *The Hare Psychopathy Checklist-Revised.* Toronto: Multi-Health Systems.

Harpur, T. J., Hakstian, A. R., & Hare, R. D. (1988). Factor structure of the Psychopathy Checklist. *Journal of Consulting and Clinical Psychology, 56,* 741–747.

Harpur, T. J., Hare, R. D., & Hakstian, A. R. (1989). Two-factor conceptualization of psychopathy: Construct validity and assessment implications. *Psychological Assessment: A Journal of Consulting and Clinical Psychology, 1,* 6–17.

Harrell, W. A. (1980). Retaliatory aggression by high and low Machiavellians against remorseful and non-remorseful wrongdoers. *Social Behavior and Personality, 8,* 217-220.

Harrell, W. A., & Hartnagel, T. (1976). The impact of Machiavellianism and trustfulness of the victim on laboratory theft. *Sociometry, 39,* 157-165.

Hegarty, W. H., & Sims, H. P., Jr. (1978). Some determinants of unethical decision behavior: An experiment. *Journal of Applied Psychology, 63,* 451-457.

Hegarty, W. H., & Sims, H. P., Jr. (1979). Organizational philosophy, policies, and objectives related to unethical decision behavior: A laboratory experiment. *Journal of Applied Psychology, 64,* 331-338.

Heineman, C. E. (1953). A forced-choice form of the Taylor Anxiety Scale. *Journal of Consulting Psychology, 17,* 447-454.

Heisler, W. J., & Gemmill, G. R. (1977). Machiavellianism, job satisfaction, job strain, and upward mobility: Some cross-organizational evidence. *Psychological Reports, 41,* 592-594.

Hollon, C. J. (1983). Machiavellianism and managerial work attitudes and perceptions. *Psychological Reports, 52,* 432-434.

Howarth, E. (1973). *Howarth Personality Questionnaire.* Edmonton, Alberta: University of Alberta Press.

Howarth, E. (1986). What does Eysenck's Psychoticism scale really measure? *British Journal of Psychology, 77,* 223-227.

Huber, V. L., & Neale, M. A. (1986). Effects of cognitive heuristics and goals on negotiator performance and subsequent goal setting. *Organizational Behavior and Human Decision Processes, 38,* 342-365.

Hunt, S. D., & Chonko, L. B. (1984). Marketing and Machiavellianism. *Journal of Marketing, 48,* 30-42.

Hunter, J. E., Gerbing, D. W., & Boster, F. J. (1982). Machiavellian beliefs and personality: Construct invalidity of the Machiavellianism dimension. *Journal of Personality and Social Psychology, 43,* 1293-1305.

Ickes, W., Reidhead, S., & Patterson, M. (1986). Machiavellianism and self-monitoring: As different as "me" and "you." *Social Cognition, 4,* 58-74.

Janisse, M. P., & Bradley, M. T. (1980). Deception, information and the pupillary response. *Perceptual and Motor Skills, 50,* 748-750.

Johnson, P. B. (1980). Need achievement and Machiavellianism. *Psychological Reports, 46,* 466.

Jones, W. H., Nickel, T. W., & Schmidt, A. (1979). Machiavellianism and self-disclosure. *Journal of Psychology, 102,* 33-41.

Kauffmann, D. R., Chupp, B., Hershberger, K., Martin, L., & Eastman, K. (1987). Learning versus grade orientation: Academic achievement, self-reported orientation, and personality variables. *Psychological Reports, 60,* 145-146.

Kerr, N. L., & Gross, A. C. (1978). Situational and personality determinants of a victim's identification with a tormentor. *Journal of Research in Personality, 12,* 450-468.

Kline, P., & Cooper, C. (1983). A factor-analytic study of measures of Machiavellianism. *Personality and Individual Differences, 4,* 569-571.

Kline, P., & Cooper, C. (1984a). A construct validation of the Objective Analytic Test Battery (OATB). *Personality and Individual Differences, 5,* 323-337.

Kline, P., & Cooper, C. (1984b). An investigation of the items in the Machiavellian scales. *Journal of Social Psychology, 124,* 251-252.

Kohn, P. M. (1972). The Authoritarian-Rebellion scale: A balanced F-scale with left-wing reversals. *Sociometry, 35,* 176-189.

Kuo, H. K., & Marsella, A. J. (1977). The meaning and measurement of Machiavellianism in Chinese and American college students. *Journal of Social Psychology, 101,* 165-173.

LaTorre, R. A., & McLeod, E. (1978). Machiavellianism and clinical depression in a geriatric sample. *Journal of Clinical Psychology, 34,* 659-660.

Leary, M. R., Knight, P. D., & Barnes, B. D. (1986). Ethical ideologies of the Machiavellian. *Personality and Social Psychology Bulletin, 12,* 75–80.

Leary, T. (1957). *Interpersonal diagnosis of personality.* New York: Ronald Press.

Levenson, H. (1974). Activism and powerful others: Distinctions within the concept of internal–external control. *Journal of Personality Assessment, 38,* 377–383.

Levenson, H., & Mahler, I. (1975). Attitudes toward others and components of internal–external locus of control. *Psychological Reports, 36,* 209–210.

Maroldo, G. K., & Flachmeier, L. C. (1978). Machiavellianism, external control, and cognitive style of American and West German co-eds. *Psychological Reports, 42,* 1315–1317.

Maroldo, G. K., Flachmeier, L. C., Johnston, L. K., Mayer, J. L., Peter, M. I., Reitan, E. J., & Russell, K. L. (1976). Relationship between Machiavellianism, external control, and cognitive style among college students. *Psychological Reports, 39,* 805–806.

Martinez, D. C. (1980). Factorial structure of the Mach V scale for Chicano and White college students. *Psychological Reports, 47,* 1139–1142.

Martinez, D. C. (1981). Group composition and Machiavellianism. *Psychological Reports, 49,* 783–793.

Mehrabian, A. (1969). Measures of achieving tendency. *Educational and Psychological Measurement, 29,* 445–451.

Mehta, P. (1969). *The achievement motive in high school boys.* New Delhi: National Council of Educational Research and Training.

Nigro, G., & Galli, I. (1985). On the relationship between Machiavellianism and anxiety among Italian undergraduates. *Psychological Reports, 56,* 37–38.

O'Hair, D., & Cody, M. J. (1987). Machiavellian beliefs and social influence. *Western Journal of Speech Communication, 51,* 279–303.

Okanes, M. M., & Murray, L. W. (1980). Achievement and Machiavellianism among men and women managers. *Psychological Reports, 46,* 783–788.

Okanes, M. M., & Murray, L. W. (1982). Machiavellian and achievement orientations among foreign and American Master's students in business administration. *Psychological Reports, 50,* 519–526.

Pandey, J. (1981). Effects of Machiavellianism and degree of organizational formalization on ingratiation. *Psychologia: An International Journal of Psychology in the Orient, 24,* 41–46.

Pandey, J., & Rastogi, R. (1979). Machiavellianism and ingratiation. *Journal of Social Psychology, 108,* 221–225.

Pandey, J., & Singh, P. (1987). Effects of Machiavellianism, other-enhancement, and power-position on affect, power feeling, and evaluation of the ingratiator. *Journal of Psychology, 121,* 287–300.

Paulhus, D. L. (1982). *Factor analyses of the Mach IV.* Unpublished studies, University of British Columbia.

Paulhus, D. L. (1983). Sphere-specific measures of perceived control. *Journal of Personality and Social Psychology, 44,* 1253–1265.

Paulhus, D. L., & Martin, C. L. (1987). The structure of personality capabilities. *Journal of Personality and Social Psychology, 52,* 354–365.

Paulhus, D. L., Molin, J., & Schuchts, R. (1979). Control profiles of football players, tennis players, and nonathletes. *Journal of Social Psychology, 108,* 199–205.

Pinaire-Reed, J. A. (1979). Personality correlates of predisposition to fashion: Dogmatism and Machiavellianism. *Psychological Reports, 45,* 269–270.

Poderico, C. (1987). Machiavellianism and anxiety among Italian children. *Psychological Reports, 60,* 1041–1042.

Prociuk, T. J., & Breen, L. J. (1976). Machiavellianism and locus of control. *Journal of Social Psychology, 98,* 141–142.

Ray, J. J. (1974). Balanced dogmatism scales. *Australian Journal of Psychology, 26,* 9–14.

Ray, J. J. (1979). The authoritarian as measured by a personality scale: Solid citizen or misfit? *Journal of Clinical Psychology, 35,* 744–747.

Ray, J. J. (1982). Machiavellianism, forced-choice formats and the validity of the F scale: A rejoinder to Bloom. *Journal of Clinical Psychology, 38,* 779–782.

Ray, J. J. (1983). Defective validity of the Machiavellianism scale. *Journal of Social Psychology, 119,* 291–292.

Ray, J. J., & Ray, J. A. B. (1982). Some apparent advantages of subclinical psychopathy. *Journal of Social Psychology, 117,* 135–142.

Richford, M. L., & Fortune, J. C. (1984). The secondary principal's job satisfaction in relation to two personality constructs. *Education, 105,* 17–20.

Rogers, R. S., & Semin, G. R. (1973). Mach V: An improved scoring system based on a triadic choice model. *Journal of Personality and Social Psychology, 27,* 34–40.

Rosenthal, S. F. (1978). The female as manipulator: A replication. *Psychological Reports, 42,* 157–158.

Rotter, J. B. (1966). Generalized expectancies for internal versus external control of reinforcement. *Psychological Monographs, 80* (No. 1, Whole No. 609), 1–28.

Russell, G. W. (1974). Machiavellianism, locus of control, aggression, performance and precautionary behaviour in ice hockey. *Human Relations, 27,* 825–837.

Shea, M. T., & Beatty, J. R. (1983). Measuring Machiavellianism with Mach V: A psychometric investigation. *Journal of Personality Assessment, 47,* 509–513.

Sheppard, B. H., & Vidmar, N. (1980). Adversary pretrial procedures and testimonial evidence: Effects of lawyer's role and Machiavellianism. *Journal of Personality and Social Psychology, 39,* 320–332.

Siegel, S. (1962). The relationship of hostility to authoritarianism. *Journal of Abnormal and Social Psychology, 52,* 368–372.

Singer, J. E. (1964). The use of manipulative strategies: Machiavellianism and attractiveness. *Sociometry, 27,* 128–150.

Skinner, N. F. (1981). Personality correlates of Machiavellianism: II. Machiavellianism and achievement motivation in business. *Social Behavior and Personality, 9,* 155–157.

Skinner, N. F. (1982a). Personality correlates of Machiavellianism: III. A simulation procedure for identifying high Machs. *Social Behavior and Personality, 10,* 197–199.

Skinner, N. F. (1982b). Personality correlates of Machiavellianism: IV. Machiavellianism and psychopathology. *Social Behavior and Personality, 10,* 201–203.

Skinner, N. F., Giokas, J. A., & Hornstein, H. A. (1976). Personality correlates of Machiavellianism: I. Consensual validation. *Social Behavior and Personality, 4,* 273–276.

Smith, C. (1976). Machiavellianism and achievement motivation. *British Journal of Social and Clinical Psychology, 15,* 327–328.

Smith, R. J., & Griffith, J. C. (1978). Psychopathy, the Machiavellian, and anomie. *Psychological Reports, 42,* 258.

Snyder, M. (1974). The self-monitoring of expressive behavior. *Journal of Personality and Social Psychology, 30,* 526–537.

Solar, D., & Bruehl, D. (1971). Machiavellianism and locus of control: Two conceptions of interpersonal power. *Psychological Reports, 29,* 1079–1082.

Spielberger, C. D., Gorsuch, R. L., & Lushene, R. E. (1970). *Manual for the State-Trait Anxiety Inventory.* Palo Alto, CA: Consulting Psychologists Press.

Steininger, M., & Eisenberg, E. (1976). On different relationships between dogmatism and Machiavellianism among male and female college students. *Psychological Reports, 38,* 779–782.

Sypher, H. E., Nightingale, J. P., Vielhaber, M. E., & Sypher, B. D. (1981). The interpersonal constructs of Machiavellians: A reconsideration. *British Journal of Social Psychology, 20,* 219–220.

Tamborini, R., Stiff, J., & Zillmann, D. (1987). Preference for graphic horror featuring male versus female victimization: Personality and past viewing experiences. *Human Communication Research, 13,* 529–552.

Touhey, J. C. (1971). Machiavellians and social mobility. *Psychological Reports, 29,* 650.

Touhey, J. C. (1973). Intelligence, Machiavellianism and social mobility. *British Journal of Social and Clinical Psychology, 12,* 34–37.

Troldahl, V., & Powell, F. (1965). A short-form dogmatism scale for use in field studies. *Social Forces, 44,* 211–214.

Turnbull, A. A., Jr. (1976). Selling and the salesman: Prediction of success and personality change. *Psychological Reports, 38,* 1175–1180.

Turner, C. F., & Martinez, D. C. (1977). Socioeconomic achievement and the Machiavellian personality. *Sociometry, 40,* 325–336.

Vleeming, R. G. (1979a). Machiavellianism: A preliminary review. *Psychological Reports, 44,* 295–310.

Vleeming, R. G. (1979b). Machiavellianism: Some problems with a Dutch Mach V Scale. *Psychological Reports, 45,* 715–718.

Vleeming, R. G. (1984). The nomothetical network of a Machiavellianism scale. *Psychological Reports, 54,* 617–618.

Weinstock, S. A. (1964). Some factors that retard or accelerate the rate of acculturation — with specific reference to Hungarian immigrants. *Human Relations, 17,* 312–340.

Wertheim, E. G., Widom, C. S., & Wortzel, L. H. (1978). Multivariate analysis of male and female professional career choice correlates. *Journal of Applied Psychology, 63,* 234–242.

White, G. L. (1984). Comparison of four jealousy scales. *Journal of Research in Personality, 18,* 115–130.

Wiggins, J. S. (1979). A psychological taxonomy of trait-descriptive terms: The interpersonal domain. *Journal of Personality and Social Psychology, 37,* 395–412.

Wiggins, J. S., & Broughton, R. (1985). The interpersonal circle: A structural model for the integration of personality research. *Perspectives in Personality, 1,* 1–47.

Williams, M. L., Hazelton, V., & Renshaw, S. (1975). The measurement of Machiavellianism: A factor analytic and correlational study of Mach IV and Mach V. *Speech Monographs, 42,* 151–159.

Wolfson, S. (1981). Effects of Machiavellianism and communication on helping behaviour during an emergency. *British Journal of Social Psychology, 20,* 189–195.

Wrightsman, L. S., Jr., & Cook, S. W. (1965). Factor analysis and attitude change. *Peabody Papers in Human Development, 3* (No. 2).

Zenker, S. I., & Wolfgang, A. K. (1982). Relationship of Machiavellianism and locus of control to preferences for leisure activity by college men and women. *Psychological Reports, 50,* 583–586.

Zook, A., II., & Sipps, G. J. (1986). Reliability data and sex differences with a gender-free Mach IV. *Journal of Social Psychology, 126,* 131–132.

Zook, A., II., & Sipps, G. J. (1987). Machiavellianism and dominance: Are therapists in training manipulative? *Psychotherapy, 24,* 15–19.

Zuckerman, M., & Lubin, B. (1965). *Manual for the Multiple Affect Adjective Checklist.* San Diego: Educational and Industrial Testing Service.

Personality and Perception: Rorschach and Luescher Correlates of Jungian Types as Measured by the Myers–Briggs Type Indicator

4

Benjamin J. Porter
Samuel Roll
University of New Mexico

It has been widely assumed since Rorschach's time that a high ratio of human movement responses to color responses reflects an introverted style, whereas a low ratio shows an extraverted tendency (Exner, 1974; Rorschach, 1942; Singer & Brown, 1977). From a Jungian point of view this is questionable, because extraversion and introversion are independent of styles of perceiving. A common belief about color preference, that extraverts tend to prefer yellow or red and introverts prefer green or blue, is doubtful for the same reason.

Jung's typology (Jung, 1971) is operationalized in the Myers–Briggs Type Indicator (Myers, 1962). This allows us to categorize people into 16 types, differing along four dimensions: extraversion–introversion, sensing–intuition, thinking–feeling, and judging–perceiving. Each person's type includes one member of each of these pairs. One may, for example, be an extraverted, sensing, thinking, perceiving type or an introverted, intuitive, feeling, judging type. The 16 possible such combinations yield 16 basic types, each with its own particular characteristics.

Extraverts tend to be more interested in what goes on outside themselves, whereas introverts are more concerned with what outside events mean to them in their private world. The introvert brings the world to him or her, whereas the extravert goes out to meet it (Shapiro & Alexander, 1975).

Each of us, whether introvert or extravert, can be said to have a preferred method of perceiving, either by intuition or sensing (Myers, 1962). The sensing person deals with relatively concrete things and facts as they actually are, whereas the intuitive lives in a world of possibility, never seeing things quite as they are, but rather as they might be. The sensing person

117

appreciates things and facts; the intuitive sees the connections first and often seems not even to need the facts. Facts and things are never ends in themselves.

Thinking and feeling refer to two alternative ways of processing perceptions. The thinking type tries to make rational sense of things, whereas the feeling type's judgments are based ultimately on a kind of fitness of feeling. Harmony between people is more important to the feeling type than strict logical consistency.

The last function, perceiving versus judging, determines which of the other two functions (intuition–sensing or thinking–feeling) is preferred. One whose judging function is dominant prefers a planned and ordered life, whereas the perceiving type is more spontaneous.

We might expect the Jungian perceiving function, intuition–sensing, to correlate most highly with Rorschach's experience type, the ratio of human movement to color responses. The fourth function, perceiving–judging, is also likely to have some relation to this, because it expresses the preference for perceiving (either intuition or sensing) or for processing the perception (thinking or feeling).

Richter and Winter (1966) have provided some evidence for this. Looking at creativity as measured on the Holtzman Inkblot Technique (HIT), they found that subjects rated highly intuitive and perceiving on the Myers–Briggs Type Indicator gave significantly more movement responses as well as color responses than did those rated high in sensing and judging.

Mayman (1977) sees the human movement response as multidetermined, which may result from one or more of five processes. Each of these processes may or may not be characteristic of a particular Jungian function. The perceiving type might respond to the perceptual imbalance of the blot; the intuitive's response might be "a fragment of arrested fantasy"; (p. 234) the kinesthetic or self-expressive aspect has no obvious Myers–Briggs correlate; nor does the interpersonal determinant, which has to do with the introjects formed; empathy might well be related to the Jungian feeling function.

There is general agreement that the Rorschach color response reveals affective responsiveness and impulsivity (Shapiro, 1977). It is just as plausible, for example, that affective responsiveness be associated with Myers–Briggs feeling.

There is much agreement among color theorists that red, orange, and yellow are extraverted colors, whereas green and blue are favored by introverts. Birren (1961) said: "When a number of people are questioned as to their predilections for color, it will be found that extroverts are inclined to favor red, while introverts are inclined to favor blue" (p. 172). Norman and Scott (1952) cite other examples of this belief: "Red and yellow are regarded by Goldstein as having an 'expansive' effect on the organism, increasing the 'effect of the external world,' while green and blue have the reverse effect, causing 'concentration' and 'contraction' . . ." (p. 217). Norman and Scott cite also Thomaschewski's study associating orange and red with teachers' ratings of sociability in their students, blue with calmness, and green with sensitivity.

On the Rorschach cards, red, yellow, and orange tend to dominate, so introverts do not get much chance to show their impulsive, affective side. There is, of course, no a priori reason why preference should translate directly into response tendency. Nevertheless, if the Rorschach is encouraging the release of primary process thinking, and if this is motivated by wish fulfillment, then what we see should be more or less what we want to see: An extravert will see the reds and yellows, but the introvert will be pulled more by formal characteristics of the blot.

Intuition–perceiving may be a more important determinant of a high human movement score than is introversion. Freedom of fantasy and imagination are evidently associated more closely with the Jungian notions of intuition and perceiving than with introversion. We should expect, therefore, a high correlation of intuition or perceiving or both with Rorschach human movement scores, and also with experience type (the relation of human movement to color determinants). If intuition is also positively correlated with color responsiveness, however, there may be no significant relationship of intuition to experience balance. Introversion could still be correlated with high experience balance, or there might be some interaction effect of introversion–extraversion with intuition–sensing or judging–perceiving of which we are not yet aware.

We designed this study to see whether experience balance in fact corresponds to Myers–Briggs and color preference measures of extraversion–introversion. At the same time we were replicating Richter and Winter's study using the Rorschach instead of the Holtzman test to see whether the same relation would be found between Myers–Briggs' intuition and human movement and color responses on the Rorschach.

METHOD

Subjects

Thirty-six students, 21 women and 15 men, were recruited as volunteer subjects from an introductory psychology class. Extra credits were added to their final course grade for their participation in this study.

Procedure

All subjects were administered the same three tests: Form F of the Myers-–Briggs Type Indicator, the Rorschach Inkblot Test, and the short version of the Luescher Color Test. Subjects were randomly assigned so that six of them took the tests in each of the six possible orders of administration.

The Rorschach was administered and scored according to the Rapaport system, details of which can be found in Allison, Blatt, and Zimet (1968) and in Rapaport, Gill, and Schafer (1968). Human movement (M) is scored for a person in movement. We scored, in addition, responses in which human-like figures (H) are in active motion as M. Humans, witches, giants, and so forth are all scored M. Movement is interpreted as including holding a posture, where the tension is explicit, as in the case of a diver poised on the end of a diving board, or a person being crushed under a tank. Looking at something is not scored M but half M (FM). According to Allison et al. (1968), this score is reserved for "weak, nonactive human movement [e.g., a person standing], to large, active part human figures, or to human-like animals in clearly human activity [e.g., bears drinking a toast, monkeys kissing]" (p. 160). The total human movement score for each protocol is the sum of strict human movements (M) and half human movements (FM), counting each M as 1 and each FM as .5. The total is referred to as human movement or M, although this is a more inclusive sense than "strict-M."

Color responses are weighted in a similar way. A response determined solely by color is assigned 1.5 points, a response dominated by color but with some formal influence gets 1.0, and a response mainly determined by form in which color also was used receives a score of .5. The total of these is Sum-C.

The ratio of human movement (M) to color (Sum-C) is the experience balance. Treating experience balance (EB) as a ratio can be a problem, because Sum-C can be zero, in which case the fraction cannot be divided because it leaves the quotient undefined. Fortunately, much of the same information can be obtained by computing the sum of M and C and the difference between the two. Although the difference between movement and color is not mathematically the same as, or linearly related to, the ratio of movement and color, in general, the ratio should tend to go up as M increases and go down as C increases.

The short version of the Luescher Color Test comprises eight cards, about $3 \times 4.5''$, each a different color (red, yellow, blue, green, brown, purple, gray, and black). The cards are laid in random order in a row in front of the subject, who is then asked to select the color that he or she likes the best. This card is then removed and the subject picks the next favorite color, and so on until only one card remains.

Luescher Color Test scores were obtained by rank ordering the preferences (1,2,3,4) for the colors red, yellow, green, and blue and summing the scores for red and yellow, then summing the scores for green and blue, and finally dividing the red–yellow sum by the green–blue sum. The result is bigger the greater the preference for the "introverted" colors.

RESULTS

All our planned comparisons of Rorschach and Luescher variables with Myers–Briggs categories failed to reach statistical significance. Thinking--feeling did correlate very highly with Luescher Color scores, although this was unpredicted. Thinking types tended to give more human movement responses than feeling types, although scoring lower on the Luescher Color Test (i.e., they preferred yellow and red to green and blue). Perceiving types gave more color responses on the Rorschach than did judging types.

Pearson product-moment correlations were computed between each pair of variables of interest (see Table 4.1). Correlations among the Myers--Briggs categories are generally small, as would be expected because all are orthogonal with each other except for sensing–intuition and judging–perceiving, which are positively correlated in the population. In this sample, sensing–intuition and judging–perceiving are positively correlated .522, significant at the .001 level. Although thinking–feeling and judging–perceiving are not correlated significantly in the population, our sample shows a significant correlation of .361 ($p = .031$). An unusually high proportion of feeling–perceiving types appear in this sample. This may be due to the type of class from which subjects were recruited, the University of New Mexico introductory psychology course that deals especially with human personality and pathology.

None of the planned correlations are significant at our stringent adjusted

TABLE 4.1
Pearson Correlation Coefficients

	EI	SN	TF	JP	M	C	M + C	M − C
EI								
SN	− .057							
	(.743)							
TF	− .281	.231						
	(.097)	(.176)						
JP	.039	.522	.361					
	(.823)	(.001)	(.031)					
M	− .095	.109	− .173	− .123				
	(.582)	(.527)	(.313)	(.476)				
C	.025	.286	.078	.204	− .264			
	(.884)	(.091)	(.653)	(.232)	(.120)			
M + C	− .069	.302	− .104	.032	.732	.464		
	(.688)	(.073)	(.546)	(.853)	(.000)	(.004)		
M − C	− .081	− .079	− .165	− .198	.851	− .731	.265	
	(.639)	(.649)	(.338)	(.247)	(.000)	(.000)	(.119)	
LC	.028	.020	.477	.251	− .256	− .050	− .271	− .154
	(.872)	(.907)	(.003)	(.140)	(.132)	(.772)	(.110)	(.370)

Note: Numbers in parentheses are *p* values.

alpha levels, nor would they have been significant at the .05 level (see Table 4.1). All extraversion–introversion correlations are lower than .1. Higher intuition scores correlate in our sample with high color (C) and movement plus color (M + C) scores (.286 and .302, respectively). Luescher color preference scores correlate negatively with M and M + C (−.256 and −.271) (i.e., subjects who preferred yellow and red also tended to give more M and M + C responses on the Rorschach). Because none of these correlations are significant, they are, of course, suggestive rather than conclusive. Table 4.1 shows one strong correlation (.477, p = .003) between thinking–feeling and Luescher color scores. Thinking types show a preference for yellow and red, whereas feeling types prefer green and blue.

If we treat the Myers–Briggs measures as categories rather than continuous scores, the results differ somewhat. T tests show no significant differences between extraverts and introverts or between sensing and intuitive types on any of the Rorschach or Luescher variables. Thinking types in our sample gave more human movement responses (M = 3.577) than did feeling types (M = 2.261), $t(34)$ = 2.59, p = .014. They also scored higher on M + C than feeling types: a mean of 5.346 as opposed to 4.109 [$t(34)$ = 2.13, p = .041]. Feeling types gained significantly higher Luescher scores (M = 1.495) than did thinking types (M = .826), $t(34)$ = 2.76, p = .009. The best predictor of thinking–feeling appears to be a standardized LC − M score: $t(34)$ = 3.61, p = .001. The mean LC − M score for thinking types is −1.143; for feeling types it is .564. Perceiving types tended to give more color (C) responses on the Rorschach (M = 2.167) than did judging types (M = 1.267), $t(34)$ = 2.32, p = .026. A t test on a standardized C + LC score shows perceiving types scoring significantly higher (M = 3.653) than judging types (M = 2.457), $t(34)$ = 2.73, p = .01.

Looking at continuous scores within categories allows us to refine our guesses somewhat. Extraversion–introversion correlate −.429 (p = .041) with M + C within the feeling types. No other significant correlations appear involving extraversion–introversion. Sensing–intuition correlates highly with C among introverts (.699, p = .008) and among thinking types (.620, p = .024). SN does not correlate significantly with M anywhere. Although judging–perceiving does not show any overall significant correlations, among introverts it correlates negatively with M (−.565, p = .044), positively with C (.610, p = .027), and negatively with M − C (−.812, p = .001). Thinking–feeling correlates with Luescher Color scores (LC) .550 (p = .007) among extraverts, .687 (p = .001) among intuitives, and .626 (p = .002) among the perceiving types.

DISCUSSION

The findings of this study do not allow any simple or straightforward interpretation. Rorschach human movement and color responses do not appear to be simply determined, nor does the experience type derived from their combination. Myers–Briggs thinking types as a group gave more human movement responses than did feeling types. It makes sense for the thinking type to tend toward form-determined "intellectual" responses and for feeling types to respond affectively with color responses. The problem is that Rorschach color responsiveness was no higher in the feeling types than it was in the thinking types. The only difference that appeared was that perceiving types tended to use color more in their responses than did judging types. Perhaps this reflects a greater openness to richer experience than the relatively constrained and rigid judging style. There is some evidence then that experience type is a function of two dimensions, or two pairs of categories: thinking–feeling and judging–perceiving.

That it is not the yellows and reds on the Rorschach that encourage high color responding is shown by the thinking types' unelevated number of color responses, together with their general preference for yellow and red on the Luescher Color Test. Feeling types preferred green and blue. It may be that the preference for less flashy colors reflects more modulated feelings than the relatively primitive feelings of the thinking type.

Our results suggest that the Rorschach, Luescher, and Jungian views of extraversion and introversion do not coincide. Our Myers–Briggs extraverts did not tend to prefer red and yellow any more than did the introverts, nor did either group favor especially green and blue. We found no significant correlation between Myers–Briggs extraversion and color, the Rorschach indicator of extraversion. Nor did any correlation appear between Myers–Briggs introversion and its Rorschach theoretical counterpart, human movement. None of the comparisons using sum or difference scores of movement and color proved fruitful either. To see extraverts as impulsive and unimaginative and introverts as able to delay gratification and resist the pull of outside events seems too simple.

We might expect rather to find intuition and perceiving, in both extraverts and introverts, correlated with imagination and fantasy; a playful and creative relation with the world rather than the fact-oriented way of the sensing–judging type. Starting with this hypothesis, Richter and Winter (1966) found strong differences. Their creative–potential group, made up of subjects selected from the upper reaches of the intuitive–perceiving types, gave substantially more human movement and color responses on the Holtzman Inkblot Test than did the extreme noncreatives (sensing–judging). There is no trade-off between the two parts of the experience type: Intuitive perceiving types scored higher in both. Our study suggests that perceiving is a more important component of color responsiveness than is intuition. We have failed to find Richter and Winter's relation of intuition–perceiving with human movement responses.

In our sample, the best predictor of thinking–feeling turns out to be a standardized score subtracting Rorschach human movement from Luescher

Color preference. A preference for green and blue along with a low movement score are the mark of the feeling type; yellow and red preference with high movement characterize the thinking type. Similarly, a standardized score combining Luescher Color preference with Rorschach color gives better predictive power of perceiving–judging than does either Luescher or Rorschach score by itself. This may mean only that in our sample feeling types tended also to be perceiving types.

Inasmuch as extraversion–introversion and thinking–feeling are orthogonal to each other, our study fails to show any evidence for experience types being related to extraversion–introversion. Our results suggest that Myers-–Briggs perceiving is a more important variable than intuition in Richter and Winter's group of creative intuitive perceiving types. This study needs to be replicated with a larger and less biassed sample; our overabundance of extraverted intuitive feeling perceiving types and the small representations of other types makes it impossible to examine thoroughly the possible interactions among the functions. At least we have clarified to some extent the main effects.

This study is a useful reminder of the difficulty of doing personality research. Ideas about extraversion and introversion that have been accepted for a long time may need to be reconsidered. The venerable experience balance may have nothing to do with extraversion and introversion. We now have a bit of evidence that thinking may be related to human movement, and thus indirectly to experience balance. Because color responsiveness appears the same in thinking and feeling types, high movement would mean higher experience balance. Myers–Briggs perceiving may be related in the opposite direction to experience balance, because it correlates positively with Rorschach color responsiveness. Because thinking and perceiving belong to two separate dimensions, future research might look at the interaction of the thinking–feeling and the judging–perceiving dimensions.

SUMMARY

The Rorschach Inkblot Test, the Luescher Color Test, and the Myers-–Briggs Type Indicator were administered to 36 undergraduate students to test hypotheses about personality variables and perception. Rorschach human movement scores (M) did not correlate significantly with introversion on the MBTI, Rorschach color (Sum-C) did not correlate with extraversion, and neither sum nor difference scores of M and Sum-C correlated with extraversion–introversion. Contrary to theory, Luescher Color preference for yellow and red failed to correlate with MBTI extraversion, and green and blue were not associated with introversion. MBTI thinking types gave more M responses than did feeling types, and perceiving types scored higher on Sum-C than did judging types, reflecting, perhaps, their tendency toward direct experience. Thinking types preferred yellow and red, whereas feeling types tended to prefer green and blue. The results of this study suggest that common beliefs about both the Rorschach and the Luescher Color Test need to be reevaluated.

REFERENCES

Allison, J., Blatt, S. J., & Zimet, C. N. (1968). *The interpretation of psychological tests.* New York: Harper & Row.

Birren, F. (1961). *Color psychology and color therapy.* Secaucus, NJ: Citadel.

Exner, J. E. (1974). *The Rorschach: A comprehensive system* (Vol. 1). New York: Wiley.

Jung, C. G. (1971). *Psychological types.* Princeton, NJ: Princeton University Press. (Original work published 1921)

Luescher, M. (1969). *The Luescher Color Test* (I. Scott, Trans. and Ed.). New York: Random House.

Mayman, M. (1977). A multi-dimensional view of the Rorschach movement response: Perception, fantasy, kinesthesia, self-representation, and object-relationships. In M. A. Rickers-Ovsiankina (Ed.), *Rorschach psychology.* (pp. 229–250). Huntington, NY: Robert Krieger.

Myers, I. B., (1962). *The Myers–Briggs Type Indicator Manual.* Palo Alto, CA: Consulting Psychologists Press.

Norman, R. D., & Scott, W. A. (1952). Color and affect: A review and semantic evaluation. *Journal of General Psychology, 46,* 185–223.

Rapaport, D., Gill, M. M., & Schafer, R. (1968). In R. R. Holt (Ed.), *Diagnostic psychological testing.* New York: International Universities Press.

Richter, R. H., & Winter, W. D. (1966). Holtzman inkblot correlates of creative potential. *Journal of Projective Techniques and Personality Assessment, 30*(1), 62–67.

Rorschach, H. (1942). *Psychodiagnostics, a diagnostic test based on perception* (P. Lemkau & B. Kronenburg, Trans.). Hans Huber. Bern: Bircher. (Original work published 1921)

Shapiro, D. (1977). A perceptual understanding of color response. In M. A. Rickers-Ovsiankina (Ed.), *Rorschach psychology* (pp. 251–301). Huntington, NY: Robert Krieger.

Shapiro, K. J., & Alexander, I. E. (1975). *The experience of introversion: An integration of phenomenological, empirical, and Jungian approaches.* Durham, NC: Duke University Press.

Singer, J. L., & Brown, S-L. (1977). The experience type: Some behavioral correlates and theoretical implications. In M. A. Rickers-Ovsiankina (Ed.), *Rorschach psychology* (pp. 325–372). Huntington, NY: Robert Krieger.

5 Susceptibility of the Rorschach to Malingering: A Schizophrenia Analogue

Glenn G. Perry
Bill N. Kinder
University of South Florida

There are many instances where individuals might desire to malinger, or to fake a mental illness, in today's society. Consequently, psychological test batteries often include the Rorschach test because it is believed to be resistant to intentional manipulation by the subject (Exner 1986; Fosberg 1938, 1941, 1943). A review of the literature specific to malingering (Perry & Kinder, 1990) revealed studies using idiographic, nomothetic, and clinical data to evaluate the ability of subjects to alter Rorschach protocols. Studies that evaluated idiographic data sets (Albert, Fox, & Kahn, 1980; Mittman, 1983) demonstrated that subjects instructed in how to fake mental illness were capable of producing Rorschach protocols that blind evaluators rated as schizophrenic.

The findings of studies using nomothetic or clinical data were inconsistent and inconclusive (Benton, 1945; Carp & Shavzin, 1950; Easton & Feigenbaum, 1967; Feldman & Graley, 1954; Fosberg, 1938, 1941, 1943; Overton, 1984; Pettigrew, Tuma, Pickering, & Whelton, 1983; Rorschach Workshops, 1987; Seamons, Howell, Carlisle, & Roe, 1981). Although malingerers seem to respond with protocols exhibiting a reduction in the number of responses *(R),* no study specific to malingering or faking on the Rorschach has controlled for such between group differences in R as suggested by Cronbach (1949) through either experimental design or appropriate statistical control procedures (Perry & Kinder, 1990). Given the reported differences in R, lack of control may have been responsible for the inconsistency in findings of Rorschach studies of malingering because a number of Rorschach variables are positively correlated with R (Fiske & Baughman, 1953).

The aim of the present study was to control for differences in responsivity and to evaluate the Rorschach protocols of control and role-informed subjects malingering schizophrenia. These groups are compared on a number of discrete scores and on some of the ratios, percentages, and derivations suggested by Exner (1986). To help control experiment-wise alpha, the variables that are evaluated were limited to those relating to the role of malingering in general, and to variables that are considered to be measures of inaccurate perception, disordered thinking, inadequate controls, and interpersonal ineptness seen in schizophrenia (Exner, 1986). Malingering was predicted to result in a guarded, defensive response set that would be reflected in (a) reductions in R, (b) increases in reaction responses, (d) and decreases in the R-$ratio$. Malingerers were further predicted to exaggerate their pathology through (e) increases in the number of dramatic responses, and (f) the failure to interpret easy popular cards.

Inaccurate perception was predicted to alter the successful malingering protocol through (a) decreases in the $X + \%$, (b) increases in the $X - \%$, and (c) decreases in P. Disordered thinking was predicted to alter the successful malingering protocol through (a) increases in the $WSUM6$, and (b) increases in the $SCZI$ index. Inadequate controls were predicted to alter the successful malingering protocol through (a) increases in the frequency of $CF + C$ responses, and (b) decreases in FC responses. Interpersonal ineptness was predicted to alter the successful malingering protocol through (a) increases in the frequency of M- responses, (b) decreases in the frequency of $H + Hd$ contents, and (c) decreases in the frequency of T responses.

The malingering process in responding to the test battery administered in this study was independently evaluated, using the MMPI $L, F,$ and K scales. The malingering group was predicted to respond to the MMPI with an increase in (a) F scores and (b) $F - K$ scores.

METHOD

Subjects

The subjects were 40 White male volunteers from undergraduate psychology classes at the University of South Florida. The sample was restricted to males to control for sex differences. The mean age was 21.2 years with a mean education level of 14.0 years.

Instruments

All subjects were administered a test battery consisting of the Rorschach and the $L, F,$ and K scales of the MMPI. The MMPI $L, F,$ and K scales have been shown to be useful in detecting deviant response sets (Graham, 1987).

Exner's Comprehensive System (Exner, 1986) was used in the administration and scoring of all the Rorschach data. Subjects were asked to respond to the blots, seated side by side with the examiner to reduce examiner cuing effects (Exner, 1986). The responses were scored according to Exner's 1986 scoring criteria by the first author. A second scoring was accomplished by a postinternship doctoral candidate with extensive training in Exner's scoring system on a random sample of eight of the protocols.

The two scorings were analyzed for the percentage of agreement between scorers and resulted in 89% overall agreement between the two scorers. Because reliability data have not been previously published concerning the variable, *Dramatic* (defined in this study as responses with a theme of depression, sex, blood, gore, confusion, mutilation, hatred, fighting, decapitation, negative emotion, or evil), a special check was made on the inter-rater agreement scoring this variable, which resulted in 81% agreement between the two raters.

Procedures

Experimental Packets that included the test materials and instructions were constructed. The experimental group subjects received a two-page typewritten description of the symptoms of schizophrenia. They were asked to malinger schizophrenia on all tests in the battery and to do so *without making it obvious that they were faking.* The control subjects were instructed to take all the tests in an open and honest manner. Research assistants randomly assigned experimental conditions to Experimental Packets, which ensured that the Rorschach examiner was blind to the experimental condition of each subject.

When the subjects arrived for the scheduled assessments, they were met by a research assistant. The research assistant (a) opened the subject's sealed Experimental Packet, (b) asked the subject to read the instructions and answered any questions the subject might have concerning the instructions, (c) administered and scored the MMPI Subscales, (d) insured that the subject signed the informed consent statement, and (e) escorted the subject to the examiner with his Experimental Packet Number for the examiner.

To insure that examiner effects were held to a minimum, a single examiner administered and scored all the Rorschach tests. The examiner was blind to the experimental condition to which the subject had been assigned. The only identifying information in the examiner's possession was the subject's Experimental Packet Number.

RESULTS

Response Selection for Data Analysis

One major methodological problem with the research on the Rorschach is that many of the Rorschach indices are correlated with R. Shaffer,

Duszynski, and Thomas (1981) used the protocols from two large samples of subjects (over 500 each) and found that, for the 24 variables analyzed, an average of 36.75% of the variance in the individual indices was accounted for by their relationship with R. Cronback (1949) was critical of the Rorschach literature because of this apparent confound and suggested that when groups differ on R analyses should be conducted by scoring a fixed equal number of responses for all subjects, constructing subgroups equated for R, or analyzing profiles of normalized scores. No research to date on Rorschach malingering has controlled for differences in R before subjecting the data to statistical tests (Perry & Kinder, 1990).

A fourth method for controlling for differences in R is statistical control through partialing or residualizing (e.g., Exner, Viglione, & Gillespie, 1984; Shaffer et al., 1981). Both approaches may produce erroneous results due to the lack of proper model specification and the linear regression on variables whose relationship is complex and nonlinear (Fiske & Baughman, 1953; Pedhazur, 1982). Further, both approaches use an additive model with the underlying assumption that data are interval or ratio in nature when most Rorschach variables are ordinal or nominal. Finally, many Rorschach variables are markedly skewed. Thus, even with R controlled for, the appropriate statistical tests will be nonparametric in many, perhaps most, instances. Because of these problems we chose to (a) equate groups on R before subjecting the data to statistical analyses, (b) analyze all distributions for skewedness, and (c) use nonparametric statistics for variables that were markedly skewed.

Two variables, the total number of responses *(R)* and the ratio of total number of responses to the last five cards and the first five cards *(R-ratio)*, were analyzed using the original total number of responses in each protocol. A third variable, the response time for the first response per card *(RT)*, was analyzed in the standard manner using the response time data for only the first response on each card.

Before analysis of the other variables, the malingering and control groups were compared to ensure that the groups did not differ systematically on the total number of responses. The control group was found to have a greater number of responses per protocol; mean number of responses were 30.9 and 22.3, respectively, Mann-Whitney $U = 120$, $p = < .05$. This difference between the fake and control groups of 8.6 responses per protocol made the analysis of the total protocols unacceptable for the remaining variables.

The first two responses for each Rorschach card were then analyzed, using the nonparametric Kruskal–Wallis Rank Test. The control group continued to have a significantly greater number of responses. The mean total number of responses for the experimental and control groups were 18.95 and 16.8, respectively, $H = 5.072$, $p = < .05$. Not only was there a significant difference in the total number of responses per protocol, but the number of responses to cards III, IV, and VI were also significantly different. Therefore, the second response on Cards III, IV, and VI were dropped from the data for the final analysis. This reduction to 17 responses per protocol for the data analysis resulted in a data set that contained no significant differences in the mean total number of responses per group, 16.51 and 15.2, respectively, Kruskal–Wallis $H = 2.118$, $p > .05$, and no significant differences in the mean number of responses per card.

Selection of Statistical Tests

Descriptive statistics and frequency distributions were generated for all the variables. For each variable, the method of statistical analysis was selected according to the normality of the distribution of the scores, which was judged on the basis of skewness as well as visual inspection of the frequency distributions. There was a natural break in the skewness data between a value of .2,910 and .6,960. Visual inspections of the frequency distributions above .6,960 confirmed their skewness. Therefore, a conservative decision was made to use nonparametric statistics on all distributions whose frequency distributions exhibited skewness of .69 or greater.

Variables that were essentially normal in distribution included the easy popular responses *(Easy P)*, the response ratio *(R-Ratio)*, the MMPI *F* and *K* scales, *SCZI*, the popular response *(P)*, *X + %*, and the sum of the human contents *(H Sum)*. These variables were statistically evaluated using an analysis of variance. The remaining variables showed severely skewed distributions, but these variables could be meaningfully ranked. They were statistically analyzed using the Mann-Whitney U test, which is designed to evaluate ordinal data, with 95% the power of a *t* test (Conover, 1980). Variables analyzed with this test included the total number of responses per protocol *(R)*, reaction time *(RT)*, dramatic responses, personalized responses *(PER)*, *Wsum6, M-, T Sum, CF +C,* and *FC*. A summary of all the following results is presented in Table 5.1.

Manipulation Check

An analysis of variance revealed that the MMPI *F* scale was affected by instructions to fake. *F* raw scores averaged 42.3 for the fake group and 6.55 for the control group; $F(1, 38) = 269.043$, $p < .0001$. The *F: K* ratio was also strongly affected by the instructions to fake; $F(1, 38) = 246.589$, $p < .0001$. *F: K* raw scores averaged 33.45 for the fake group and -5.45 for the control group.

General Malingering Variables

Dramatic. As predicted, the *dramatic* special score occurred with greater frequency among faking subjects than for the control group, as

TABLE 5.1
Means, Standard Deviations, and Significant Test Values of the Rorschach
Variables as a Function of Instructional Set

| Variable | Testing Condition | | Significance Value | |
	Fake	Control	F (1.38)	Mann-Whitney U
General Malingering				
Dramatic	4.800	1.050		45.5***
	(3.156)	(0.999)		
RT	13.055	8.030		96.0**
	(5.841)	(3.955)		
R	22.300	30.900		120.0*
	(8.511)	(12.548)		
Easy P	2.550	3.250	4.811*	
	(1.050)	(0.967)		
R-Ratio	1.125	1.091	.112	
	(0.326)	(0.306)		
PER	0.450	0.300		190.0
	(1.146)	(0.733)		
Manipulation Check				
F	42.300	6.550	269.043****	
	(8.743)	(4.310)		
F − K	33.450	− 5.450	246.589****	
	(9.076)	(6.353)		
Disordered Thinking				
SCZI	3.650	1.750	52.16****	
	(0.988)	(0.639)		
Wsum6	8.350	1.550		99.0**
	(10.184)	(2.605)		
Inaccurate Perception				
P	3.750	4.950	6.617*	
	(1.333)	(1.605)		
X − %	0.331	0.171	25.583****	
	(0.116)	(0.080)		
X + %	0.384	0.498	13.605***	
	(0.090)	(0.105)		
Interpersonal Ineptness				
M −	1.450	0.200		86.0**
	(1.538)	(0.410)		
Tsum	0.450	0.600	1.566	
	(0.605)	(0.821)		
Hsum	5.000	4.100		188.0
	(2.695)	(1.774)		
Inadequate Controls				
CF + C	1.750	1.550		144.0
	(1.251)	(1.701)		
FC	0.800	1.500		171.0
	(1.005)	(1.469)		

Note: Standard deviations are given in parentheses.
*p .05; **p .01; ***p .001; ****p .0001.

determined by the Mann-Whitney *U* test, $U = 45.5$, $p < .001$. The mean number of dramatic scores was 4.80 for the faking group and 1.05 for the control group.

Reaction Time.   The *RT* increased for the faking group as compared to the control group; $U = 96.0$, $p < .01$. The mean reaction time was 13.05 seconds for the faking group and 8.03 seconds for the control group.

Responses.   *R* was lower among the faking group than the control group; $U = 120$, $p < .05$. The mean number of responses for the faking group was 22.3; the mean for the control group was 30.9 responses.

Easy Popular Responses.   The faking group produced fewer *Easy P* responses than the control group: $F(1, 38) = 4.81$, $p < .05$. The mean number of *Easy P* responses for these groups were 2.55 and 3.25, respectively.

R-Ratio.   The ratio of the responses to the first five and the last five cards did not differ significantly between the faking group and the control group. The mean *R–Ratio* for the faking group was 1.125; this ratio for the control group was 1.091.

PER.   The number of personalized responses did not differ significantly as predicted. The mean *PER* for the faking group was .450, whereas the mean for the control group was .300.

Disordered Thinking Variables

SCZI.   As predicted, the *SCZI* fake group mean of 3.65 was significantly greater than the control mean of 1.75; $F(1, 38) = 52.16$, $p < .0001$.

Wsum6.   The mean *Wsum6* score of the fake group was significantly greater than for the control group: $U = 99.0$, $p < .01$. The respective means were 8.35 for the fake group and 1.55 for the control group.

Inaccurate Perception Variables

P.   As predicted, the fake group produced significantly fewer popular responses than the control group; $F(1, 38) = 6.617$, $p < .05$. The faking group mean was 3.75; the control group mean was 4.95.

X − %.   The fake group mean for $X - \%$ was significantly higher than the control group mean; $F(1, 38) = 25.583$, $p < .0001$. The means were .331 for the fake group and .171 for the control group.

$X + \%$.   The fake group mean $X + \%$ of .384 was significantly lower than the control group mean of .498 $F(1, 38) = 13.056, p < .001$.

Interpersonal Ineptness Variables

M-.   The fake group produced a greater number of M- responses than the control group; $U = 86.0, p < .01$. The respective means were 1.45 and .20.

$T\ sum$.   The sum of the texture responses was not significantly different for the fake and control groups. The means were .45 for the fake group and .60 for the control group.

$H\ sum$.   The sum of the human content responses did not differ significantly between the fake and control groups. The means were 5.0 for the faking group and 4.1 for the control group.

Inadequate Controls Variables

$CF + C$.   The sum of CF and C did not differ significantly between the fake and control groups. The mean for these groups were 1.75 and 1.55, respectively.

FC.   The number of FC responses did not differ significantly between the fake and control groups. The mean for the faking group was .80 as compared to 1.50 for the control group.

DISCUSSION

The aim of this study was to compare the protocols of subjects malingering schizophrenia with a control group, after controlling for responsivity, in order to determine if the role-informed subjects could consciously alter their Rorschach protocols in a manner suggestive of malingering schizophrenia. The results indicated that the role-informed subjects could consciously alter their Rorschach protocols when 17 responses per protocol were analyzed, consisting of the first response to Cards III, IV, and VI, and the first two responses to the remaining cards.

The results indicated that college students, with minimal training in the definition of schizophrenia, were able to manipulate the Rorschach variables most commonly considered to be indicative of reality testing and the accurate perception of the stimulus ($X - \%$, $X + \%$, and P). Further, this manipulation was in the direction expected in schizophrenic protocols. The reduction in P in the malingering group appears robust, supporting the reduction reported in many studies (Bash, 1978; Easton & Feigenbaum, 1967; Feldman & Graley, 1954; Overton, 1984), but is contradicted by some previous research (Exner, 1978; Seamons et al., 1981).

Perhaps the strongest evidence supporting the malingering groups' ability to alter the Rorschach protocol in the area of inaccurate perception and–or poor reality testing was found in the ability of this group to substantially increase their $X - \%$. The malingering group were not only able to provide unique responses to the stimulus cards but were also able to respond in a manner that seriously distorted the stimuli. This ability to increase $X - \%$ has not been reported in the literature to date, possibly because the variable has not been examined because it was thought that such structural variables were resistant to manipulation (Exner, 1978, 1986).

The results indicated that the malingering group clearly were able to alter the $SCZI$ index in the direction of pathological-disordered thinking. In the malingering group, 55% were able to obtain a $SCZI$ of 4 or greater. This finding supports the Rorschach Workshops 1987 Alumni Newsletter that reported that 20% to 25% of informed subjects could obtain a $SCZI$ value of 4 and that 33% of nonschizophrenic inpatients, who had contact with schizophrenics, could obtain a $SCZI$ value of 4. Further, 20% of the malingering group subjects in the present study were able to obtain a $SCZI$ value of 5. This finding differs from the 1987 Rorschach Newsletter preliminary finding because they report that almost none of the informed subjects could obtain a value of 5 and that none of the nonschizophrenic psychiatric inpatients could produce $SCZI$ value of 5. This difference could have developed because the two studies gave their malingering subjects different instructions.

The disparity between the control and malingering groups in the six weighted special scores *(Wsum6)* indicated that the malingering group was able to malinger difficulties in the thinking process. These findings concur with those of Seamons et al. (1981), who reported an increase in two of the special scores (*INCOM* and *FABCOM*). Because both the $SCZI$ and *Wsum6* are additive, these increases are especially noteworthy given they were calculated on a mean R of only 17.

On the variables most commonly associated with interpersonal ineptness (*M-, H, + Hd,* and *T-sum*), the malingering group could only alter the *M*-variable. Given the malingering group's large increase in the $X - \%$, this finding was expected and suggests that the distorted projection of movement involving human forms is vulnerable to intentional manipulation. The difference in *T sum* means were neither statistically nor clinically significant. The nature of cards IV and VI appear to "pull" for texture responses at a higher rate than the other cards. Therefore, it is possible that by limiting the analysis to only one response on these cards in the database, the analysis might not have evaluated a sufficient range of texture responses. Alternatively, the subjects may have found it difficult to alter their texture responses. The ability to alter the texture response should be further explored in a design more specific to this hypothesis that allows a greater range of responsivity in the data to be analyzed.

Significant differences in the $H + Hd$ were not found between groups. These differences were reported by Overton (1984) but were likely a function of his instructions that specifically asked informed fakers to "Avoid reporting human figures or animals performing human behaviors" (p. 104). The subjects in the present study, who had no specific instructions on how to malinger, were unable to alter the amount of human content in their responses. Alternatively, the failure to find a significant reduction in either the $T\ sum$ or $H + Hd$ could be the result of equating on R prior to analyzing the data. It is possible that previously reported reductions were artifacts of responsivity because both variables are positively correlated with responsivity. The malingering group was unable to alter the color responses in the direction suggestive of inadequate controls, as previously reported by Overton (1984). Again, Overton's instructions were specific to the scoring of the Rorschach in that the informed faker group was instructed "Whenever possible, report objects or animals which color alone would bring to mind" (p. 104). It appears that subjects were able to alter the balance between their FC and $CF + C$ responses when specifically instructed what to report but were unable in the present study to alter this balance when instructed on the symptoms of schizophrenia while remaining naive to specific Rorschach scoring variables.

Graham (1987) suggested that a fake bad MMPI profile can be differentiated from a severely disturbed psychotic profile through the extreme elevation of the fake bad F scale (usually well above a T score of 100 as compared to the range of 70:90 for those clinically diagnosed as psychotic). In the malingering group the minimum T score was 100, whereas 18 of the 20 subjects' T scores were in excess of the maximum T score of 110 (raw score 31) indicated in the commonly used T score conversion charts (Dahlstrom, Welsh, & Dahlstrom, 1972). The malingering group scores did not overlap the control group scores. The highest control group score was a T score of 84 (raw score of 18). Using a T score of 100 as a cutting score, 100% of the malingering group were correctly identified with no false positive or false negative placements. Using a raw score of 15 as a cutting score, 100% of the malingering group were correctly identified with one false positive from the control group incorrectly classified.

Similarly, the $F-K$ scores revealed nonoverlapping scores between the control and malingering groups. The control scores ranged from -14 to $+12$, whereas the malingering $F-K$ scores ranged from 16 to 49. Using an $F-K$ of 7 as a cutting score, 100% of the malingering group were correctly identified whereas one subject in the control group was falsely identified. With this group of well-educated subjects attempting to malinger schizophrenia, the MMPI *F* and *K* scale scores appeared to be powerful indicators that the malingering manipulation instructions were successful.

Two of the four Rorschach variables most commonly associated with a defensive response set were significantly different when comparing the malingering and control groups, *R* and *RT*, whereas *PER* and *R–Ratio* were not significantly different. The reduction in *R* replicates the findings of Bash (1978), Benton (1945), Easton and Feigenbaum (1967), Feldman and Graley (1954), Henry and Rotter (1956), and Meisner (1984), whereas contradicting the results of Overton (1984) and Seamons et al. (1981). The increase in *RT* for the malingering group supports the work of Benton (1945). Although the two groups were overlapping in response times and some malingering subjects were able to respond very quickly to all cards, the response time disparities between the two groups were statistically significant.

Both the Rorschach variables associated with the exaggeration of psychopathology, *Easy P* and *Dramatic,* were significantly different between the malingering and control groups. The malingering subjects seemed determined not to report the perceptions reported by over 80% of Exner's normative sample. This finding again corresponds with the findings of Bash (1978) and suggests that male subjects attempting to malinger report an excessively low percentage of the percepts most easily seen in the inkblots, as though they were avoiding the normal response as suggested by Feldman and Graley (1954). Similarly, the malingering group repeatedly responded in an overly dramatic manner using melodramatic intonations in describing heinous situations in their responses.

The process of administering a Rorschach is an interpersonal process that is ripe with opportunity for a clinical evaluation of the subject's affect, linguistic skills, and interpersonal skills. Each of these areas is often seen to be deficient in the presentations of individuals diagnosed with schizophrenic symptoms. The malingering group's affect appeared to be in the normal range with no sign of the blunted, flat, or inappropriate affect often seen in psychotic states. Linguistically, there was little evidence of word distortions, blocking, or clanging. Speech appeared to flow normally without disruption or the loosening of associations frequently witnessed in individuals in a psychotic state. Furthermore, their responses were usually clearly articulated and appeared goal directed. This goal-directed behavior again contradicts the behavior seen in schizophrenia where there is nearly always a disturbance in volition. Finally, the malingering subjects seemed to enjoy interacting with the examiner before, during, and after the Rorschach administration. They reacted to stimuli presented by the examiner, failing to demonstrate the autistic detachment from environmental stimulation often observed in schizophrenia. Furthermore, they also appeared eager to interact interpersonally with the examiner, revealing strong interpersonal skills and failing to demonstrate the withdrawal from interpersonal involvement encountered in schizophrenia.

CONCLUSIONS

The results of this study suggest it was possible for college students, trained in the symptoms of schizophrenia, to alter their Rorschach protocols in a direction suggestive of schizophrenia. Of particular concern was the apparent ease in which the malingering group altered the variables thought to be strongly indicative of schizophrenia including P, $X - \%$, $M-$, and the $SCZI$ index. Although the malingering subjects were able to manipulate these variables, they were unable to manipulate variables involving texture (T), human content $(H + Hd)$, or the Color–Form balance $(FC, CF + C)$. Although these protocols were altered in a direction suggestive of schizophrenia, it would be unprofessional to infer that a diagnosis of schizophrenia should result from the blind interpretation of the Rorschach in the absence of historical data, behavioral data, other test instruments, and self-report data. When some of these data were entered into the evaluation, a different picture evolves.

The Rorschach protocols of the malingering group may have appeared schizophrenic, but their MMPI F and K scale data indicated an excess of psychopathology; pathology at levels far exceeding the levels reported by most subjects diagnosed with schizophrenia. These excesses in self-reported pathology appeared to compliment their intratest data involving the use of an unreasonably dramatic response set that avoided common percepts during the Rorschach.

Perhaps even more important was the complete disparity between their Rorschach data and their behavioral presentation. The malingering subjects were unable to behaviorally demonstrate the affective restrictions, linguistic difficulties, and lack of interpersonal skills that would have been suggested by an interpretation of their Rorschach protocols. When viewed together, the Rorschach protocols, MMPI data, and behavioral observations of the malingering subjects lacked internal consistency. If these findings are replicated, practicing clinicians might use these same 17 responses along with MMPI data and behavioral observations to evaluate future protocols where the detection of malingering is warranted.

The Rorschach protocols of malingering male college students appear to be distinguishable from the protocols of students asked to respond openly and honestly, but this finding does little to assist in discriminating between malingering clinical subjects and diagnosed schizophrenics. Future research is needed that includes a schizophrenic group that can be compared directly with a malingering group. Bash (1978) was a beginning, but replication is required using Exner's comprehensive system. Research is also needed to define and examine the behavioral differences reported as clinical observations in the literature. Such research could greatly assist in developing a set of decision rules to assist in distinguishing malingerers from schizophrenics. Finally, the results of this project, along with the misdiagnoses reported by Albert, Fox, and Kahn (1980) and Mittman (1983), strongly suggest that a single testing procedure used in a vacuum for diagnosis is a risky business. The most reliable diagnosis will be arrived at using test data from multiple sources along with appropriate behavioral observations.

SUMMARY

The ability to deliberately alter Rorschach responses in a direction suggestive of schizophrenia was investigated. Forty male undergraduate student volunteers were randomly assigned to one of two conditions, informed malingerer or control, and were administered the MMPI *L, F,* and *K* scales and the Rorschach, using Exner's Comprehensive System, by a single examiner blind to experimental condition. Differences between the groups in *R* were controlled. On the Rorschach, the malingering group was able to alter *SCZI, Wsum6, P, X − %,* and *M-* in the schizophrenic direction. Further, the malingering group increased dramatic themes and response time whereas decreasing the total number of responses and easy popular responses. Their MMPI *F* and *K* scale data served as a manipulation check and indicated an overabundance of psychopathology, suggesting a fake bad response set. However, malingering subjects were not able to alter significantly Rorschach indicators of inadequate control *(FC, CF, C)* and did not demonstrate behaviorally the level of psychopathology suggested in their Rorschach protocols. These inconsistencies between the Rorschach and MMPI data and the behavioral observations appeared to provide a meaningful framework for the detection of malingering.

REFERENCES

Albert, S., Fox, H., & Kahn, M. (1980). Faking psychosis on the Rorschach: Can expert judges detect malingering? *Journal of Personality Assessment, 44,* 115–119.

Bash, I. Y. (1978). A study designed to differentiate between schizophrenic offenders and malingerers. *Dissertation Abstracts International, 39,* 2973B.

Benton, A. L. (1945). Rorschach performances of suspected malingerers. *Journal of Abnormal and Social Psychology, 40,* 94–96.

Carp, A. L., & Shavzin, A. R. (1950). The susceptibility to falsification of the Rorschach psychodiagnostic technique. *Journal of Consulting Psychology, 14,* 230–233.

Conover, L. J. (1980). *Practical nonparametric statistics.* New York: Wiley.

Cronbach, L. J. (1949). Statistical methods applied to Rorschach scores: A review. *Psychological Bulletin, 46,* 393–429.

Dalstrom, W. G., Welsh, G. S., & Dalstrom, L. E. (1972). *An MMPI handbook* (Vol. 1). Minneapolis: University of Minnesota Press.

Easton, K., & Feigenbaum, K. (1967). An examination of an experimental set to fake the Rorschach test. *Perceptual and Motor Skills, 24,* 871–874.

Exner, J. E. (1978). *The Rorschach: A comprehensive system* (Vol. 2). New York: Wiley.

Exner, J. E. (1986). *The Rorschach: A comprehensive system* (Vol. 1, 2nd ed.). New York: Wiley.

Exner, J. E., Viglione, D. J., & Gillespie, R. (1984). Relationship between Rorschach variables as revelant to the interpretation of structural data. *Journal of Personality Assessment, 48,* 65–70.

Feldman, M. J., & Graley, J. (1954). The effects of an experimental set to simulate abnormality on group Rorschach performance. *Journal of Projective Techniques, 18,* 326–334.

Fiske, D. W., & Baughman, E. E. (1953). Relationships between Rorschach scoring categories and the total number of responses. *Journal of Abnormal and Social Psychology, 48,* 25–32.

Fosberg, I. A. (1938). Rorschach reactions under varied instructions. *Rorschach Research Exchange, 3,* 12–30.

Fosberg, I. A. (1941). An experimental study of the reliability of the Rorschach psychodiagnostic technique. *Rorschach Research Exchange, 5,* 72–84.

Fosberg, I. A. (1943). How do subjects attempt to fake results on the Rorschach test? *Rorschach Research Exchange, 7,* 119–121.

Graham, J. R. (1987). *The MMPI: A practical guide.* New York: Oxford University Press.

Henry, E. M., & Rotter, J. B. (1956). Situational influences on Rorschach responses. *Journal of Consulting Psychology, 6,* 457–462.

Meisner, J. S. (1984). Susceptibility of Rorschach depression correlates to malingering. *Dissertation Abstracts International, 45,* 3951B.

Mittman, B. L., (1983). Judges' ability to diagnose schizophrenia on the Rorschach: The effect of malingering. *Dissertation Abstracts International, 44,* 1248B.

Overton, M. N. (1984). An examination of naive and role informed faking on Rorschach performance. *Dissertation Abstracts International, 45,* 683B.

Pedhazur, E. J. (1982). *Multiple regression in behavioral research.* New York: Holt Rinehart & Winston.

Perry, G. G., & Kinder, B. N. (1990). The susceptibility of the Rorschach to malingering: A critical review. *Journal of Personality Assessment, 54*(1 & 2), 47–57.

Pettigrew, C., Tuma, J., Pickering, J., & Whelton, J. (1983). Simulation of psychosis on a multiple-choice projective test. *Perceptual and Motor Skills, 57,* 463–469.

Rorschach Workshops. (1987). *Alumni Newsletter.* Asheville, NC.

Seamons, D. T., Howell, R. J., Carlisle, A. L., & Roe, A. V. (1981). Rorschach simulation of mental illness and normality by psychotic and non-psychotic legal offenders. *Journal of Personality Assessment, 45,* 130–135.

Shaffer, J. W., Duszynski, K. R., & Thomas, C. B. (1981). Orthogonal dimensions of individual and group forms of the Rorschach. *Journal of Personality Assessment, 45,* 230–239.

6

Empirical Assessment of Marital Distress: The Marital Distress Scale for the MMPI-2

Stephen Hjemboe
University of Minnesota

James N. Butcher
University of Minnesota

Moshe Almagor
University of Haifa

The importance of assessing marital relationship quality in the context of psychological assessment has arisen in recent years from at least two trends. First, there is a growing appreciation for the critical role played by an individual's primary attachment relationship in mediating psychological health and disorder (Hafner & Spence, 1988; Kumar & Robson, 1984; Waring, 1983; Waring, Patton, Neron, & Linker, 1983; Yassa, Nastase, & Camille, 1988). Knowledge of an individual's functioning in this area that can aid the test interpreter in assessing an individual's interpersonal functioning, general life adjustment, and social resources is critical in facilitating and maintaining treatment gains. Second, practitioners of marital therapy in recent years have become increasingly aware of the need for personality assessment as a part of treatment planning. Growing awareness of the limitations of family systems perspectives among family and marital therapists has prompted new interest in individual psychology, and with this trend is expected a renewed interest in individual assessment.

This chapter describes an attempt to develop a scale for an individual assessment instrument, the Minnesota Multiphasic Personality Inventory (MMPI), which provides the best possible measure of marital functioning. Interest in using the MMPI in marital assessment in both counseling and research is not new; indeed, it spans almost the life of the instrument (see Arnold, 1970; Barrett, 1973; Cookerly, 1974; Hjemboe, 1991; Hjemboe & Butcher, 1991; Snyder & Regts, 1990; Swan, 1953, 1957). However, its ability to reliably identify marital distress or to distinguish counselees from others has been rather modest. The clinical Scale 4 (Psychopathic deviate, Pd) has consistently proven to be the most significant index differentiating individuals with marital problems. Pd is a very heterogeneous scale, however, with a wide range of clinical meanings, and its relationship to dyadic problems is inconsistent at best. Arnold (1970) found Pd (not necessarily clinically elevated) in the 2-point codetypes of 55.2% and 62% of his female and male counselees, respectively; Cookerly (1974) found 51% and 50% of his samples had Pd-related codes. Snyder and Regts (1990) found 42.5% of high scorers on Snyder's Marital Satisfaction Inventory (MSI) Global Distress Index had elevated Pd scores and noted as well that many with high Pd scores appeared maritally satisfied. Modest correlations have been found between Pd and two measures of marital adjustment: .43 with the MSI Global Distress Scale (Snyder & Regts, 1990) and $-.41$ with the DAS (Hjemboe & Butcher, 1991). Pd also tends to misclassify many people who show no marital distress (Hjemboe, 1991; Snyder & Regts, 1990). The recently developed Family Problems (FAM) Content Scale (Butcher, Graham, Williams, & Ben-Porath, 1989), although less heterogeneous than the Pd scale, operates in a similar manner in identifying marital distress, also misclassifying individuals at both ends of the marital distress continuum. Its correlation with the DAS was found to be $-.41$, about as strong as that of Pd (Hjemboe & Butcher, 1991). Whereas designed to be homogeneous in content, the domain of family problems covered by FAM is somewhat broader than that of relationship distress.

The research described in this chapter was undertaken to develop the most efficient scale possible for identifying relationship maladjustment on the basis of the MMPI-2 item pool. In order to attain the highest possible discriminant validity, it was decided to develop a cross-validated set of items relevant in content to the domain of dyadic adjustment, from among those items that were most highly correlated with a measure of marital adjustment.

METHOD

The subjects were 150 couples in marital counseling and 776 couples from the MMPI-2 Restandardization sample (Butcher, Dahlstrom, Graham, Tellegen, & Kaemmer, 1989); of the latter sample, 384 couples were reserved for cross-validation. Counselees were obtained from therapists and marriage counselors, who themselves were initially selected through telephone directory listings of psychologists, private clinics specializing in marital and family therapy, and community mental health settings primarily in the Minneapolis–St. Paul metropolitan area and in Scottsdale, Arizona. From 45 sites initially contacted, 21 clinicians, primarily private practitioners, elected to participate. The control sample was designed to obtain a representative sample of the United States adult population with respect to geographic distribution, age, race, income, marital status, and residential setting (urban vs. rural), using 1980 census figures as guidelines. They were not screened for absence of psychopathology or marital distress. These subjects were randomly solicited and paid a small fee for their participation. The average age of the counselees was 37 years whereas controls averaged 41 years of age.

All subjects completed a 704-item adult experimental version (Form AX) of the MMPI on which the MMPI–2 was developed. Only those items used in the new test were used for scale development. A number of other personal information forms were also completed, including the Dyadic Adjustment Scale (DAS; Spanier, 1976), a 31-item inventory assessing areas of relationship consensus, cohesion, affection, and satisfaction. Higher scores on the DAS indicate better adjustment.

Subjects were excluded from the study who obtained a raw F- scale score greater than 30, a Back-F score greater than 25, or a Cannot Say greater than 30. All couples were heterosexual spouses or living partners (for stylistic brevity, the term marital is used in reference to all subjects).

Development of the Marital Distress Scale

The initial item pool for the scale was chosen by computing Pearson Product–Moment correlations between each MMPI–2 item and the DAS score among both counselee males and females. These items were then checked against the normal development sample. Seventeen items were found that correlated $p < .001$ among both sexes among the counselees, which also correlated significantly with both normal males and females. In the course of the selection procedure, it was clear that a great many more MMPI–2 items showed significant correlations to the DAS among normals, due in large measure to the less restricted range of DAS scores in the normal sample. The content of these items involved primarily anxiety and depression, whereas those strong in all four groups (male–female, counselee––normal) were those related more specifically to interpersonal functioning. This inspection raised the confidence of the investigators that using counselees for initial item selection was a profitable step for ensuring discriminant validity, because the group factor appeared to attenuate much of the significance of association of items less focal to relationship concerns. The 17 items then were correlated with the cross-validation sample only in order to exclude items with nonreplicating correlations. This step eliminated two items. In an attempt to increase the size of the item pool and to capture any variance remaining at large, all MMPI–2 items were then correlated to the provisional 15-item scale in all four development subsamples. Ten items correlated highly in at least three of these subsamples were retained for tentative scale inclusion. When entered as a group, however, scale correlation with the DAS declined markedly. Item inspection indicated, again, that many of the new items addressed depression and anxiety, and, whereas the nature of these items was intuitively related to marital distress, they were clearly lowering discriminant validity. The strongest of these new items were then entered into the original group one at a time, but none were found that increased scale correlation with the DAS. Previously chosen items were then removed one at a time and the scale retested with each removal. Three items were identified whose removal did improve the scale. At this point item content was again inspected; one of these detracting items was eliminated on the basis of extraneous content, whereas the two others were retained, trading a small degree of correlational strength for an increase in scale length. Because uniform T scores were to be computed for the scale, sufficient items were included to allow an adequate distribution of scores, as well as good reliability. Correlations between the final set of 14 items with the DAS were $-.52$ and $-.62$ for males and females, respectively, in the development sample, and $-.52$ and $-.54$ in the cross-validation sample, respectively. Cronbach's Alpha reliability coefficient was .65 in the development sample and .60 in the cross-validation sample. Although Alpha had approached .90 with the inclusion of the 10 extra items, it was decided to accept the lower alpha in favor of greater discriminant validity.

The final set of items (Hjemboe, Almagor, & Butcher, 1991) with their direction of scoring, and membership on other scales, is provided in Appendix A. As indicated, a number of the items also appear on Pd and FAM: As expected, the correlations of the MDS with these scales are quite high, as shown in Table 6.1. These correlations also indicate that, whereas sharing considerable variance, their domains have some degree of independence. Uniform T scores for the MDS, shown in Appendix B, were computed on the scale in the same manner as for MMPI-2 clinical and content scales (Butcher et al., 1990). This allows direct comparability between the elevation of the MDS scale and other MMPI-2 scales.

TABLE 6.1
Pearson Product-Moment Intercorrelations between Dyadic Adjustment Scale
(DAS) and Four MMPI-2 Predictors of Marital Distress

	DAS	MDS	Pd	Pdl
MDS	$-.55$			
Pd	$-.41$	.63		
Pdl	$-.43$	.62	.63	
FAM	$-.41$	.69	.55	.66

Note: Tabled values reflect pooled correlations across the entire sample.

RESULTS

In order to evaluate the relative efficacy of the Marital Distress Scale, we compared it with the three other MMPI-2 scales; Pd, FAM, the Harris-Lingoes (Harris & Lingoes, 1955) content scale Pd1 (Familial Discord) (scored with a linear *T* transformation). Scale comparisons were carried out through the use of multiple regression techniques with the DAS serving as the criterion.

The six-item overlap among the four scales necessitated the use of the following procedure in scale comparisons: First, the stepwise multiple regression technique was applied where the three scales entered the regression equation with no a priori set order. Second, in separate analyses, each of the scales entered the equation first followed by the others. The latter step allowed us to examine the unique contribution of each scale.

In the first regression equation, the four scales served as predictors for the DAS scores. This analysis was carried out for the total sample (n = 1,858). Table 6.2 indicates that MDS appeared as the best predictor with Pd1 following by a significant .01 increase in multiple R. The contribution of any scale other than MDS was significant but marginal in terms of multiple R increase (a final increase of .013 in R). In the second stage the entry order was set so that Pd1 was the first predictor entering the equation. The results indicated that Pd1 entered first with a multiple R value of .48 and all the scales contributed significantly to criterion prediction.

However, Pd1 and MDS contributed more substantially than both FAM and Pd. In the third step the order was set so that FAM entered the equation first. The results of this analysis indicated that MDS was the best predictor of DAS scores (R = .59; B = -4.72; β = $-.50$; t = 16.72; p < .000), whereas the contribution of the other scales, albeit significant, was marginal, adding only .013 to multiple R value. In these three analyses MDS emerged as the best predictor of DAS scores, whereas the contribution of the other three scales appeared negligible.

In addition to scale comparisons for the total sample, we compared their performance for the clinical and nonclinical subsamples. For this purpose, the preceding analyses were repeated.

TABLE 6.2
Regression Equation for the Total Sample with no a Priori Set Order of Entry

Variable	Multiple R	B	Beta	t	p
MDS	.592	-4.72	$-.50$	-16.74	.001
Pd	.602	$-.33$	$-.15$	-5.25	.001
Pd1	.604	$-.33$	.06	2.30	.02
FAM	.605	$-.11$	$-.05$	2.00	.05

When the nonforced regression equation was applied to the clinical sample ($n = 304$), MDS and FAM were the only scales in the final equation. Multiple R value when MDS entered the equation was .52 ($B = -5.08$; $\beta = -.63$; $t = -8.73$; $p < .000$). The addition of FAM led to a .01 increase in R ($R = .53$; $B = .31$; $\beta = .16$; $t = 2.2$; $p < .03$). In the next stage, the entry order was set first to enter Pd1 as the first predictor, then to enter FAM as the first predictor entering the regression equations. In both equations, MDS emerged as the best predictor ($R = .52$; $B = -5.06$; $\beta = -.63$; $t = -7.64$; $p < .000$) when Pd1 entered first, and $R = .55$ ($B = -4.07$; $\beta = -.55$; $t = 25.7$; $p < .000$) when FAM was the first to enter the equation.

The results of the analyses concerning the clinical sample demonstrated that MDS was the best predictor of marital distress. The same analyses were performed on the nonclinical sample ($n = 1,552$). The results of the non-forced regression analysis indicated that FAM entered the equation first with R value of .31 ($B = .4$; $\beta = .21$; $t = 2.6$; $p < .01$). The addition of MDS led to a .21 increase in R ($R = .52$; $B = -5.06$; $\beta = -.63$; $t = -7.64$; $p < .00$). The contribution of the other scales led to a .02 increase in R. When Pd1 was the first to enter the equation, the value of R was .43 ($B = -.26$; $\beta = -.13$; $t = -3.99$; $p < .00$), and the addition of MDS increased the value of R to .56 ($B = -3.86$; $\beta = -.43$; $t = -13.30$; $p < .00$). The contribution of FAM when it entered first was nonsignificant although R value was .41 ($B = -.02$; $\beta = -.01$; $t = -.24$; $p < .81$). The contribution of MDS that entered next was significant with a .14 increase in R ($R = .55$; $B = -4.04$; $\beta = -.45$; $t = -14.72$; $p < .00$). Again the contribution of the other scales was negligible although significant.

The results of the analyses concerning the normal sample corroborate the results of the earlier analyses demonstrating MDS as the best predictor of DAS scores.

The ability of the MDS to differentiate maritally distressed counselees from nondistressed normal subjects, compared with the other scales, was tested by means of a series of contingency tables (see Table 6.3). Counselees scoring 100 or below on the DAS and controls scoring above 100 were used for these comparisons: This multimethod strategy of group selection gave a high assurance of obtaining pure groups of well-adjusted and poorly adjusted subjects, avoiding the assumption of adjustment level on the basis of either group membership or adjustment score alone.

The efficiency of the scales at their cutting score were compared on three criteria: (a) the percentage of correct classification, (b) the percentage of correct positive judgments, and (c) the percentage of true cases identified. The first criterion indicates whether the scale as a whole improves on base rates. The second, the ratio of valid positives to all high scorers, indicates the probability of a condition being present given a positive diagnostic sign; it also indicates the scale's tendency to over-report distress. The third is the

TABLE 6.3
Comparisons of *Pd, Pd1, FAM,* and *MDS* Scale Elevations as
Measures of Dyadic Adjustment.[a]

Dyadic Adjustment	Scale T score		
	< 60	> 60	Total
Pd			
Poor	123	95	218
Good	1138	129	1267
			1485
Total	1261	224	
Pd1			
Poor	127	91	218
Good	1175	92	1267
			1485
Total	1302	183	
FAM			
Poor	138	80	218
Good	1143	124	1267
			1485
Total	1281	204	
MDS			
Poor	130	88	218
Good	1216	51	1267
Total	1346	139	1485

[a]Poor adjustment: DAS < 100; good adjustment: DAS > 100.

ratio of true positives to the total number of distressed individuals, and it also gauges the tendency of the scale to under-report. These tests are derived from methods proposed by Meehl and Rosen (1955).

The T score for the comparisons shown in Table 6.3 was set according to the base rate of .18 for marital distress in the normative sample, as measured by a DAS score less than 100. A T score cutoff of 60 was used, which theoretically permits 16% of the normal population to fall above the cutoff; a higher T score would necessarily result in an excessive number of false negatives. The asymmetry of sample sizes also approximately reflects this purported population distribution of marital distress, although in a clinical setting more equal numbers of distressed and nondistressed would be expected.

On the first criterion, only the MDS exceeds the base rate of 85% in correct classification: It correctly classifies 88% of the subjects. The Pd scale classifies 83% correctly, Pd1 classifies 85%, and FAM classifies 82%. On the MDS, scores at 60 indicated true distress 63% of the time. The MDS is the only scale on which a positive diagnostic judgment has a better than even chance of being correct. FAM does the worst in this regard, identifying many more who do not show distress than those who do. On the third criterion, no scale identifies more than half of the distressed at a T score of 60. The Pd scale actually identifies a greater number, but with much less discrimination between true and false negatives.

Further tests indicated that sample members misclassified by the MDS sample differ significantly in degree of distress from correctly classified sample members. A one-way analysis of variance on the four cells of the MDS contingency table indicated that their mean DAS scores differed significantly, $F(3, 1481) = 802.70$, $p < .0001$; Scheffe's multiple comparison procedure indicated that any pairwise comparison of group scores would be significant at the .01 level. From these tests it is clear that the mean adjustment score of the valid positives was significantly lower than that of the false negatives (with mean DAS scores of 72.5 and 83, respectively), and that the valid negatives had a significantly higher mean adjustment score than the false positives (121 and 111, respectively).

Lowering the cutting score of the MDS to 58 (raw score of 5) permitted the identification of 53% of the distressed, while reducing the overall correct classification rate from 88% to 86%, and the true positive rate to 54% – still providing a greater than even probability that a positive judgment would be correct. These number could be expected to improve in a clinical outpatient setting, in which the base rate for marital distress typically would be much higher. Although the actual functioning of the scale in such settings awaits the results of clinical trials, it seems likely that this lower score would be an appropriate point to begin to interpret.

CONCLUSION

The aim of this study has been to develop the most effective index of relationship distress possible on the basis of MMPI–2 items. The items were derived empirically on the basis of their correlation with a known measure of marital adjustment within a sample of marital counselees, separately for males and females. Use of counselees for initial item selection appeared to highlight and distinguish those items related in content to relationship distress from closely associated anxiety and depression items. These items were validated against a split sample of normal subjects, separately for males and females; hence, each item ultimately demonstrated its association with marital adjustment in both in sexes in three separate samples.

Comparison of the scale with the Pd, Pd1, and the FAM scales indicated its stronger correlation with the DAS scale, although multiple regression analyses indicate that it does not absorb all the variance in DAS scores. Although the current study did not analyze the meaning of these independent contributions, previous analyses of the meaning of Pd and FAM (Hjemboe & Butcher, 1991) among marital counselees suggested that the former tends to indicate more characterological disturbance, whereas the latter has somewhat greater sensitivity to a broad range of past and current family issues. External validation research is still required to delineate the domain tapped by the MDS, and to refine the distinctions between elevations on this scale and on the other scales here considered.

At a T score of 60, the MDS proves superior to any of the other scales in identifying more distressed subjects with the fewest false positives, and it made both types of discriminations efficiently. Although it identified just less than half of all subjects acknowledging substantial relationship problems, and well over half the subjects identified at that elevation were indeed in the distressed group. These tests were conducted with an attempt to approximate the antecedent probability of marital distress in the population. This approach probably underestimated the predictive strength of the scale in clinical use, because it probably overrepresents the proportion of individuals without relationship disturbance (and hence of false–positives) in the typical clinical setting. It awaits future research to test the scale on outpatients with sample sizes more representative of clinical base rates.

Although the demonstrated hit rate for positive scores on the MDS of 63% (Criterion 2) is not as high as might be wished for, it should be noted that unlikely base-rate assumptions can distort comparisons of its performance with that of other scales. For example, in the development of the MacAndrew alcoholism scale (MAC; MacAndrew, 1965), equal-sized groups of alcoholics and normal outpatients were used, which probably overestimates the prevalence of alcoholism among outpatients. Consequently, the expectable number of false–positives is probably underestimated. Hence, whereas MacAndrew's data show that positive judgments on the MAC at the cutting score would be 80% correct, that percentage is probably much lower in actual clinical use: If a still generous but more likely base rate of one alcoholic in five outpatients were assumed, its accuracy rate would be only 50%.

The low number of true cases identified (Criterion 3) is a second difficulty of the MDS. However, the current study does suggest that scores even at a T score of 58 (raw score of 5) may be useful in identifying most significant distress in a clinical situation, although its false–positive rate in a clinical situation is unknown. In spite of the brevity of the MDS, small numbers of items apparently can be quite diagnostic. Inspection of item content suggests intuitively that endorsement of even a few items would be unlikely in the absence of significant relational problems. Finally, it must be said that although the computation of cutting scores is useful in scale development and in indicating the probability of a correct clinical judgment, it is not well used as an absolute indicator of whether or not to interpret a scale score. As with other MMPI-2 scales, the MDS is most appropriately used as a continuous scale, with greater elevations indicating greater likelihood and extent of relationship maladjustment.

Another limitation of the MDS is that it is intrinsically limited in its sensitivity by the content of the MMPI-2 item pool. Because all MMPI-2 items must apply universally, items specific to a subject's mate relationship are precluded; hence, the MDS must approach the identification of relationship distress somewhat indirectly, and error must be expected in so doing. For the same reason the MDS can provide no specific information on types of relationship problems: Hypotheses of this kind must be generated in connection with other scale elevations. Although the limited information the scale does provide might be obtained quickly via interview, the clinician may not so inquire or have the opportunity to do so, particularly if the interpretation is blind.

Further research on the MDS is clearly called for in three areas. First, the performance of the MDS against a different measure of dyadic distress should be studied, because the DAS was involved in both test development and its validation. Second, more needs to be known concerning its extratest behavioral and personality correlates, particularly because not all maritally distressed individuals appear to score highly on the MDS. Finally, more discriminant validation work is required: Studies are needed in mixed outpatient groups to validate its ability to discriminate relationship maladjustment from other forms of psychological maladjustment.

In summary, The MDS is an empirically constructed scale intended to aid the clinician working with MMPI-2 in assessing relationship functioning. The MMPI-2 is used to generate hypotheses based on empirical correlates concerning a person's behavior, emotional state, response to therapy, and so forth. Accumulated knowledge on family and marital functioning has shown that, in some cases, an individual's difficulties may be associated with discord in one's primary relationship. However, the assessment techniques (both projective and objective) traditionally used in the assessment of psychological distress, as well as the current classifications of mental disorders (e.g., DSM-III-R), focus on the individual person. Although the nature and content of the MMPI-2 does not ideally suit it to the assessment of relationships, the use of the MDS, in conjunction with the standard Pd and FAM scales, will alert the MMPI-2 user to the possibility of marital or family discord, as well as provide an index of the level of relationship adjustment. It is hoped that this measure will provide a valuable utility in the process of case formulation and treatment planning.

ACKNOWLEDGMENTS

We thank the many marital therapists who collected data from their clients for this study: especially Joyce Anderson, Annette Brandes, Ralph Earle, Marlene Feldman, Mick Hunter, Pat Lilligren, and Gail Ross. Thanks are also extended to Yossef

Ben-Porath for his discussions on data analysis, to Brad Roper for the computation of Uniform *T* scores for the Marital Distress Scale, and to Karen Gayda and other members of the MMPI office staff in the Department of Psychology at the University of Minnesota for many hours of assistance in data collection and handling. We also acknowledge the University of Minnesota Press, National Computer Systems, and Academic Computing Services and Systems at the University of Minnesota for their support of this research.

REFERENCES

Arnold, P. D. (1970). *Marriage counselee MMPI profile characteristics with objective signs that discriminate them from married couples in general.* Unpublished doctoral dissertation, University of Minnesota, Minneapolis.

Barrett, R. K. (1973). *The relationship of emotional disorder to marital maladjustment and disruption.* Unpublished doctoral dissertation, Kent State University, OH.

Butcher, J. N., Dahlstrom, W. G., Graham, J. R., Tellegen, A., & Kaemmer, B. (1989). *Minnesota Multiphasic Personality Inventory-2 (MMPI-2): Manual for administration and scoring.* Minneapolis: University of Minnesota Press.

Butcher, J. N., Graham, J. R., Williams, C. L., & Ben-Porath, Y. S. (1990). *Development and use of the MMPI-2 Content Scales.* Minneapolis: University of Minnesota Press.

Cookerly, J. R. (1974). The reduction of psychopathology as measured by the MMPI clinical scales in three forms of marriage counseling. *Journal of Marriage and the Family, 36,* 332.

Hafner, R. J., & Spence, N. S. (1988). Marriage duration, marital adjustment and psychological symptoms: A cross-sectional study. *Journal of Clinical Psychology, 44,* 309–316.

Harris, R. E., & Lingoes, J. C. (1955). *Subscales for the MMPI: An aid to profile interpretation* (mimeographed). San Francisco: Department of Psychiatry, University of California.

Hjemboe, S. (1991). *MMPI-2 measured personality characteristics associated with marital distress.* Unpublished doctoral dissertation, University of Minnesota, Minneapolis.

Hjemboe, S., Almagor, M., & Butcher, J. N. (1991). In J. N. Butcher (Ed.), *User's guide to the Minnesota report for alcohol and drug treatment* (p. 92). Minneapolis: National Computer Systems.

Hjemboe, S., & Butcher, J. N. (1991). Couples in marital distress: A study of personality factors as measured by the MMPI-2. *Journal of Personality Assessment, 57,* 216–237.

Kumar, R., & Robson, K. M. (1984). A prospective study of emotional disorders in childbearing women. *British Journal of Psychiatry, 144,* 35–47.

MacAndrew, C. (1965). The differentiation of male alcoholic outpatients from nonalcoholic psychiatric outpatients by means of the MMPI. *Quarterly Journal of Studies on Alcohol, 26,* 238–246.

Meehl, P. E., & Rosen, A. (1955). Antecedent probability and the efficiency of psychometric signs, patterns or cutting scores. *Psychological Bulletin, 52,* 194–215.

Snyder, D. K., & Regts, J. M. (1990). Personality correlates of marital satisfaction: A comparison of psychiatric, maritally distressed, and nonclinic samples. *Journal of Sex and Marital Therapy, 16,* 34–43.

Spanier, G. B. (1976). Measuring dyadic adjustment: New scales for assessing the quality of marriage and similar dyads. *Journal of Marriage and the Family, 38,* 15–28.

Swan, R. J. (1953). *The application of a couple analysis approach to the MMPI in marriage counseling.* Unpublished doctoral dissertation, University of Minnesota, Minneapolis.

Swan, R. J. (1957). Using the MMPI in marriage counseling. *Journal of Counseling Psychology, 4,* 239–244.

Waring, E. M. (1983). Marriages of patients with psychosomatic illness. *General Hospital Psychiatry, 5,* 49–53.

Waring, E. M., Patton, D., Neron, C. A., & Linker, W. (1983). Types of marital intimacy and prevalence of emotional illness. *Canadian Journal of Psychiatry, 31,* 720-726.

Yassa, R., Nair, V., Nastase, C., & Camille, D. (1988). Prevalence of bipolar illness in a psychogeriatric population. *Journal of Affective Disorders, 14,* 197-201.

Appendix A
MMPI-2 Marital Distress Scale Items: Key Direction, and Scale Memberships

12	My sex life is satisfactory. (False)	F, 4, 8 (False)
21	At times I have very much wanted to leave home. (True)	4, 8, 9, FAM (True)
22	No one seems to understand me. (True)	4, 6, 8, TRT (True)
83	I have very few quarrels with members of my family. (False)	K, 4, ASA (True)
95	I am happy most of the time. (False)	2, 3, 4, 6, DEP (False)
125	I believe my home life is as pleasant as that of most people I know. (False)	3, 4, FAM (False)
135	I have often lost out on things because I couldn't make up my mind soon enough. (True)	3, 0, OBS, WRK, A (True)
195	There is very little love and companionship in my family as compared to other homes. (True)	4, FAM (True)
219	I have been disappointed in love. (True)	4, 5 (True)
382	I often have serious disagreements with people who are close to me. (True)	FAM (True)
484	People are not very kind to me. (True)	No scales
493	When I have a problem it helps to talk it over with someone. (False)	TRT (False)
494	My main goals in life are within my reach. (False)	TRT (False)
563	In most marriages one or both partners are unhappy. (True)	FAM (True)

Note: from Hjemboe, Almagor, & Butcher (1991).

Appendix B
Uniform *T* scores for the Marital Distress Scale

Raw Score	Males	Females
0	36	36
1	42	42
2	47	47
3	51	51
4	55	55
5	59	58
6	64	62
7	69	67
8	73	71
9	78	76
10	82	80
11	87	84
12	91	89
13	96	93
14	101	97

Note: T Scores have been derived on 1,138 men and 1,462 women in the MMPI-2 Normative Sample.

7

Angina Pectoris and Personality: Development and Validation of the Anginal Syndrome Questionnaire

Anthony F. Greene
University of Florida

Douglas D. Schocken
Charles D. Spielberger
University of South Florida

Chest pains characterized by intense pressure, heaviness, tightness, and pressure radiating to the neck, jaw, and left arm have been linked to cardiac disease since Heberden's original description of this syndrome, known as angina pectoris (AP), more than 200 years ago. Through the evaluation of autopsy results of patients with such complaints, Parry (1799) established an association between AP and "ossification" of the coronary arteries. Subsequent epidemiological and angiographic studies have shown that coronary artery disease (CAD) is the most common underlying cause of AP (Chaitman et al., 1981; Diamond & Forrester, 1979).

Angina pectoris has also been linked to other physical causes, such as coronary spasm, in patients with normal coronary arteries (Cannon, Leon, Watson, Rosing, & Epstein, 1985; Magarian & Hickam, 1986; Masseri et al., 1979; Silverman & Grossman, 1984). In addition, psychological factors have been found to contribute to AP symptoms in patients with normal arteries (Almeida, Stanford, Lutz, & Wenger, 1985; Katon et al., 1988). It is estimated that as many as 30% of patients with chest pains suspected of having ischemia are subsequently found to be free of clinically significant CAD (Chaitman et al., 1981; Gazes, 1988).

As the criteria for the diagnosis of AP have become more clearly defined, the research literature on nonanginal and atypical chest pain has also increased. Clinical investigators have recently suggested that atypical chest pain reflects an underlying psychiatric disorder resulting from a dynamic interaction between biological and psychosocial factors. It has been suggested by Mayou (1989), for example, that "psychiatric disorder is a major cause of atypical non-cardiac chest pain and psychological mechanisms frequently contribute to continuing symptoms, emotional distress and disability" (p. 403).

A biopsychosocial orientation seems to be gaining broader acceptance in medicine and cardiology, but divergent interpretations of the relation between psychological factors and the presentation of cardiovascular symptoms contribute to diagnostic uncertainty. Given increasing recognition of the important contribution of psychosocial and behavioral factors to the etiology of coronary heart disease, more sophisticated methods for assessing personality and clinical symptom presentation are needed to improve the diagnosis of coronary artery disease and the management of chest pain. To the degree that such methods can provide for a more differentiated evaluation of biological and psychosocial symptoms, confidence in the diagnosis of CAD will be enhanced.

Although relatively few studies have investigated the relation between chest pain and personality, those that used well-validated objective measures of psychological factors and operational procedures for assessing chest pain have reported findings with critical clinical implications for patient care. For example, Jenkins, Stanton, Klein, Savageau, and Harken (1983) interviewed 204 men awaiting bypass surgery and evaluated their reports of anginal chest pain and other symptoms. Poor sleep patterns and life crisis events were found to be the best predictors of AP symptoms precipitated by strong emotion. In commenting on the diagnostic implications of their findings, these authors concluded that it is essential to take emotional factors into account in diagnosing chest pain symptoms.

Evaluation of the contribution of emotions to the etiology of coronary disease also requires consideration of the gender and personality characteristics of the interviewer who takes the medical history, as well as the content and phrasing of the questions. Response biases of the patient in responding to personality tests may also contribute to differences in diagnostic outcome. Thus, the methods employed in evaluating emotions, personality, and chest pain symptoms are influenced by many factors that may, in turn, influence the observed relations of psychosocial and personality measures to AP and CAD.

This chapter begins with a brief review of the research literature on the relation between reports of chest pain symptoms and measures of emotion and personality traits in angiographic studies of coronary artery disease. The development and validation of the Anginal Syndrome Questionnaire (ASQ), a self-administered survey of AP symptoms, is then described in detail, and the psychometric properties and factor structure of this measure are reported. Research on the relation of the ASQ to measures of anxiety, anger, hostility, and cynicism, and to CAD as determined by angiography, is also presented. Finally, implications of the findings for the diagnosis and treatment of cardiovascular disorders are discussed.

ANGINAL SYMPTOMS, NEUROTIC TRAITS, AND CORONARY DISEASE

Early clinical studies of the relation between AP and cardiovascular pathology relied almost entirely on patients' reports of the nature and history of their chest pain symptoms, rather than on objective procedures for diagnostic classification of AP. More recent investigations have taken advantage of technological advances in diagnosis, such as the use of angiography for the assessment of obstruction due to atherosclerotic coronary artery disease. But the patient's symptom presentation and the history of AP are considered of great importance by cardiologists and internists in ordering angiographic tests, and in the management of cardiac problems.

Diagnostic uncertainty regarding the relation between chest pain and underlying disease results from the fact that AP is a descriptive symptom syndrome with features that are neither necessary nor sufficient to make the diagnosis of coronary atherosclerosis. According to the New York Heart Association (1979), in its most common form, AP is defined as "pain in the chest (usually localized to the retrosternal area), neck, shoulder, or left arm in patients with organic heart disease which is usually produced by effort and relieved by rest or nitrites" (p. 289). Atypical angina may be diagnosed where definite classical features are present along with unusual or nontypical symptoms. When complaints of intense discomfort in the upper body are reported but no classic AP features are presented, nonanginal chest pain may be diagnosed.

The New York Heart Association (1979) has developed a differentiated classification of AP patients based on limitations in physical activity that are presumed to generally reflect the *severity* of the underlying CAD. This system classifies patients into the following four classes: Class I includes patients with AP leading to the diagnosis of cardiac disease, but without any resulting limitation of physical activity; Class II includes patients with a slight limitation of physical activity; Class III patients are considered to have cardiac disease that results in marked limitation of physical activity; Class IV patients are unable to carry out any physical activity and may experience symptoms at rest, presumably due to severe cardiac disease.

Patients may also be classified on the basis of their *pattern* of chest pain as having Stable, Unstable, or Variant (Prinzmetal's) Angina (Hurst, 1978). In Stable Angina, the symptoms typically remain constant in quality, intensity, and precipitating factors and usually do not exceed 2 to 10 minutes in duration. The symptoms of Unstable Angina, also referred to as Crescendo, are characterized by prolonged attacks that become more frequent and intense as time passes. Variant, or Prinzmetal's, Angina usually occurs at rest or during sleep.

Research has shown that both the NYHA severity classification and the pattern method of classifying AP symptoms provide useful information for treatment and prognosis (Chaitman et al., 1981; Jenkins, 1976; Proudfit, Shirey, & Sones, 1966), but there are nevertheless large diagnostic error rates. For example, in the Coronary Artery Surgery Study (CASS) of 8,157 patients (Chaitman et al., 1981), disease prevalence as evaluated by angiography of patients with definite angina, chronic stable chest pain and no history of myocardial infarction, was 93% in men and 72% in women. Thus, 28% of the women with chronic, definite angina did not have clinically significant disease. Also noteworthy, the disease prevalence was 66% for men and only 32% for women in patients classified as having "probable" angina.

In addition to the problems in the reliability of the diagnosis of AP, there are serious limitations in the validity of AP symptoms as a predictor of the incidence and mortality of CAD. For example, in a study of 1,921 patients who had survived myocardial infarctions (Friedman & Byington, 1985), physicians diagnosed three times as many patients as having AP as were diagnosed using the Rose Questionnaire, a brief seven-item anginal screening device derived from a questionnaire by the London School of Hygiene (Rose, 1962). Relative risk of coronary heart disease (CHD) mortality, however, was somewhat better for the Rose Questionnaire (14.4%) than for diagnosis of AP by the physicians (11.4%). When patients with atypical AP were excluded, this did not improve the prediction of CHD mortality, but when the diagnosis of AP was positive for both procedures, mortality risk was slightly higher (15.4%).

Although the presence of AP symptoms is considered important in the diagnosis of cardiac disease, the absence of CAD is not synonymous with the absence of functional impairment due to chest pain. For example, in a follow-up study of 159 patients whose coronary angiograms had shown narrowing or occlusion of less than 30%, Pasternak, Thibault, Savoia, DeSanctis, and Hutter (1980) found that nearly half these patients reported some limitation of activity. Moreover, 22% had either stopped working or changed jobs because of chest pain. Similarly, Almeida et al. (1985) reported that 32% of chest pain patients with normal coronary arteries subsequently stopped work due to their pain.

Diagnostic information about chest pain symptoms may be influenced during history taking by the questions asked and the depth of inquiry during the diagnostic interview, and by the empathic support provided by the physician. Engel, Baile, Costa, Brimlow, and Brinker (1985) found that physicians often overestimated patients' symptoms based on patients' own reports, especially regarding severity of pain. These findings raise questions about the conventional belief that physicians' ratings of symptoms reflect both the presence of a disease process and the sensitivity of the patient's nervous system to experiencing that process (Hurst, 1978).

It is now generally accepted that emotions can make severe demands on cardiac capacity, especially when there is already some physical limitation of function (Deanfield & Selwyn, 1986; Rozanski et al., 1989). Based on his extensive review of research findings on anxiety and neuroticism as precursors of coronary disease, Jenkins (1971) noted that these traits were particularly important risk factors for AP, and that somatic preoccupation and lower pain thresholds seemed be to characteristic of chest pain patients. Although the diagnosis of AP, myocardial infarction (heart attack), and sudden cardiac death were generally grouped together as a common endpoint for coronary heart disease, at the time of his review, Jenkins suggested that the precursors of these disease states might be quite different. In a later review of psychosocial risk factors for coronary disease, Jenkins (1976) concluded that anxiety, depression, neuroticism, and personal dissatisfaction were consistently reported as precursors of AP, but not of the other CHD endpoints.

In one of the earliest studies of the personality correlates of AP and CAD, as assessed by coronary angiography, Zyzanski, Jenkins, Ryan, Flessas, and Everist (1976) found that men with AP symptoms and more severe CAD scored *higher* on measures of anxiety, neuroticism, and depression than those with less severe CAD. In contrast, recent angiographic studies have consistently reported that patients with chest pain and angiographic evidence of CAD score *lower* in anxiety and neuroticism than those with chest pain but no CAD (Costa et al., 1985; Elias, Robbins, Blow, Rice, & Edgecomb, 1982; Schocken, Greene, Worden, Harrison, & Spielberger, 1987). Such findings raise questions concerning the appropriateness of using patients undergoing coronary angiography to evaluate behavioral risk factors for CHD (Pickering, 1985).

Whereas Mayou (1989) contends that temperament and personality play a causal role in the development of chest pain, Costa, Fleg, McCrae, and Lakatta (1982) have proposed that neuroticism leads to the diagnosis of AP because this syndrome influences patients' health perceptions and symptom reports. Greene, Lindholm, Kolb, and Pepine (1990) found that patients who reported angina with documented ischemic episodes (as assessed by EKG) were rated as more hostile, interrupted the interviewer more often, and spoke more rapidly during a stressful interview than patients without chest pain. Similarly, Schocken et al., (1990) found that patients with AP, with or without ischemia, had greater anger than patients with silent myocardial ischemia. Thus, patients with AP were rated as more hostile and neurotic than patients who did not report chest pain, even when the latter had angiographically documented CAD.

In summary, the relation between personality and chest pain symptoms seems to be both dynamic and bidirectional. Furthermore, nonatherosclerotic origins of chest pain have yet to be rigorously investigated, a serious shortcoming that limits the conclusions that may be drawn from the present literature. Hopefully, the development of more objective and sophisticated procedures for assessing chest pain can contribute to teasing apart the interactive influence on CAD of personality factors and patients' presentations of anginal symptoms.

DEVELOPMENT OF THE ANGINAL SYNDROME QUESTIONNAIRE

The ASQ is a self-administered questionnaire that was developed to provide an objective, unbiased assessment of patients' perceptions of their chest discomfort. The initial set of ASQ items were selected on the basis of previous efforts at diagnostic enumeration of anginal symptoms. Primary sources for identifying symptoms traditionally associated with AP included Heberden's (1772) classical description of AP, the NYHA diagnostic criteria (1979), the CASS criteria (Chaitman et al., 1981), studies of anginal histories by Rose (1962), Frank, Weinblatt, and Shapiro, (1973), Costa et al. (1985), and Engel et al. (1985), and extensive consultation with practicing cardiologists.

In developing the ASQ, the full range of information and symptom description required for the differential diagnosis of chest pain was compiled into a comprehensive survey of 43 traditional AP symptoms. The Rose Questionnaire, a section of the London School of Hygiene Questionnaire that focuses on angina pectoris (Rose, 1962), was used to define the central set of symptoms of classical angina pectoris. These symptoms, which have been extensively researched in field trials and clinical populations, include sensations of pressure or heaviness in the chest that are precipitated by exertion and relieved by rest. The pattern of symptoms and relief assessed by the Rose Questionnaire have achieved prominence in the literature as reflecting the typical pattern of ischemic chest pain in persons with coronary artery disease. Other common variants of this pattern, such as chest discomfort experienced as squeezing or tightness, are also included in the subset of 43 traditional AP symptoms.

A number of Atypical AP symptoms and nonanginal or "bogus" chest pain symptoms were added to the initial ASQ item pool in order to provide a balanced questionnaire that reflected noncoronary chest pains and neurotic complaints, as well as AP symptoms. Symptoms descriptive of pains associated with gastric disturbances or arthritic conditions clearly unrelated to CAD are examples of the nonanginal items included in the

ASQ. The preliminary ASQ was comprised of 27 Atypical AP symptoms and 39 items describing nonanginal symptoms. The symptom features comprising the ASQ Traditional AP, Atypical AP, and Nonanginal symptom subsets are listed in Appendix A.

Five parameters of chest discomfort are assessed by the ASQ: (a) quality and intensity; (b) location and radiation; (c) duration, frequency, and pattern of recurrence; (d) precipitating, aggravating, and relieving factors; and (e) accompanying signs and symptoms. In responding to the ASQ, patients are asked to check the symptom features that describe any chest discomfort they had experienced in the last 2 to 3 months. For each ASQ symptom feature reported by the patient, 1 point is scored on the appropriate ASQ scale. One or 2 additional points are scored on the basis of the patient's endorsement of greater intensity (mild, moderate, intense) or frequency (sometimes, often, almost always). Additional points are also scored if the patient reports that the symptoms had persisted for a longer period of time. Thus, ASQ scores are based on ratings by the patient of the quality, intensity, duration, and relief of chest pain symptoms, as well as the number of complaints.

Psychometric Properties of the ASQ

The psychometric properties of the final form of the ASQ, which can be found in Appendix B, were evaluated in a sample of medical patients (87 males, 57 females) scheduled to undergo coronary angiography for evaluation of chest discomfort. The questionnaire was administered the afternoon or evening preceding the angiography procedure. Participating cardiologists evaluated the percentage of stenosis for each of the four major coronary arteries. The collaborative project from which these patients are a subset has been described in detail elsewhere (Greene, 1986, 1988; Schocken et al., 1987).

The means and standard deviations for the ASQ Traditional AP (ASQ-AP) and Nonanginal (ASQ-N) subscales for patients with and without disease (75% or greater occlusion of one or more arteries) are reported in Table 7.1. The alpha coefficients for the ASQ-AP subscale for the total sample were .81 for males and .87 for females, and somewhat lower for the NonAnginal subscales. In general, the findings for the Atypical AP symptoms were similar to those obtained for the Nonanginal symptoms and are not reported in this chapter.

Differences in the AP and Nonanginal symptoms as a function of gender and the presence or absence of disease were evaluated in separate 2 × 2 factorial ANOVAs. The disease main effects were statistically highly significant for both symptom subsets ($p < .001$). Surprisingly, both male and female patients with no clinically significant disease reported substan-

TABLE 7.1
Means and Standard Deviations for the ASQ Traditional AP (ASQ-AP) and
Nonanginal (ASQ-N) symptoms for Males and Females With and Without CAD

		Males		Females	
		CAD	No CAD	CAD	No CAD
		(72)	(15)	(24)	(33)
ASQ-AP	Mean	42.1	50.5	41.9	49.5
	SD	11.6	12.6	13.7	11.0
ASQ-N	Mean	31.4	36.4	31.2	38.1
	SD	7.0	8.6	10.1	11.6

tially more symptoms than those with CAD. There were no significant differences between men and women nor Gender by Disease interactions in the number of symptoms reported for either the ASQ-AP or ASQ-N subscales. Thus, reporting a larger number of symptoms was associated with the *absence* of CAD, regardless of gender or the nature of the symptoms.

Gender and ASQ subscale scores were entered in regression analyses as predictors of *severity* of disease for the total sample. CAD severity was defined by the number of arteries with 75% or greater occlusion. Contrary to our expectations, but consistent with the findings previously reported for presence or absence of disease, patients reporting *more* symptoms were evaluated by cardiologists as having *less* severe disease. In these analyses, gender was the strongest predictor of disease; being male accounted for approximately 13% of the variance in disease severity.

Factor Structure of the ASQ

Given our focus in developing the ASQ on CAD as the primary index of criterion validity, we explored the underlying factor structure for the 43 ASQ items describing symptom features classically associated with AP in the literature. Separate principle components factor analyses were performed for male and female patients. The ASQ responses of 176 patients (131 males, 75 females) were available for these analyses. Considering eigenvalues greater than unity, along with Cliff and Hamburger's (1967) "breaks" criterion, the three-factor solution was considered optimal for both sexes in terms of simple structure. This solution yielded the highest number of nonoverlapping factor loadings, with the fewest number of items with salient loadings of less than .30 for at least one factor. Goodness-of-fit tests for the two-, four-, and five-factor solutions confirmed the selection of the three-factor solution as optimal.

In order to minimize the influence of neuroticism on the factor structure of the ASQ, correlations of each of the 43 traditional AP items with trait anxiety scores, and with the presence or absence of CAD, were used as exclusion criteria. Those items that were both significantly positively correlated with anxiety and negatively correlated with CAD were eliminated, except that items from the Rose Questionnaire were given immunity from exclusion in order to retain the ability to derive a diagnosis of AP comparable to that which might be obtained using the Rose Questionnaire. The following five symptoms (items) that correlated significantly and positively with anxiety ($p < .05$) and negatively with CAD ($p < .05$) were eliminated: discomfort when angry, when upset, or when eating a large meal; a pattern of increasing severity; and frequent choking sensations.

A second set of exclusion criteria was based on individual factor loadings for each item in separate oblique, three-factor solutions for males and females. Although individual item loadings were similar in the orthogonal and oblique solutions for both sexes, the oblique solutions were selected as the criterion for item exclusion for two reasons: (a) Factor loadings were stronger in the oblique solution, and (b) two of the three factors showed high intercorrelations. Any item that did not have a salient loading of .30 or greater on at least one of the three factors for either males or females was eliminated. In accordance with these criteria, the following four items were eliminated: Dizziness, size of the discomfort, origin in right chest, and feeling tense.

A principle components factor analysis was performed on the remaining 34 items. Review of the loadings for the two- and four-factor solutions reaffirmed the optimal goodness-of-fit for the oblique three-factor solution, which was used as the final criterion for exclusion. Those items that did not have a factor loading of at least .30 for *both* males and females, rather than for *either* males or females, were eliminated. This more stringent criterion was chosen to avoid gender bias. The four items that were excluded on the basis of this criterion were prompt relief from nitroglycerin, having sex prior to an episode, frequency of episodes, and radiations to right chest.

The simple structure of the resulting factors for the remaining 30 items, which we refer to as the ASQ–30, was relatively clear. Alpha coefficients for the 30 item ASQ–30 for males and females were .81 and .77, respectively. The items and their loadings on the three ASQ–30 factors are reported in Table 7.2. Factor I is comprised of pain descriptors and symptoms of respiratory distress; Factor II consists primarily of descriptors of chest pain that radiates to the neck and the left side of the body; the items in Factor III describe chest pain features evoked by exertion. The Rose Questionnaire items area are marked by asterisks; double asterisks indicate marginal loadings for these items.

TABLE 7.2

Factor Loadings for ASQ–30 Items for Males (M) and Females (F)

	FACTOR LOADINGS					
	I		*II*		*III*	
Items	*M*	*F*	*M*	*F*	*M*	*F*
1. Frequent tightness in the chest	.73	.28	−.09	.29	.05	−.09
2. Intense tightness in the chest	.69	.54	−.06	.28	.12	.03
*3. Frequent heaviness in the chest	.68	.77	.04	−.03	−.06	−.01
*4. Intense heaviness in the chest	.67	.84	.16	.09	−.06	−.08
5. Associated with difficulty breathing	.62	.66	−.29	.01	.16	.18
6. Frequent squeezing in the chest	.57	.36	.11	.29	−.07	−.15
7. Intense squeezing in the chest	.56	.39	.22	.29	−.16	−.01
8. Associated with a loss of energy	.53	.28	.08	.37	.10	.17
*9. Frequent pressure in the chest	.50	.74	.23	−.17	−.25	.06
10. Tries sitting for relief	.48	.46	−.04	.08	.02	.15
*11. Intense pressure in the chest	.47	.64	.36	.01	−.02	−.02
**12. Tries resting for relief	.34	.04	.08	.33	−.03	−.16
**13. Resting brings prompt relief	−.30	.27	.28	−.01	−.32	.12
14. Intense aching in the chest	.10	−.20	.66	.59	.11	.23
15. Frequent aching in the chest	.01	−.13	.64	.60	.08	.20
16. Number of nitroglycerin tablets used	−.02	.12	.57	.33	.10	−.22
*17. Discomfort radiates to the left arm	−.07	.01	.55	.54	−.08	.09
*18. Discomfort radiates to the left chest	.14	−.04	.49	.60	.02	.15
*19. Discomfort lasts ten minutes or less	−.01	.20	.48	.33	−.39	−.30
20. Discomfort radiates to neck and jaw	.03	.20	.43	.49	.05	−.01
**21. Tries nitroglycerin tabs for relief	.12	.01	.40	.08	.20	−.05
*22. Discomfort when walking hurriedly	−.07	.17	.02	−.17	.71	.77
*23. Discomfort when walking uphill	.01	.20	.14	−.16	.69	.73
24. Discomfort when mowing the lawn	.09	.17	−.15	.04	.64	.56
25. Discomfort when lifting weight	.04	−.03	.15	−.24	.61	.59
26. Discomfort working with arms overhead	−.03	−.06	.34	.23	.57	.55
27. Discomfort in cold weather activity	−.01	−.10	.12	.19	.50	.60
28. Each occurrence is similar in pattern	−.02	−.13	−.11	−.37	.35	.31
29. Discomfort when exercising	−.17	.01	.22	.19	.33	.52
**30. Discomfort when walking normally	.16	.09	.19	.29	.08	.19

*Indicates items from the Rose Questionnaire that met the inclusion criteria for retention in the factor analysis.

**Indicates items from the Rose Questionnaire that were allowed immunity from exclusion from the factor analysis.

Several gender differences may be noted in the three-factor solutions for the ASQ–30 reported separately for males and females in Table 7.2. For most items, the factor loadings were generally stronger for the males. The second strongest factor for males was comprised of items that described radiation of chest pain to the left side of the body (Factor II), whereas the factor relating to exertional precipitation (Factor III) was second strongest for females. Because the traditional AP symptoms that comprise the ASQ-30 were originally identified in predominantly male patients, it is perhaps not surprising that the factor loadings were stronger for males than females.

Examination of the individual ASQ-30 item loadings in Table 7.2 reveals that most of the Rose Questionnaire items had salient loadings on one of the three factors, even without the predetermined immunity from exclusion. The ASQ items with the weakest and least consistent loadings were related to the failure to obtain relief of AP symptoms from rest or nitroglycerin. The response to these items may be influenced by a noncardiac chest pain component because there would be little basis for expecting that rest or nitroglycerin would relieve the discomfort experienced by patients with noncardiac pain. It is also possible that the total number of pain-relief items was not sufficient to define a viable factor.

Relation of the ASQ to Neurotic Traits and CAD

Scores on the ASQ-30 of patients with and without disease were compared, and the relations of trait anxiety, anger expression, and cynical hostility to disease status were evaluated. Although patients with CAD were expected to report more classical AP symptoms than those without disease, the findings reported earlier in this chapter indicated that the opposite was, indeed, the case (i.e., patients without CAD reported more ASQ symptoms, including classical AP symptoms). A similar relationship was also found for the items adapted from the Rose Questionnaire, as well as for the subset of items rated by cardiologists as "probably" related to CAD (Greene, Schocken, & Spielberger, 1991).

In order to take age into account in evaluating the relation between the personality measures and CAD, the patients were divided into three age groups. Because there were substantially more male than female patients in the study sample, comparable cell sizes for evaluating age and gender differences were created by defining the age groups on the basis of the 30th and 70th percentiles of the age distribution for the female patients. The resulting age ranges and the number of male and female patients in each age group were as follows: younger, age range = 30 to 59 (41 males, 25 females); middle, age range = 60 to 67 (41 males, 26 females); older, age range = 68 to 81 (39 males, 25 females).

Multivariate analyses of variance were performed with the presence or absence of CAD, gender, and age groups as the independent variables and scores on trait anxiety, anger expression, hostility, and the ASQ-30 as the dependent variables. The multivariate findings using Wilks' criterion indicated significant main effects for CAD [$F(4,182) = 2.58, p < .04$], Gender

$[F (4,182) = 3.30, p < .02]$, and age $[F (8,364) = 2.99, p < .01]$, but no statistically significant interactions.

The statistical findings in the multivariate analyses were clarified in univariate analyses in which age, gender, and CAD were independent variables and trait anxiety, anger expression, cynical hostility, and AP complaints were the dependent variables. As in the preceding analyses, patients without CAD scored significantly higher on the ASQ-30 than those with disease, which was reflected in the main effect for CAD $[F (1,185) =$ 7 to 71, $p < .01]$. This was true for the younger and middle-age groups, but not for the older males; older men with CAD reported more symptoms than those without CAD. A significant main effect of age was also found; younger patients reported more chest pain symptoms than the middle-age group $[F (2,185) = 4.50, p < .02]$, with the older group reporting an intermediate number of symptoms.

There were no significant differences in trait anxiety associated with age, gender, or disease. Male patients without CAD had significantly higher hostility scores than males with CAD $[F (1,185) = 6.55, p < .05]$, and males also scored higher in cynical hostility than females $[F (1,185) = 8/81, p < .01]$. No other differences in cynical hostility were found, but the middle-age group scored higher in anger expression than the older group $[F (2,185) = 4.01, p < .02)]$.

The results of the present study suggest that the relation between personality traits and CAD is complex and strongly influenced by age and gender differences, as was previously reported for the anxiety scores in a related sample of angiography patients (Schocken et al., 1987). In general, age shared overlapping variance with anger expression (older patients were less angry) and with chest pain (younger patients reported more symptoms). Although anger–hostility was related to CAD for males independent of age, the observed relations were opposite in direction to those reported in a majority of the studies cited in the literature. For women, older age and lower ASQ-30 scores were both significantly related to the presence of disease.

DISCUSSION AND CONCLUSIONS

In the present study, the ASQ-30 was significantly and inversely related to the presence of CAD for both male and female patients undergoing angiography for evaluation of their chest pain complaints. Moreover, an inverse relation between symptoms and angiographic evidence of CAD was found across several different methods of scoring both symptoms and CAD. This consistent tendency for patients without CAD to endorse more ASQ-30 symptoms than those with disease was not influenced by either age or gender. A possible explanation for these paradoxical findings may relate to a selection bias in the study sample. The patients in the study were known to have been referred for diagnostic coronary angiography to evaluate chest pain. For such patients, there is clinical uncertainty regarding the basis and severity of their complaints, which may be a function of mixed disease manifestations.

Costa et al. (1982, 1985) reported that anginal symptoms and angiographic evidence of CAD were essentially unrelated. In the present study, patients' reports of symptoms were inversely related to CAD. For women personality features were unrelated to CAD, but for men cynical hostility was inversely related to CAD. These findings suggested that patients' reports of chest pain are more strongly associated with nonatherosclerotic factors such as neurotic tendencies, and that age, gender, and sampling procedures should be considered in research on the relation between AP symptoms, personality and disease.

Analysis of the anxiety scores of patients evaluated in the first 2 years of this study revealed that the women scored significantly higher in anxiety than the men (Schocken et al., 1987). However, as more subjects were added to the sample, this gender difference in anxiety lost significance, due primarily to the higher anxiety scores of the younger males entering the study. Comparison of the mean anxiety scores of our patients to those of working adults revealed that the anxiety level of the female patients were within the normal range, whereas the anxiety scores of the male patients were elevated due primarily to the higher scores of the younger males without CAD. The fact that the younger men without CAD were more anxious and more hostile may have contributed to their referral for angiography.

Pickering (1985) observed that most angiography studies report comparable disease prevalence rates, but he questioned the findings of relations between personality and CAD based on studies of patients undergoing angiography because of possible sampling bias. Empirical support of this need for caution was provided by Matthews (1988). Based on a meta-analytic review of studies of high-risk and population-based samples, Matthews reported that negative emotions were unrelated to CHD in studies of high-risk patients but significantly related in population-based investigations. Our findings provide further evidence that sample characteristics may influence the relations among symptom presentation, personality characteristics, and CAD.

The factor analyses of the traditional AP symptoms in this study identified three factors that were intuitively consistent with the organic pathology presumably associated with anginal pain. The observed inverse relation of traditional AP symptoms with disease defies clear explanation and merits further study with other patient samples. The findings of the present study suggest that it will be important to take relevant personality factors into account when evaluating the nature of the symptoms reported by patients referred for angiography. It seems reasonable, for example, that AP symptoms related to labored breathing and precipitated by exertion would be highly correlated, but do more stoic individuals endorse fewer pain descriptors? Do individuals with chest pain from noncardiac causes endorse fewer symptoms from the exertion domain?

The delineation of traditional AP symptoms in the ASQ-30 along with the findings presented in this chapter provide a starting point for the systematic investigation of the personality correlates of the anginal syndrome. Clearly, there is much more to be learned about the presentation of the features of chest pain and discomfort, and how these relate to personality and demographic variables.

SUMMARY

The essential features of angina pectoris have maintained their prominence in the practice of cardiology for many years and are widely used as clinical markers of coronary artery disease. Recent investigations have suggested that personality factors, such as anxiety and neuroticism, may significantly influence the report of chest pain. The Rose Questionnaire, which focuses on the presence or absence of the traditional primary symptoms of myocardial ischemia, has been used extensively in epidemiological studies but rarely in clinical practice.

The Anginal Syndrome Questionnaire (ASQ) was developed to sample a broad range of chest symptoms in addition to the traditional features of angina pectoris. This questionnaire was designed for research on AP and potential use as a supplementary diagnostic tool. Exploratory factor analyses of the ASQ have identified three distinct components or factors that underlie the clinical features of chest pain. Two of these factors, respiratory difficulties and exertional precipitation of discomfort, reflect traditional symptoms of underlying cardiac ischemia. The individual ASQ items with the weakest loadings on these factors were related to minimal exertion as a precipitant of AP and to various methods for the relief of chest pains. The third factor, which included symptoms relating to pain descriptors and locations, may turn out to be most influenced by neurotic traits.

In the present study, patients without angiographic evidence of CAD consistently reported more traditional chest pain symptoms in responding to the ASQ-30, regardless of age or gender. This was also true for reports of nonanginal symptoms, and even for the Rose Questionnaire symptoms. Contrary to expectation, males without CAD were higher in hostility than those with CAD; personality was otherwise unrelated to CAD. When considered along with the results of previous studies, these findings suggest that the endorsement of chest pain complaints in responding to the ASQ-30 may be substantially influenced by neurotic personality traits. Whereas the relationship between personality and AP is multidetermined, neurotic individuals who "protest too much" appear to be less likely to have CAD.

REFERENCES

Almeida, D., Stanford, J., Lutz, J., & Wenger, N. (1985). Chest pain with normal coronary arteries. *Journal of Cardiopulmonary Rehabilitation, 5,* 364–372.

Cannon, R. O., Leon, M., Watson, R., Rosing, D., & Epstein, S. (1985). Chest pain and "normal" coronary arteries—role of small coronary arteries. *American Journal of Cardiology, 55,* 50B–60B.

Chaitman, B., Bourassa, M., Davis, K., Rogers, W., Tyras, D. H., Berger, R., Kennedy, J. W., Fisher, L., Judkins, M. P., Mock, M. B., & Killip, T. (1981). Angiographic prevalence of high-risk coronary artery disease in patient subsets (CASS). *Circulation, 64,* 360–367.

Cliff, N., & Hamburger, C. D. (1967). The study of sampling errors in factor analysis by means of artificial experiments. *Psychological Bulletin, 68,* 430–455.

Costa, P. T., Fleg, J. L., McCrae, R. R., & Lakatta, E. G. (1982). Neuroticism, coronary artery disease, and chest pain complaints: Cross-sectional and longitudinal studies. *Experimental Aging Research, 8,* 37–44.

Costa, P. T., Zonderman, A. B., Engel, B. T., Baile, W. F., Brimlow, D. L., & Brinker, J. (1985). The relation of chest pain symptoms to angiographic findings of coronary artery stenosis and neuroticism. *Psychosomatic Medicine, 47,* 285–293.

Deanfield, J. E., & Selwyn, A. P. (1986). Character and causes of transient myocardial ischemia during daily life. *The American Journal of Medicine, 80(Supplement 4C),* 18–24.

Diamond, G. A., & Forrester, J. S. (1979). Analysis of probability as an aid in the clinical diagnosis of coronary artery disease. *New England Journal of Medicine, 300,* 1350–1358.

Elias, M. F., Robbins, M. A., Blow, F. C., Rice, A. P., & Edgecomb, J. L. (1982). A behavioral study of middle-aged chest pain patients: Physical symptom reporting, anxiety and depression. *Experimental Aging Research, 9,* 45–51.

Engel, B. T., Baile, W. F., Costa, P. T., Brimlow, D., & Brinker, J. (1985). A behavioral analysis of chest pain in patients suspected of having coronary heart disease. *Psychosomatic Medicine, 47,* 274–284.

Frank, C. W., Weinblatt, E., & Shapiro, S. (1973). Angina pectoris in men: Prognostic significance of selected medical factors. *Circulation, 47,* 509–517.

Friedman, L. M., & Byington, R. P. (1985). Assessment of AP after MI: Comparison of the "Rose Questionnaire" with physician judgment in the Beta-Blocker Heart Attack Trial. *American Journal of Epidemiology, 121,* 555–562.

Gazes, P. C. (1988). Angina pectoris: Classification and diagnosis, part 2. *Modern Concepts of Cardiovascular Disease, 57,* 25–27.

Greene, A. F. (1986). *Anxiety, anginal symptoms and coronary artery disease.* Unpublished master's thesis, University of South Florida, Tampa.

Greene, A. F. (1988). *Coronary heart disease in anxious angry hearts.* Unpublished doctoral dissertation, University of South Florida, Tampa.

Greene, A. F., Lindholm, L., Kolb, R., & Pepine, C. (1990, April). Verbal stylistics during a structured anger assessment interview in symptomatic and asymptomatic ischemia patients. *Eleventh Annual Proceedings: Session Abstracts and Meeting Information.* Society of Behavioral Medicine, Chicago.

Greene, A. F., Schocken, D. D., & Spielberger, C. D. (1991). Self-report of chest pain symptoms and coronary artery disease in patients undergoing angiography. *Pain, 47,* 319–324.

Heberden, W. (1772). Some account of a disorder of the breast. *Medical Transcripts of the Royal College of Physicians, 2,* 59–67.

Hurst, J. W. (1978). *The heart: Arteries and veins.* New York: McGraw–Hill.

Jenkins, C. D. (1971). Psychologic and social precursors of coronary disease. *New England Journal of Medicine, 284,* 244–255, 312–317.

Jenkins, C. D. (1976). Recent evidence supporting psychologic and social risk factors for coronary disease. *New England Journal of Medicine, 294,* 987–994, 1033–1038.

Jenkins, C. D., Stanton, B., Klein, M., Savageau, J., & Harken, D. (1983). Correlates of angina pectoris among men awaiting coronary by-pass surgery. *Psychosomatic Medicine, 45,* 141–153.

Katon, W., Hall, M. L., Russo, J., Cormier, L., Hollifield, M., Vitaliano, P. P., & Beitman, B. (1988). Chest pain: Relationship of psychiatric illness to coronary arteriographic results. *The American Journal of Medicine, 84,* 65–80.

Magarian, G. J., & Hickam, D. H. (1986). Noncardiac causes of angina-like chest pain. *Progress in Cardiovascular Disease, 29,* 65–80.

Masseri, A., L'Abbate, A., Chierchia, S., Parodi, O., Sereri, S., Biagini, A., Distante, A., Marzilli, M., & Ballestra, A. M. (1979). Significance of spasm in pathogenesis of ischemic heart disease. *American Journal of Cardiology, 44,* 788–792.

Matthews, K. A. (1988). Coronary heart disease and Type A behaviors: Update on and alternative to the Booth-Kewley and Friedman (1987) quantitative review. *Psychological Bulletin, 104,* 373–380.

Mayou, R. (1989). Invited review: Atypical chest pain. *Journal of Psychosomatic Research, 33,* 393–406.

New York Heart Association. (1979). *Nomenclature and criteria for diagnoses of diseases of the heart and great vessels.* Boston: Little, Brown.

Parry, C. H. (1799). *An inquiry into the symptoms and causes of the syncope anginosa, commonly called angina pectoris.* Bath, England: R. Crutwell.

Pasternak, R., Thibault, G., Savoia, M., DeSanctis, R., & Hutter, Jr., A. (1980). Chest pain with angiographically insignificant coronary arterial obstruction. *American Journal of Medicine, 68,* 813–817.

Pickering, T. G. (1985). Should studies of patients undergoing coronary angiography be used to evaluate the role of behavioral risk factors for CHD? *Journal of Behavioral Medicine, 8,* 203–213.

Proudfit, W. L., Shirey, E. K., & Sones, F. M. (1966). Selective cine coronary arteriography: Correlation with clinical findings in 1,000 patients. *Circulation, 33,* 901–910.

Rose, G. A. (1962). The diagnosis of ischaemic heart pain and intermittent claudication in field surveys. *Bulletin of the World Health Organization, 27,* 645–658.

Rozanski, A., Bairey, C. N., Kranz, D. S., Friedman, J., Resser, K. J., Morell, M., Hilton-Chalfenm, S., Hestrin, L., Bietendorf, J., & Berman, D. S. (1988). Mental stress and the induction of silent myocardial ischemia in patients with coronary artery disease. *New England Journal of Medicine, 318,* 1005–1012.

Schocken, D. D., Greene, A. F., Worden, T. J., Harrison, E. E., & Spielberger, C. D. (1987). Effects of age and gender on the relationship between anxiety and coronary artery disease. *Psychosomatic Medicine, 49,* 118–126.

Schocken, D. D., Rickman, R. L., Greene, A. F., West, T. W., Glasser, S. P., & Spielberger, C. D. (1990, April). *Greater anger in patients with symptomatic versus silent myocardial ischemia.* Poster presented at the 11th Annual Meeting of the Society for Behavioral Medicine, Chicago.

Silverman, K. J., & Grossman, W. (1984). Angina pectoris: Natural history and strategies for evaluation and management. *The New England Journal of Medicine, 310,* 147–148.

Zyzanski, S. J., Jenkins, C. D., Ryan, T. J., Flessas, A., & Everist, M. (1976). Psychological correlates of coronary angiographic findings. *Archives of Internal Medicine, 136,* 1234–1237.

APPENDIX A

ASQ Traditional AP, Atypical AP and Nonanginal Symptoms

I. ASQ Traditional AP Symptoms
1. Walking hurriedly
2. Walking uphill
3. Exercising
4. Having sex
5. Eating a large meal
6. Working with arms overhead
7. Lifting weight
8. Mowing the lawn
9. Cold weather activity
10. Angry
11. Tense
12. Upset
13. Once-a-week recurrence
14. 5–10 minutes duration
15. Similar each time
16. Becoming more severe
17. Frequent aching
18. Frequent tightness
19. Frequent pressure
20. Frequent heaviness
21. Frequent squeezing
22. Frequent choking
23. Difficulty breathing
24. Feeling tired
25. Dizziness
26. Intense aching
27. Intense tightness
28. Intense pressure
29. Intense heaviness
30. Intense squeezing
31. Rest for Relief
32. Sitting for relief
33. Nitroglycerin for relief
34. Prompt relief by rest
35. Prompt relief by nitroglycerin
36. 1–2 nitro tablets bring relief
37. Substernal location
38. Sensation in left chest
39. Sensation in right chest
40. Radiates to left chest

41. Radiates to right chest
42. Radiates to neck and jaw
43. Radiates to left arm

II. ASQ Atypical AP Symptoms

1. Walking normally
2. Lying down
3. Sleeping
4. Other precipitants specified
5. Afraid
6. Annoyed
7. Frustrated
8. Worried
9. Nervous
10. Occurs less than once-a-week
11. Lasts more than 30 minutes
12. Only one episode
13. Discomfort less severe
14. Discomfort more often
15. Discomfort less often
16. Frequent burning
17. Other discomfort
18. Palpitations
19. Bowel pressure
20. Other symptoms specified
21. Intense burning
22. Intense choking
23. Other medications used
24. Prompt relief with other medications
25. 3–4 nitro tablets bring relief
26. Sensation in left arm
27. Sensation in right arm

III. ASQ Nonanginal Symptoms

1. Discomfort while sitting
2. Discomfort from bending
3. Not related to activity
4. Happy
5. Content
6. Laughing
7. Calm
8. Lasts more than 15 mins.

9. Different each time
10. Frequent tingling
11. Frequent stabbing
12. Frequent numbness
13. Frequent tearing
14. Frequent pinching
15. Frequent cutting
16. Fainting
17. Belching
18. Dizziness
19. Sighing
20. Nausea
21. Soreness
22. Urinary urgency
23. Intense tingling
24. Intense stabbing
25. Intense numbness
26. Intense tearing
27. Intense pinching
28. Intense cutting
29. Eating for relief
30. Antacid for relief
31. Prompt relief by sitting
32. Prompt relief by eating
33. Prompt relief by antacids
34. Nitro does not bring relief
35. Generalized location
36. Sensation in neck or throat
37. Sensation in stomach
38. Radiation to right arm
39. Radiation to stomach

APPENDIX B

ANGINAL SYNDROME QUESTIONNAIRE (ASQ)

Name:_____   ID #:_____

Age: _____   Sex: _____   Race: _____   Today's Date:_____

DIRECTIONS:

To help your doctor understand the underlying cause of your chest discomfort, please try to describe it as accurately as possible. Please try to recall:

DATE OF FIRST EPISODE: (Month/Date/Year) _____/_____/_____
DATE OF MOST RECENT EPISODE: (Month/Date/Year) _____/_____/_____

Think about the episodes (attacks) of discomfort that you have experienced in the past two or three months in responding to the following questions, and check all items that apply to you.

PART ONE

A.   At the time of the episode I am usually:

☐ At home
☐ At work
☐ Other

B.   Check the activities in which you have been involved just before or at the time of your chest discomfort:

☐ 1.   Walking (slowly or normally)
☐ 2.   Walking hurriedly
☐ 3.   Walking uphill or up stairs
☐ 4.   Exercise (Specify _____)
☐ 5.   Lying down (side, back, stomach)
☐ 6.   Having sex
☐ 7.   Sleeping
☐ 8.   Eating a large meal
☐ 9.   Working with arms overhead
☐ 10. Lifting heavy weight
☐ 11. Mowing the lawn, sweeping, mopping
☐ 12. Cold weather activity
☐ 13. Sitting (reading, watching TV)
☐ 14. Bending over or reaching down
☐ 15. Not related to activity
☐ 16. Other _____

C. Check the words that best describe your feelings just before or at the time of an episode of chest discomfort:

☐ 1.	Happy	☐ 5.	Tense	☐ 9.	Frustrated
☐ 2.	Afraid	☐ 6.	Content	☐ 10.	Nervous
☐ 3.	Angry	☐ 7.	Worried	☐ 11.	Calm
☐ 4.	Annoyed	☐ 8.	Laughing	☐ 12.	Upset

PART TWO

A. Approximately how often does the discomfort occur?

☐ 1. Less than once a month
☐ 2. Once or twice a month
☐ 3. Once or twice a week
☐ 4. Three to five times a week
☐ 5. Once or twice a day
☐ 6. Three to five times a day
☐ 7. Six or more times a day

B. When the discomfort occurs, how long does it last?

☐ 1. Less than 30 seconds
☐ 2. 30 seconds to one minute
☐ 3. 1-4 minutes
☐ 4. 5-10 minutes
☐ 5. 11-15 minutes
☐ 6. 16-30 minutes
☐ 7. More than 30 minutes

C. Is the discomfort similar to or different from chest discomfort you may have had in the past?

☐ 1. No discomfort since the first episode
☐ 2. Discomfort has been similar each time
☐ 3. Discomfort becoming more severe
☐ 4. Discomfort becoming less severe
☐ 5. Occurs more often than before
☐ 6. Occurs less often than before
☐ 7. Each episode is different and unpredictable

PART THREE

A.   Patients have used the following words to describe their chest discomfort. Please tell how you would generally describe your chest discomfort or pain by circling the appropriate number.

		Almost Never	Some-times	Often	Almost Always
1.	Burning	1	2	3	4
2.	Aching	1	2	3	4
3.	Tightness	1	2	3	4
4.	Pressing, Crushing	1	2	3	4
5.	Tingling, Pinpricking	1	2	3	4
6.	Heaviness	1	2	3	4
7.	Squeezing	1	2	3	4
8.	Stabbing	1	2	3	4
9.	Strangling, Choking	1	2	3	4
10.	Numbness	1	2	3	4
11.	Tearing	1	2	3	4
12.	Pinching	1	2	3	4
13.	Cutting, Knifelike	1	2	3	4
14.	Other _____	1	2	3	4

B.   At the time you are experiencing chest discomfort, indicate the extent to which you experience any of the following related symptoms.

		Almost Never	Some-times	Often	Almost Always
1.	Breathlessness or shortness of breath	1	2	3	4
2.	Fainting or feeling faint	1	2	3	4
3.	Fatigue or energy loss	1	2	3	4
4.	Belching	1	2	3	4
5.	Dizziness	1	2	3	4
6.	Sighing	1	2	3	4
7.	Palpitations ("skipped beats")	1	2	3	4
8.	Stomach upset, nausea, or vomiting	1	2	3	4
9.	Soreness of muscle or skin	1	2	3	4
10.	Sweating	1	2	3	4
11.	Urinary urgency	1	2	3	4
12.	Pressing bowels	1	2	3	4
13.	Other _____	1	2	3	4

C.   People have used the following words to describe their chest discomfort. Please indicate how severe you would rate each sensation in describing your discomfort or pain by circling the appropriate number.

		None	Mild	Moderate	Intense
1.	Burning	1	2	3	4
2.	Aching	1	2	3	4
3.	Tightness	1	2	3	4
4.	Pressure	1	2	3	4
5.	Tingling	1	2	3	4
6.	Heaviness	1	2	3	4
7.	Squeezing	1	2	3	4
8.	Stabbing	1	2	3	4
9.	Strangling/Choking	1	2	3	4
10.	Numbness	1	2	3	4
11.	Tearing	1	2	3	4
12.	Pinching	1	2	3	4
13.	Cutting, Knifelike	1	2	3	4

PART FOUR

A.   What methods have you tried for relief from your discomfort?

		Almost Never	Some- times	Often	Almost Always
1.	Resting (lying down)	1	2	3	4
2.	Sitting down	1	2	3	4
3.	Eating or drinking	1	2	3	4
4.	Antacids	1	2	3	4
5.	Nitroglycerin	1	2	3	4
6.	Other medications	1	2	3	4

B.   How long before relief occurs?

		1 min. or less	1-4 mins.	5-10 mins.	11-15 mins.	longer, no relief, never used
1.	Resting	1	2	3	4	5
2.	Sitting down	1	2	3	4	5
3.	Eating or drinking	1	2	3	4	5
4.	Antacids	1	2	3	4	5
5.	Nitroglycerin	1	2	3	4	5
6.	Other medication	1	2	3	4	5

C.   How many nitroglycerin tablets bring relief?

0   1   2   3   4   5   more   never used

PART FIVE

Using the diagram below, place a dot or a circle to show the area most often affected during
your episode of discomfort. Also, if it moved to another location, draw an arrow or arrows to
show where it moved during the episode.

<u>EXAMPLES</u>

8 Trait Anger: Theory, Findings, and Implications

Jerry L. Deffenbacher
Colorado State University

In endeavoring to refine and clarify the nature of anger as a psychological construct, Spielberger, Jacobs, Russell, and Crane (1983) adapted and applied Trait–State Anxiety Theory (Spielberger, 1966, 1972) to the concept of anger and developed scales for measuring state and trait anger (Spielberger, 1988) and anger expression (Spielberger, Krasner, & Solomon, 1988). State anger (S-Anger) refers to a transitory emotional–physiological condition consisting of subjective feelings of anger and activation of the autonomic nervous system, either at a particular moment or over a short period of time. S-Anger can vary in intensity, from little or no anger to mild or moderate emotional states (e.g., annoyed, irritated, frustrated), to intense levels of affective arousal (e.g., furious, enraged); and from minimal physiological arousal to marked levels of sympathetic activation, increased skeletal and facial muscle tone, and release of adrenal hormones. S-Anger may also fluctuate over time as a function of perceived affronts, injustice, insults, and–or frustration.

Trait anger (T-Anger), on the other hand, refers to a relatively stable personality dimension of anger proneness (i.e., individual differences in the tendency to experience state anger more frequently and–or more intensely; Spielberger, 1988; Spielberger et al., 1983, 1988). Although Trait–State Anger Theory does not specifically address the issue of response duration, by analogy with the earlier Trait–State Anxiety Theory (e.g., Spielberger, 1966, 1972), individuals high in T-Anger would be expected to experience more lengthy states of anger as well. Thus, trait anger reflects individual differences in the frequency, intensity, and duration with which state anger is experienced over time.

Consistent with the foregoing definitions of the constructs of state and trait anger, Spielberger (1988) and his colleagues (Spielberger et al., 1983) developed the State–Trait Anger Scale (STAS), which is analogous in conception and format to the *State–Trait Anxiety Inventory* (STAI; Spielberger, 1983). The STAS State Anger Scale asks individuals to respond according to how they feel right at the moment, or at a particular time. The STAS Trait Anger Scale requires individuals to respond according to how they generally feel or react.

The findings of studies in which our research group evaluated predictions derived from Trait–State Anger Theory (Spielberger et al., 1985) are presented in this chapter. In addition, we assessed a number of personality correlates and behavioral characteristics associated with trait anger. The chapter is comprised of five major sections. The first explores the relation of T-Anger to anger expression (i.e., how individual differences in the disposition to experience anger relate to general tendencies to express anger). The second summarizes studies in which predictions from Trait––State Anger Theory are evaluated. Studies of correlates of trait anger are reported in the third section. The final two sections draw together research findings that have significant implications for theory, clinical assessment, and intervention.

RELATION OF TRAIT ANGER TO STYLE OF ANGER EXPRESSION

Research on the relation of trait anger to styles of anger expression reveals two general findings (Spielberger, 1988; Spielberger et al., 1985). First, trait anger is positively related to anger suppression and negative expressive styles and inversely associated with anger control. Second, anger suppression is unrelated to negative outward expression of anger and anger control, which are significantly and inversely related to each other.

Two of our studies endeavored to replicate and extend the previous research findings (Deffenbacher & Ball, 1988; Deffenbacher & Shepard, 1991). In the first study, students in an abnormal psychology course completed the STAS T-Anger Scale and the Anger Expression (AX) Scale (Spielberger et al., 1985), in addition to other measures. The AX subscales measure tendencies to hold in or suppress anger (AX-I), to express it outwardly (AX-O), typically in negative ways such as cursing or throwing things, or to control anger (AX-C) in socially acceptable ways, such as being calm or patient. We found that the STAS T-Anger Scale correlated significantly with AX-I, AX-O, and AX-C (rs = .18, .59, and − .55). Tests of the differences between these dependent correlations revealed that the relation of the STAS T-Anger Scale with AX-O and AX-C were significantly stronger than with AX-I. AX-I scores were minimally correlated with AX-O and AX-C (rs = $-.07$ and $-.16$), whereas the correlation between AX-O and AX-C was substantially stronger (r = $-.59$).

In the second study, introductory psychology students completed the STAI Trait Anxiety (T-Anxiety) Scale (Spielberger, Gorsuch, & Lushene, 1970) in addition to the STAS T-Anger and AX Scales. The T-Anger Scale correlated significantly with AX-I, AX-O, AX-C, and T-Anxiety (rs = .26, .60, $-.55$, and .32), and T-Anxiety correlated positively with AX-I, AX-O, and AX-C (rs = .44, .15, and .16). As in the previous study, AX-I did not correlate significantly with AX-O or AX-C (rs = .01 and .03), which were significantly and inversely related (r = $-.47$). Tests for differences in the dependent correlations revealed two interesting findings. First, as in the prior study, AX-O and AX-C were more strongly associated with T-Anger than was AX-I. Second, AX-I was more strongly correlated with T-Anxiety than with AX-O, AX-C, or T-Anger.

Both studies replicated the findings of prior research in which T-Anger was more strongly related to the negative outward expression and control of anger than to anger suppression, and anger suppression was minimally related to anger control and the outward expression of anger. Thus, high trait anger, as measured by the STAS T-Anger Scale, consistently reflects a stronger tendency to express anger outwardly in a negative, less controlled, and less constructive manner, than to suppress anger. The findings in the second study also indicated that anger suppression was more strongly related to T-Anxiety than to T-Anger and other styles of anger expression, suggesting that general or neurotic anxiety inhibits the experience and expression of anger.

Research in behavioral medicine and health psychology should take note of the evidence of a stronger linkage between anger suppression and anxiety, than between suppressed anger and other forms of anger expression. Such findings suggest that measures of both anger expression and anxiety should be included in research on cardiovascular phenomena so that results are not attributed to different processes when, in fact, the processes are linked. Work in areas such as depression may also benefit from this research strategy (e.g., Biaggio & Goodwin, 1987; Riley, Treiber, & Woods, 1989).

Parenthetically, the findings for the AX Scale in our studies and those of other investigators (e.g., Spielberger, 1988; Spielberger et al., 1985) provide evidence of the discriminant validity of self-report methodologies. The AX-I subscale correlated consistently but minimally with AX-O and AX-C, despite the shared method variance of the AX Scale items resulting from the fact AX-I, AX-O, and AX-C items are intermixed and rated on the same scale. Because all AX items involve ratings of how the individual generally deals with anger, one might expect some degree of correlation. However, subjects responded to the AX-I and AX-O questions in an independent manner, providing a form of discriminant validity for the AX Scale.

TESTS OF TRAIT–STATE ANGER THEORY

Prediction of State Anger Frequency

Trait–State Anger Theory, as previously noted, posits that trait anger reflects individual differences in the frequency and intensity with which state anger is experienced over time. This general premise leads to a series of predictions with logical and theoretical implications. If Trait–State Anger Theory is valid, then T-Anger should be (a) positively correlated with the frequency of experience of state anger, and (b) more strongly associated with S-Anger than with other emotions such as anxiety and depression, or with behaviors such as becoming intoxicated; that is, trait anger ought to predict the frequency of S-Anger better than it predicts the frequency of other common emotions and behaviors.

These two predictions were evaluated by Deffenbacher, Bane, and Thwaites (1991) in a study involving over 800 introductory psychology students. These students completed the STAS T-Anger Scale and rated the number of times, on a 6-point scale (0 to 5 or more), they had been angry, anxious, depressed, or drunk in the last month. Preliminary analyses revealed gender effects, with men reporting higher T-Anger and drunkenness and women reporting being more frequently anxious and depressed. However, these gender effects accounted for less than 1% of the variance on the T-Anger and T-Anxiety scales, and less than 3% of variance in the number of times depressed or drunk. T-Anger correlated positively with the number of times anger (S-Anger) was experienced in the past month for both men ($r = .56$) and women ($r = .48$). A test of the difference between these independent correlations revealed that the correlation for men was stronger than for women. Tests for differences in the dependent correlations of the T-Anger Scale with S-Anger frequency indicated that these correlations were significantly stronger than the correlations of T-Anger with anxiety, depression, and drunkenness for men ($rs = .23, .29,$ and $.18$) and women ($rs = .17, .25,$ and $.08$).

The finding that T-Anger was positively associated with frequency of S-Anger over the past month, and that this relation was stronger than the correlations of T-Anger with the frequency of other common emotions and behaviors, supported Trait–State Anger Theory and provided evidence of the discriminant validity of the STAS T-Anger Scale. This study also found gender differences in T-Anger scores, but not in the frequency of anger experiences in the past month. In addition, the strength of the correlation between T-Anger and anger frequency in the past month was stronger for males, suggesting that men generally experience more anger than women, and that their T-Anger scores are more predictive of their anger. It should be noted, however, that the impact of gender differences on the STAS was relatively minor, accounting for less than 1% of the variance; furthermore, most studies have found no sex differences for this measure.

Comparisons of High and Low Trait Anger Individuals

Four studies (Deffenbacher, Demm, & Brandon, 1986; Deffenbacher & Eiswerth-Cox, 1991; Deffenbacher & Sabadell, in press; Story & Deffenbacher, 1986) evaluated a series of predictions derived from Trait-State Anger Theory concerning differences between persons high or low in trait anger. It was hypothesized that high T-Anger individuals, as compared to persons low in T-Anger, would exhibit (a) greater anger across a wide range of provocative situations, (b) greater anger in ongoing provocative situations, (c) greater intensity and frequency of day-to-day anger, (d) stronger general tendencies to express and suppress anger and less anger control, and (e) self-reports of greater anger-related physiological arousal. It was further predicted that, when provoked, high T-Anger individuals would experience (f) greater physiological arousal, (g) higher levels of state anger, and (h) more dysfunctional coping, as manifested in physical and verbal antagonism and in less constructive coping.

Deffenbacher and Eiswerth-Cox (1991) tested several of these predictions, using a contrast group design in which the high-low anger groups were operationally defined by scores in the upper or lower quartiles of the STAS T-Anger scale. The hypotheses were further tested in three studies, using a clinical analog design in which the high T-Anger subjects not only scored in the upper T-Anger quartile but also reported personal problems with anger for which they desired help (Deffenbacher, Demm, & Brandon, 1986; Deffenbacher & Sabadell, in press; Story & Deffenbacher, 1986). The low anger groups in these studies scored in the lower quartile of the T-Anger scale and also reported that they had no problems with anger. Comparison of the client-like, high T-Anger students, who recognized that they had anger problems for which they needed help, with students who did not perceive themselves as having anger problems provided a test of the potential utility of the T-Anger scale as a brief screening device for identifying individuals who might benefit from treatment.

The high and low T-Anger contrast groups in the four studies completed the following instruments and assessment procedures, which were selected or designed for testing each of our eight hypotheses:

1. Novaco's (1975) Anger Inventory was used to assess anger across a wide range of situations. In responding to this self-report scale subjects rated, on a 5-point scale, the degree of anger elicited by 90 different, potentially provocative, situations.

2. Anger experienced in provocative situations was evaluated with the Anger Situation Scale (Deffenbacher et al., 1986). In responding to this instrument, subjects describe their worst ongoing angering situation and then rate the intensity of the anger they experienced in this situation on a 100-point scale (0 = no anger, 100 = maximal anger).

3. Intensity of daily anger was measured by the Anger Log (Deffenbacher et al., 1986). This instrument requires subjects to track, for a period of 7 days, the worst anger experience of each day, and rate the intensity of this daily anger-provoking situation on a scale of from 0 to 100. In addition, Deffenbacher and Eiswerth-Cox (1991) also required their subjects to track the daily frequency of all angering events.

4. General anger expression styles (i.e., tendencies to express, suppress, or control anger) were assessed with the AX-O, AX-I, and AX-C subscales. Note, however, that the AX subscales were not administered in the Deffenbacher et al. (1986) study, and that the AX-C subscale was not available for use in the investigations reported by Deffenbacher and Sabadell (in press) and Story and Deffenbacher (1986).

5. Anger-related physiological arousal was assessed with the Anger Symptom Index (Deffenbacher et al., 1986). In responding to this measure, the individual is asked to specify the physiological symptom that he or she experiences most often when angry, and then to rate the severity of this symptom on a 100-point scale (0 = no problem at all; 100 = extremely severe).

Predictions 6, 7, and 8 were evaluated in analog provocation studies in which the participants were trained to monitor wrist or carotid pulse. They then visualized a specified anger-provoking event as though it were happening to them at that moment. After a 2-minute visualization of the specified event, a party at which the individual was criticized and put down, the subjects took their own 15-sec pulse rate (Hypothesis 6) and completed the STAS S-Anger Scale (Hypothesis 7). A 6-item Coping Strategies Measure (Novaco, 1975), which requires the individual to indicate the probability of coping via physical antagonism, verbal antagonism, or constructive coping, was then administered to evaluate Hypothesis 8. The subjects in these studies also completed the *State–Trait Anxiety Inventory* (STAI Form X) T-Anxiety Scale (Spielberger et al., 1970) prior to the analog task.

Anger by Gender MANOVAs revealed that gender did not interact with T-Anger level in any study, nor did it produce consistent main effects across the other dependent variables. In contrast, individual differences in trait anger produced significant multivariate effects and a highly consistent pattern of findings. Except for heart rate when provoked, the anger main effects were significant for all variables. The high T-Anger subjects reported responding with greater anger to a wide range of potential provocations, greater anger in ongoing personally provocative situations, more frequent and intense daily anger reactions, and more intense anger-related physiological symptoms.

Also, the high T-Anger subjects spontaneously reported additional anger-related physiological symptoms two to four times more often than low anger subjects. In terms of anger expression style, subjects with high trait anger reported stronger tendencies to suppress and negatively express anger, and less anger control. Assessment of state anger in the analog provocation revealed more intense S-Anger and more dysfunctional coping, as reflected in higher reported probabilities for physical and verbal antagonism and lower instances of constructive coping. The high T-Anger subjects also reported a significantly higher level of trait anxiety than the low anger subjects.

The findings comparing high and low T-Anger subjects have been clarified and extended by additional analyses and further studies. For example, the failure to find differences in heart rate in the analog provocation may have been due to the ineffectiveness of the imagery manipulation in evoking physiological arousal, despite its ability to do so in previous studies (e.g., Roberts & Weerts, 1982; Schwartz, Weinberger, & Singer, 1981). However, consistent main effects for trials were found in repeated measures ANOVAs (Anger × Sex × Trials), but no statistically significant interactions. These findings indicated that the experimental procedures increased heart rate (6 to 8 beats per minute), but not differentially as a function of level of T-Anger. Because the analog imagery event produced at least a modest increase in arousal, the failure to find physiological differences between the high and low T-Anger subjects cannot be attributed to the weakness of the experimental provocation.

Reaction of High and Low T-Anger Individuals to Different Situations

Because the analog studies just described employed only a single provocation, namely, a negative interaction at a party, the generality of this provocation was examined in an independent study (Stark & Deffenbacher, 1986a). The analog provocation employed by Stark and Deffenbacher was similar to the one used in the previous studies, except for the scene content. The new scene involved a nonverbal interaction in a grocery store in which an individual rudely bumps into the subject's cart and pushes ahead without apology (Novaco, 1975). The results were similar to those of prior studies: High T-Anger subjects reported more intense state anger, greater verbal and physical antagonism, and less constructive coping tendencies. However, no differences in heart rate were found between the high and low T-Anger subjects. Thus, the findings in the prior studies were confirmed with a different type of anger provocation.

The greater anger reported by the high T-Anger subjects across a wide range of anger-provoking situations, as measured by the Anger Inventory, could have resulted from two sources. First, the high T-Anger subjects may have experienced anger more often across many situations, but they might not differ from low anger subjects in terms of the frequency of their high-intensity anger responses. Second, high T-Anger individuals may experience more frequent, high-intensity anger reactions than persons low in T-Anger. Of course, they might do both. To examine these possibilities, differences in the number of high-intensity anger responses (ratings of 4 or 5 on a 5-point scale) reported by the high and low T-Anger subjects in the Deffenbacher–Eiswerth-Cox (1991) study were evaluated in a Gender by T-Anger ANOVA. The Gender and Anger main effect was significant: no interaction was found. The high T-Anger subjects gave more high-intensity anger ratings than the low T-Anger subjects (i.e., they reported that they would respond more often with intense anger to a greater number of situations). Females also consistently reported more high-intensity anger reactions than males.

Observed differences between high and low T-Anger subjects might also have resulted from their reacting differently to different situations, or in qualitatively different ways to the same situation. Data from several studies were pooled to examine the effects of qualitatively different situations on the self-report and physiological responses of 168 high and 199 low T-Anger subjects. Anger Situations and Anger Log entries were examined for the following general types of situations: Family relationships, nonfamily interpersonal relationships, self, school, work, and other (Deffenbacher, Eiswerth, & Stark, 1986). Physiological reactions on the Anger Symptom Index were coded according to type of reaction.

Analysis of anger reactions on the Anger Situation Scale revealed the following distributions of these reactions: 15% family provocations; 53% nonfamily interpersonal interactions (e.g., roommates and friends); 10% stemming from one's own behavior; 6% work; 6% school; and 9% other situations, such as driving incidents and inanimate objects. Anger Log breakdowns by category were somewhat similar: 5% family; 40% other interpersonal interactions; 22% self-referenced sources; 7% school; 3% work; and 22% other.

The high anger subjects consistently reported that they reacted with more intense anger to a wide range of provoking situations, but Chi-square analyses indicated no significant differences between the high and low T-Anger groups in the types of situations that angered them the most (Anger Situation), or that angered them on a daily basis (Anger Log). High and low anger subjects differed in the intensity of their anger reactions, but not in terms of the type of provocation to which they reacted; the anger-provoking situation ratings and anger log entries were quite similar for the two groups. These findings suggested that low T-Anger individuals occasionally experienced intense anger reactions though not as often, nor in as many situations, as persons high in T-Anger.

The dominant physical symptoms (Anger Symptom) were 19% clenched jaw, 10% general shaky feelings, 9% sweating, 7% each, high blood pressure and flushed face, 4% headaches, and 13% other symptoms. Although there were no significant differences between high and low T-Anger subjects in physical symptom patterns, the high anger subjects reported more severe symptoms. Thus, high and low T-Anger subjects did not appear to differ in the type of situations that evoked anger nor in the physiological reactions they experienced, but rather in the intensity and the frequency of their anger reactions.

In the three studies (Deffenbacher & Eiswerth-Cox, 1991; Deffenbacher & Sabadell, in press: Story & Deffenbacher, 1986), in which the AX-I and AX-O scales were administered, the high and low T-Anger subjects did not differ on these measures. Correlations between the AX-I and AX-O scores ranged from .08 to .31. Tests of differences in the dependent correlations between these measures and STAS T-Anger scores in the analog provocation revealed that the AX-O subscale was consistently more strongly related to T-Anger and verbal antagonism than was AX-I. Additionally, AX-O correlated more strongly with physical antagonism, Anger Log Intensity, and the Anger Inventory in at least one study. In the single study that included the AX-C subscale (Deffenbacher & Eiswerth-Cox, 1991), the strength of the correlations of this measure with T-Anger, Anger Inventory, Anger Situation, and verbal antagonism were similar in magnitude but opposite in direction to those for AX-O, but much stronger than for AX-I. Taken together with earlier findings, the results for the extreme T-Anger groups showed that AX-I was minimally related to AX-O and AX-C, and that the latter two modes of anger expression were more strongly related to a number of anger indices than was AX-I.

In order to identify the best combination of predictors of trait anger, a series of stepwise multiple regressions were run (Deffenbacher et al., 1986; Deffenbacher & Eiswerth-Cox, 1991; Deffenbacher & Sabadell, in press; Story & Deffenbacher, 1986). In all three studies that included the AX-O and AX-I measures, the AX-O scale was consistently the first variable to enter the regression equations, with AX-I entering all equations as the second or third variable. Other variables that entered several of the equations were the STAI T-Anxiety Scale, the Anger Situation, and the Anger Inventory. When the AX Scales were dropped from the regressions to eliminate possible conceptual overlap with the T-Anger measure, trait anxiety and verbal antagonism entered into all the equations, along with Anger Log intensities and Anger Situations. The high trait anger individuals, in addition to their style of anger expression, were characterized by high levels of trait anxiety and verbal antagonism.

Finally, the mean STAI T-Anxiety scores of the high T-Anger students were compared to the college freshmen norms for T-Anxiety reported in the STAI (Form X) Manual (Spielberger et al., 1970). The high T-Anger males scored above the 75th percentile for trait anxiety; high T-Anger females scored between the 80th and 90th percentile for trait anxiety. Thus, high T-Anger individuals reported that they frequently experienced anxiety as well as anger.

Assessing the Consequences of High Levels of Trait Anger

Most of the predictions derived from Trait–State Anger Theory were supported by the findings in the studies previously reported, but anger-related outcomes were not addressed in these studies (i.e., what are the consequences of the experience and expression of anger). Averill (1983) observed that only a small percentage of anger incidents resulted in aggressive or destructive negative consequences, but his findings did not take into account individual differences in level of trait anger. In a treatment study of students with anger problems, Hazaleus and Deffenbacher (1986) found that these high T-Anger students experienced many negative consequences of their anger, but comparative base rates for anger-related consequences for low anger students were not available.

Consistent with Trait–State Anger Theory, it might be expected that high T-Anger individuals would experience more frequent and–or more intense negative consequences from the experience or expression of their anger. In a pilot study of anger consequences, Deffenbacher and Thwaites (1991) had 175 abnormal psychology students report their two worst anger-related incidents during the past year (Anger in Last Year Questionnaire) and then describe the consequences resulting from their anger. The students also rated the overall costs of their anger on a 5-point scale of severity. From the students' responses, seven types of anger consequences were identified: (a) physical destruction or damage to an object; (b) physical damage to self (injury or disease resulting from one's anger); (c) physical damage or injury to another person; (d) damage to interpersonal relationships (anger damaged, interfered with, or terminated one or more relationships); (e) vocational or school problems (anger-damaged relationships and performance at work or school); (f) legal or quasi-legal actions (anger contributed to involvement with police, courts, or quasi-legal systems such as campus disciplinary agents); and (g) anger resulted in negative feelings about self (i.e., loss of self-esteem).

Unfortunately, the students' descriptions were not sufficiently detailed to allow reliable ratings of the severity of the consequences that resulted from their anger. In order to solicit greater detail about anger consequences, students were asked whether or not they had experienced an anger consequence in each of the preceding categories, and, if so, to describe it in detail. The revised questionnaire was given to 92 high and 102 low T-Anger students in introductory psychology courses.

Descriptions of consequences were then rated by trained raters using the Consequence Rating Scale (CRS) that was designed to evaluate the severity of each anger-related consequence. In developing the CRS, a large number of protocols were reviewed and the severity of the responses in each anger-consequence category was rated on a 4-point scale (0 = no consequence; 1 = mild; 2 = moderate; 3 = severe). The criteria that seemed most helpful in distinguishing among the severity ratings were then identified. For example, in formulating the criteria for physical damage to self, the number of physical symptoms suffered, the intensity of pain experienced, and the extent to which medical attention was required were consistently found to be associated with the rated severity of the consequences. Weightings for each of these factors were then formulated for each level of consequence severity.

In formulating the severity criteria, three general principles seemed to underlie the ratings. The first was a *conservative* principle (i.e., if the consequence was vague or incomplete, the rater was instructed to code the less severe consequence). The second was a *reality* principle (i.e., only real or actual outcomes should be rated). For example, if an individual drove wildly, potentially endangering him or herself or others, but did not actually hurt anyone, then no consequence was scored for physical damage to self or others. Finally, because moderate and severe self-esteem consequences could not be reliably distinguished, the ratings for these consequences were collapsed to form a 3-point rating scale.

The reliability (objectivity) of CRS ratings was established by having 3 raters each rate 100 protocols, of which 25 protocols were randomly selected from the 4 male–female, high–low T-Anger combinations. Inter-rater reliabilities for pairs of raters were .92 or greater for all categories, except for 1 rater pair in the relationship category for whom the reliability coefficient was .88. Given these high reliabilities, the CRS was subsequently applied to the consequences of all anger incidents.

The Gender by Anger MANOVA of the consequences for the worst anger incident in the past year revealed significant Anger and Gender main effects, but no interactions. The high T-Anger subjects reported significantly higher overall cost ratings and more severe consequences in all categories, except for work–school and legal consequences; legal consequences were infrequently reported by all subjects. The Gender effects were due mainly to males reporting more severe damage to objects and other people.

In the Gender by Anger MANOVA of the consequence ratings for the second worst anger incident, only the main effect of trait anger was significant. For this incident, the univariate ANOVAs revealed that the high T-Anger subjects reported significantly more severe damage to physical objects, personal relationships, and self-esteem, and that their overall cost ratings were higher.

From the preceding analyses, it was difficult to determine whether the anger consequences resulted from a few high T-Anger individuals reporting very negative consequences, a larger number of high anger subjects reporting more mild to moderate consequences, or both. To explore these alternatives, the proportion of individuals reporting at least some type of anger-related consequence for each category (i.e., consequence ratings ≥ 1) were analyzed, along with the intensity ratings of these anger consequences.

The analyses for the worst anger incident indicated that a higher proportion of the high T-Anger subjects reported negative consequences in all categories, except legal consequences. For example, 45% of the high T-Anger subjects reported physical damage to self as compared to only 17% of the low anger subjects. Similarly, 20% of the high anger subjects reported damage to others, 26% reported physical damage to objects, 80% reported relationship damage, and 35% reported work–school consequences. In contrast, the percentages of anger consequences reported by the low T-Anger subjects in these same categories were 4%, 8%, 60%, and 25%, respectively. Univariate Gender by Anger ANOVAs for the anger severity ratings did not reveal any significant sex or interaction effects, but significant Anger main effects indicated that the high T-Anger subjects experienced more severe relationship damage and greater overall negative consequences.

The analyses for the second worst incident during the previous year yielded similar results to those found for the worst incident. In addition, univariate Anger main effects were found for damage to self-esteem and overall cost ratings, with high T-Anger subjects again experiencing more severe consequences. Thus, although the multivariate anger effects for most variables were due to more high T-Anger subjects reporting that they experienced more frequent mild to moderate consequences, the high T-Anger subjects also reported more severe overall negative consequences and relationship damage and, in some cases, more severe negative self-esteem consequences than the low anger subjects.

Additional Correlates of Trait Anger

In two studies (Deffenbacher & Ball, 1988; Deffenbacher & McClintock, 1988), students in an abnormal psychology class completed the STAS T-Anger and AX Scales, a 6-item stress coping scale (e.g., coping in general with tests, speeches, same and opposite sex social situations, and university life), and a 12-item stress symptom questionnaire (e.g., headaches, stomach problems, fatigue). They also responded to a questionnaire inquiring about common chemical use (e.g., cigarettes, marijuana, alcohol, tranquilizers), and an inventory that assessed health status and the utilization of medical facilities (e.g., number of times sick, physician visits, etc.).

In stepwise multiple regressions with T-Anger and anger expression style (AX subscales) as predictors, successful coping with the six stressful events was consistently predicted by the AX-I and AX-C subscales. The T-Anger Scale failed to enter these equations, and AX-O entered only as the third variable in the prediction of coping with social interactions. In general, individuals who reported coping more successfully with stress were lower in anger suppression and more controlled in the expression of anger.

The finding by Deffenbacher and Ball (1988) that trait anger was unrelated to coping is at odds with Schill, Ramanaiah, and O'Laughlin (1984), who found that total scores on the Buss–Durkee Hostility Inventory (BDHI) were inversely related to coping. This apparent discrepancy might be accounted for by the moderate positive relationship of suppressed anger with trait anger noted earlier (i.e., the BDHI correlations with coping may reflect the relation of T-Anger with inhibited anger expression). The findings in the present study suggest that successful stress coping is determined more by the manner in which an individual deals with anger (AX-I and AX-C) than with the frequency that anger is experienced (T-Anger). To enhance our understanding of the personality structure of individuals who are stress resistant, future research should endeavor to clarify the negative effects of anger suppression on stress coping, as well as the positive influence of anger control on successful coping.

Anger suppression (AX-I) was the only measure to enter into the regression equation for predicting the total number of physical stress symptoms. However, the prediction equations for individual symptoms revealed a more complex picture. For example, fainting, fatigue, and two sleep-related symptoms (fitful sleep, difficulty falling asleep) were best predicted by AX-I, whereas the T-Anger Scale was the best predictor of sensitive skin, memory loss, and three types of stomach symptoms (nausea, upset stomach, ulcers). Although limited by the number and type of physical symptoms that were sampled in our study, as well as the rating format of the stress symptom questionnaire, these findings strongly suggest that the relations between measures of the experience and expression of anger and specific symptoms and symptom clusters deserve further exploration. Our findings also suggest that caution should be exercised in interpreting previously reported correlations between anger measures and physical symptoms that are based on total symptom scores.

In our studies, suppressed anger (AX–I) was the best single predictor of all health variables except severity of illness, which was unrelated to any of the anger measures. Although there was no relation between most of the anger measures and the use of drugs and alcohol, frequency and amount of alcohol use were associated with higher AX-O scores. Moreover, the correlations of the AX-O subscale with alcohol use for our university students were similar to those reported between a measure of anger and alcohol use for high school students (Oetting, Swaim, Edwards, & Beauvais, 1988). Because Oetting et al. did not employ anger expression measures in their study, their findings might reflect the underlying relation between T-Anger and anger expression style as measured by the AX-O subscale, which has been frequently replicated in our research.

In summary, when the anger expression subscales were included in the regression equations, trait anger (i.e., how often an emotional state of anger is experienced) did not predict stress coping, chemical substance use, stress symptoms, or health status. Further, the anger predictors of stress coping and chemical use showed little overlap, and the predictors of specific types of stress symptoms were quite different from the predictors of total symptoms. These findings indicate that future investigations of the correlates and consequences of trait anger should include measures of anger expression. Assessing how people deal with their anger contributes to a richer, more differentiated, understanding of the influence of various components of anger on coping and health.

Trait Anger, Irrational Beliefs, Self-Concept, and Psychopathology

Story and Deffenbacher (1985) administered the STAS T-Anger Scale and the Irrational Beliefs Test (Jones, 1969) to introductory psychology students. They found that the irrational beliefs of catastrophizing, need for personal perfection, blame proneness, and dependency (with a negative beta weight) entered a stepwise regression equation for predicting T-Anger scores, in the order indicated. Negative events such as failure appear to have a devastating (catastrophizing) impact on T-Anger. Believing that one must be perfect in order to be worthwhile (personal perfection) seems to impose unrealistic pressures on an individual that heighten vigilance, especially for potential threats that evoke anger reactions. Blame proneness and dependency appear to enhance frustrations that channel perceptions of threat into the emotion of anger.

The relation between trait anger and self-concept was the focus of an investigation by Stark and Deffenbacher (1986b). In this clinical analog study, introductory psychology students completed the STAS T-Anger Scale and the Tennessee Self-Concept Scale (Fitts, 1964). Inverse relationships were found between T-Anger and general self-concept, and between T-Anger and all specific self-concept dimensions (e.g., physical, moral, social, family, and personal self). High T-Anger students did not like themselves as much as low anger subjects, nor did they feel as worthwhile and confident. They also reported more negative views of their basic identity and behavior and were less self-accepting than the low anger students. Further evidence that individuals with high trait anger have low self-esteem was reported in a recent treatment study by Deffenbacher and Stark (1990), who found that high T-Anger subjects scored a full standard deviation below the mean on a measure of self-esteem.

Stark and Deffenbacher (1987) compared the MMPI scale scores and profiles of introductory psychology students who were high or low in T-Anger. Mean scores on the individual MMPI scales were all within normal limits, none exceeding T scores of 70 for any group. However, the Anger by Gender MANOVA of students' scores across all 13 standard MMPI validity and clinical scales revealed significant Anger, Sex, and interaction effects. High anger subjects had significantly higher D, Pd, Pa, Pt, Sc, Ma, and Si scores, and lower F and K scores than low anger subjects. Although gender effects were found for the F, Hs, D, Hy, Mf, and Pt scales, when the clinical scale means were plotted as MMPI profiles, the gender differences tended to disappear (i.e., the profiles for males and females were roughly similar in shape). The significant interaction effect was due primarily to the low anger males; these students had lower scores on the Pa Scale than the other three groups, which did not differ on this scale.

Although the MMPI findings were generally characteristic of groups without extreme pathology, the low anger students tended to present themselves in a more socially favorable manner whereas the high anger students tended to exhibit greater moodiness, restlessness, and dissatisfaction. Taken together, the statistically significant differences on the MMPI clinical scales indicated that the high anger students showed greater anxiety, worry, depression, turmoil, dissatisfaction, resentfulness, and irritability than low anger subjects. Thus, whereas the high T-Anger subjects showed relatively little severe pathology, they were somewhat more tense, high strung, and irritable. These trends need to be cautiously interpreted, however, because the differences between high and low anger students, although statistically significant, were generally small and not meaningful in a clinical sense (i.e., the observed differences reflected tendencies within fairly normal limits for a college population).

It is possible that clinically important differences in the Stark and Deffenbacher (1987) study were masked by grouping together students with very different MMPI profiles. For example, high anger subjects with 4–9 and 9–4 profiles, reflecting more aggressive acting out styles, were mixed with students with 3–1, 1–3, and 2–6–7 profiles, which indicate more repressive and suppressive ways of dealing with anger. Within the limits of the procedures used in this study, however, the findings suggested that students reporting high levels of trait anger do not have a clinically unique profile, even though as a group they showed signs of greater stress, anger, and turmoil.

IMPLICATIONS FOR ANGER THEORY AND FUTURE RESEARCH

A consistent finding in our studies of the correlates and consequences of trait anger was that gender had a relatively limited impact on the results. There were few sex main effects and those that were found were not consistent across samples, suggesting that the observed gender differences were relatively unstable. Moreover, gender never interacted with anger level, suggesting that there were no differences between males and females with high or low anger. Thus, the results appear generalizable to both men and women, at least for college populations.

It is not suggested that men and women do not differ in the experience or expression of anger, for they certainly may. But the findings reported in this chapter suggest that men and women may be more alike regarding anger than current conceptions of sex-role stereotypes appear to suggest. To be more specific, we found that men and women were similar in the frequency and the intensity of their anger experiences, reacted in a similar manner to the same anger-provoking situations, and expressed anger in similar ways as was found by others (e.g., Averill, 1983). Although there may well be sex-linked patterns in the experience and expression of anger, theory and research on sex roles will need to integrate the results of studies such as those reported in this chapter in which no such differences were found.

Spielberger's Trait–State Anger Theory (Spielberger et al., 1983, 1985, 1988) was strongly supported by our research findings. Trait anger predicted recent state anger experiences better than this measure predicted other common emotions, such as anxiety and depression. Moreover, high T-Anger individuals, as compared to those with low anger, consistently reported more frequent and intense state anger across provocative situations, in personally relevant ongoing provocations, and in day-to-day living. Further, the observed differences between high and low T-Anger individuals did not appear to be attributable to differences in the kinds of situations to which they were exposed. When high and low anger students were exposed to similar situations, the high T-Anger subjects reacted with greater anger, as was also found by Lopez and Thurman (1986).

High T-Anger individuals also reported more intense anger-related physiological arousal than low anger individuals, and more anger-related physical symptoms. When confronted with an analog provocation, the high T-Anger individuals reported higher levels of state anger, and stronger tendencies to become verbally and physically antagonistic and less constructive. Further, a larger proportion of the high anger subjects suffered more negative, anger-related consequences, which were also more severe in some cases. In sum, Trait–State Anger Theory was quite robust, and the construct validity of the STAS T-Anger Scale received considerable support.

A consistent negative result in our studies was the failure to find physiological differences between high and low T-Anger individuals in the analog provocation. Although the experimental procedures produced a significant increase in heart rate for all subjects, the physiological arousal evoked by the analog manipulation may not have been strong enough to reveal the between-group differences predicted by Trait–State Anger Theory. However, the Anger Symptom data, for which support was found for the predicted physiological differences, suggested another, more plausible, alternative. The findings for this variable, which were based on assessments of a variety of physiological systems, indicated that accelerated heart rate accounted for only 18% of the primary symptoms. Thus, physiological differences in response to the analog provocation might have been found if multiple physiological measures were included and–or the individual's most reactive physiological system was assessed.

Correlations and regression analyses consistently showed that trait anger was predicted by AX-I, AX-O, and AX-C, which makes intuitive sense in that an association would be expected between general anger and the ways it is expressed. Other findings suggested, however, that trait anger was more strongly related to AX-O and AX-C (inversely) than AX-I, which was more strongly related to anxiety. When the effects of the anger expression measures were removed from the analyses, trait anger was consistently associated with trait anxiety and verbal antagonism. These findings suggest that high T-Anger individuals are marked by substantial elevations of trait anxiety (above the 75th percentile for both sexes), and by a tendency to be verbally abrasive and antagonistic when provoked.

Explanation of the covariation of trait anger and trait anxiety is not entirely clear. Anger is one of the most taboo emotions in our society and may therefore have a history of being associated with punishment. Consequently, angry feelings may elicit anxiety in anticipation of negative physical and social consequences (Spielberger, 1988; Spielberger et al.,

1983). Conversely, anger might eventuate from chronic frustration and its aversive consequences that result in feeling generally tense, anxious, and fearful; that is, an individual may become chronically angry because of the vulnerability and consequences of chronic anxiety. A third alternative may be that both trait anxiety and trait anger reflect general negative affectivity (Watson & Clark, 1984), wherein high anger individuals are prone to greater negative emotionality of varying types. This view was supported by our findings that high anger individuals had lower self-esteem (Deffenbacher & Stark, 1990; Stark & Deffenbacher, 1986b), MMPI patterns reflective of more stress, anxiety, and turmoil (Stark & Deffenbacher, 1987), and lowered coping with common stressors (Deffenbacher & Ball, 1988), all indicating that high anger covaries with other negative, stressful emotions.

The covariance in general anxiety and general anger may be due to overlapping or shared cognitive processes. Although cognitively oriented theorists such as Beck (1976) emphasize specificity in the cognitive processes for different emotions, this does not rule out the possibility of commonalities as well. For example, irrational beliefs of catastrophizing and personal perfection were found to regress on both trait anger (Story & Deffenbacher, 1985) and trait anxiety (Zwemer & Deffenbacher, 1984); that is, both trait anger and anxiety shared common cognitive themes. However, blame proneness was more predictive of anger (Story & Deffenbacher, 1985; Zwemer & Deffenbacher, 1984), whereas problem avoidance predicted anxiety (Zwemer & Deffenbacher, 1984). Thus, shared dysfunctional cognitions and biased information processing may predispose the individual toward heightened vulnerability and emotionality, whereas the specific situation and the nature of its cues may elicit problem avoidance (anxiety) or externalizing, blaming (anger) tendencies. This would account for the emotion of the specific moment and the relatively strong covariation of the two emotional propensities, especially at the extremes of the distributions where the strongest relationships were found. Thus, individuals can honestly and accurately report high levels of both emotions because they experience high levels of both, perhaps linked by common cognitive denominators.

The findings in regard to habitual styles of dealing with or expressing anger initially appear to be confusing. High anger subjects reported both expressing (AX-O) and suppressing (AX-I) anger at nearly equal levels. How can an individual both suppress and express anger habitually? There may be two answers to this question. First, contrary to popular conceptualization, anger expression and suppression do not appear to be opposite poles of the same continuum. As found in the studies reported in this chapter and by others (e.g., Spielberger, 1988; Spielberger et al., 1983), the two constructs are unrelated and orthogonal. An individual is thus free to fall anywhere along either dimension and may employ both anger expressions styles at high levels. Second, because high anger individuals experience anger more frequently than their less angry peers, they may quite accurately report using both styles more often because they have more opportunities to use them.

The choice of outward expression, suppression, or a controlled anger style, may depend heavily on the nature of a particular situation, the individual's history with such situations, his or her skills in reading and coping with such situations, and his or her immediate preanger state (Berkowitz, 1990). Thus, an individual may behave constructively at one time, negatively at another, or express or suppress anger, depending on subtle differences in situational cues and–or the internal preanger state of the individual. Given the regression findings linking trait anger to verbal antagonism, high anger individuals seem more likely to engage in verbal antagonism, and other less constructive options, which may be due to social and communication skills deficits in handling inevitable frustration and conflict. Because anger expression and suppression have been implicated in cardiovascular arousal and disease (e.g., Diamond, 1982), health-related research would benefit from using measures of state and trait anger and preferred anger expression style, such as the *State–Trait Anger Expression Inventory* (STAXI; Spielberger, 1988).

IMPLICATIONS FOR CLINICAL ASSESSMENT AND TREATMENT

Although the research findings that we have reported were relevant to theory testing, they also have important implications for clinical assessment and treatment. For example, the consistent finding of minimal gender differences suggests that men and women are similar enough that they can be treated in the same therapy groups. An added benefit of having mixed-sex treatment groups would be to help break down sex-role stereotypes, at least in regard to anger. Having men and women share similar anger-related experiences and styles of anger expression in treatment groups would provide naturalistic examples of how similar situations anger them, whereas also providing opportunities for feedback from the opposite sex. Mixed-gender treatment groups would also facilitate discussion and role play in which members of both sexes could participate.

The findings that high anger subjects reported heightened arousal on a daily basis, in ongoing situations, in the analog provocation, and on the Anger Symptom index indicated that these students were experiencing considerable anger-related physiological arousal. Targeting this arousal for treatment with an applied relaxation coping skills program (e.g., Deffenbacher et al., 1986; Deffenbacher & Stark, 1990; Hazaleus & Deffenbacher,

1986) would help clients learn to lower anger by self-initiated relaxation exercises. Successful treatment would then free them to use problem-solving and social skills already in their response repertoires that have been previously disrupted by unpleasant and distracting physiological arousal associated with heightened states of anger.

The finding that high anger individuals experienced anger across a wide range of ongoing daily situations has several important clinical implications. First, the significant parameters of situations that evoke anger should be carefully evaluated. Even though the high T-Anger individuals generally experience more intense anger in a number of situations, there are wide individual differences in the kinds of situations that trigger anger, in the topography of their anger experience, and in associated behaviors. There may also be major differences within the same individual in similar situations at different times.

The emotional state of anger can be conceptualized as a complex psychophysiological-cognitive phenomenon embedded in a specific situational context. All aspects of this phenomenon need careful assessment, along with the behaviors triggered by anger or associated with it. A number of different measurement strategies should be used in assessing anger and the situations that evoke this emotion, such as interviewing, roleplays, simulations, imagery recall, and self-monitoring, so that the range of real and potential sources of anger may be mapped. Reliance on a single assessment strategy is likely to miss the complexity and richness of the experience of anger and its expression. The need for multiple intervention strategies is perhaps obvious; a single strategy is unlikely to be appropriate for all situations, especially for group interventions, where substantial individual differences are to be expected. Moreover, given the frequency and intensity of daily anger experiences, it is important to train clients for transfer to day-to-day living. In the latter stages of therapy, it may be appropriate to use self-monitoring, in vivo probes, and–or simulations to provide opportunities for assessment, rehearsal, and transfer of skills and insights.

As noted previously, persons high in trait anger tend to interpret a wide range of situations as frustrating or insulting, or as trespasses into their personal domain (Beck, 1976). Themes of catastrophizing, personal perfection, anxious overconcern, and blaming, which were particularly evident in high anger individuals (Hazaleus & Deffenbacher, 1985; Hogg & Deffenbacher, 1986; Story & Deffenbacher, 1985; Zwemer & Deffenbacher, 1984), should be targeted with psychodynamic, self-explorative, cognitive, or behavioral interventions to help clients perceive the world in less ego-threatening ways. Such interventions should help the individual feel less vulnerable, thus reducing the likelihood to experience frustration, perceived injustice, personal affronts, and insults, and thereby decreasing the frequency and intensity of the client's anger reactions.

The observed tendencies for high anger individuals to suppress anger and to express it negatively and in less controlled, socially desirable ways require careful clinical assessment in treatment programs. Further, because elevated AX-O and lowered AX-C were associated with a greater probability of physical and verbal antagonism, these anger expression styles should also receive special attention. Exploration of when, where, and why clients employ different anger expression strategies will not only contribute to clarifying the nature of anger and its expression but may also help to identify adaptive cognitions and strategies that can be used effectively in angering situations.

In addition to the previously noted findings that high anger individuals reported stronger tendencies toward verbal and physical antagonism and less constructive behavior, verbal antagonism was a consistent predictor of trait anger after the anger expression measures were removed. These findings suggest that high anger individuals are generally more abrupt, abrasive, and intimidating. The verbal and nonverbal cues associated with such behavior may elicit anger in others, leading them to withdraw or counterattack, which may then stimulate further anger and aggression in the high T-Anger individual, resulting in a vicious cycle.

Although the source of the negative coping characteristics of high T-Anger individuals is not clear, there are at least three distinct possibilities: emotional interference, skill deficit, and role–identity consonance. Each of these has different treatment implications. With regard to emotional arousal, even though the high anger individual may have adequate coping skills for dealing with provocation, these skills would be disrupted by anger arousal, much as anxiety disrupts performance in a skilled individual. In such cases, treatment should focus on cognitive restructuring (e.g., Deffenbacher, Story, Brandon, Hogg, & Hazaleus, 1988; Hazaleus & Deffenbacher, 1986; Moon & Eisler, 1983; Novaco, 1975), arousal reduction (e.g., Deffenbacher et al., 1986; Deffenbacher & Stark, 1990; Hazaleus & Deffenbacher, 1986; Schlichter & Horan, 1981), or their combination (e.g., Deffenbacher et al., 1988; Deffenbacher, Story, Stark, Hogg, & Brandon, 1987; Deffenbacher & Stark, 1990; Novaco, 1975; Schlichter & Horan, 1981). As clients alter their anger-eliciting cognitions and experience less emotional arousal, more effective coping skills can emerge that will result in calmer, more socially appropriate, behavior.

For the high T-Anger individuals who have deficits in interpersonal, social, communication, or problem-solving skills needed to handle inevitable conflict, such deficits may be addressed in specific skills training programs. Training in areas such as basic listening, time out–leave taking, social problem solving, nonjudgmental communication, conflict resolution, and assertion (e.g., Deffenbacher et al., 1987; Moon & Eisler, 1983) can be adapted for working with clinically angry individuals.

The third possibility (i.e., that anger and associated intimidating and aggressive behavior may be consonant with the individual's role and–or personal identity) is based on the assumption that these characteristics are part of the person and how he or she perceives his or her role and not ego alien or undesired. This type of ego-syntonic character structure may require interventions aimed at exploring the negative consequences of the anger-motivated behaviors, and framing constructive alternatives so that they can then become role or identity consonant. For example, the belief of an adolescent male that "taking no crap off anybody and fighting" might be reframed as weak and cowardly, whereas being calm, cool, and negotiative is strong, powerful, and male. Similarly, an angry, intimidating, demanding supervision style might be reframed within the role of how different behaviors constitute being a good supervisor. Once role or identity ref-raming takes place, then emotional control, skill building, and insight approaches will be more applicable and less resisted.

Finally, high anger individuals had elevated trait anxiety scores, and anxiety was a consistent predictor of trait anger in the regression equations. These findings suggest that overlap in the emotional and cognitive processes associated with anger and anxiety might be profitably targeted for clinical intervention. For example, the common dysfunctional cognitions that appear to be shared by anxiety and anger could be targeted with cognitive restructuring interventions (e.g., Deffenbacher et al., 1988; Hazaleus & Deffenbacher, 1986; Moon & Eisler, 1983; Novaco, 1975). Similarly, the high levels of physiological arousal characteristics of both anger and anxiety might be targeted with applied relaxation programs (e.g., Deffenbacher & Stark, 1990; Deffenbacher et al., 1986; Hazaleus & Deffenbacher, 1986). To the extent that certain social skill deficits are associated with both high anger and anxiety (e.g., low assertiveness), both emotions could be targeted with skill building and social problem-solving applications (e.g., Deffenba-cher et al., 1987; Moon & Eisler, 1983). The point here is not to compile an exhaustive list of covarying problems and interventions, but to emphasize the need for careful assessment of them and the importance of training for the transfer of skills, strategies, and insights from treatment to real-life coping with anger-provoking situations.

SUMMARY AND CONCLUSIONS

This chapter reported research findings that focused on theoretical issues relating to the nature, correlates, and consequences of trait anger and, clinically, on high trait angry individuals. Persons high in trait anger frequently experience intense state anger in a number of situations, and in many parts of their lives. This largely overlooked group is, on the average, more angry than counseling center clients, even those clients who sought counseling, at least in part, because of their anger problems (Hazaleus & Deffenbacher, 1986). They also experience frequent and sometimes severe consequences resulting from their anger and are generally high in anxiety, low in self-esteem, less likely to cope well with stress, and more likely to misuse alcohol.

There is as yet no clear DSM category for diagnosis of the chronically angry person. An individual can be chronically worried and anxious (generalized anxiety disorder) or chronically moderately depressed (dysthymia or neurotic depression), but chronically, moderately angry individuals are difficult to diagnose unless they have significant impulse control problems or anger clearly impacts their health. But such persons do exist in relatively large numbers. Because many of them fail to realize their potential and some suffer intensely, perhaps the time has come for applied psychology to begin to pull together information for formulating a general anger syndrome so that chronically high levels of this forgotten (Averill, 1983) or misunderstood (Tavris, 1982) emotion can be recognized as a meaningful, diagnosable, and treatable emotional disorder.

REFERENCES

Averill, J. R. (1983). Studies on anger and aggression: Implications for theories of emotion. *American Psychologist, 38,* 1145–1160.

Beck, A. (1976). *Cognitive therapy and the emotional disorders.* New York: International Universities Press.

Berkowitz, L. (1990). On information and regulation of anger and aggression: A cognitive-neoassociationistic analysis. *American Psychologist, 45,* 494–503.

Biaggio, M. K., & Goodwin, W. H. (1987). Relation of depression to anger and hostility constructs. *Psychological Reports, 61,* 87–90.

Deffenbacher, J. L., & Ball, S. L. (1988, April). *Anger, coping with stress, and common chemical use in college students.* Paper presented at Rocky Mountain Psychological Association, Snowbird, UT.

Deffenbacher, J. L., Bane, A., & Thwaites, G. (1991, April). *A test of state-trait anger theory.* Paper presented at Rocky Mountain Psychological Association, Denver, CO.

Deffenbacher, J. L., Demm, P. M., & Brandon, A. D. (1986). High general anger: Correlates and treatment. *Behaviour Research and Therapy, 24,* 480–489.

Deffenbacher, J. L., Eiswerth, L. E., & Stark, R. S. (1986, April). *Situations and physiological symptoms in general anger.* Paper presented at Rocky Mountain Psychological Association, Denver, CO.

Deffenbacher, J. L., & Eiswerth-Cox, L. (1991, April). *An empirical evaluation of state-trait anger theory.* Paper presented at Rocky Mountain Psychological Association, Denver, CO.

Deffenbacher, J. L., & McClintock, C. M. (1988, April). *Anger in the prediction of stress symptoms and health variables.* Paper presented at Rocky Mountain Psychological Association, Snowbird, UT.

Deffenbacher, J. L., & Sabadell, P. M. (in press). Comparing high trait anger individuals with low anger individuals. In M. Muller (Ed.), *Anger and aggression in cardiovascular disease.* Germany: Hans Huber Verlag.

Deffenbacher, J. L., & Shepard, J. (1991, April). *Relationship of trait to anger expression style and trait anxiety.* Paper presented at Rocky Mountain Psychological Association, Denver, CO.

Deffenbacher, J. L., & Stark, R. S. (1990). *Relaxation and cognitive-relaxation treatments of general anger.* Manuscript submitted for publication, Department of Psychology, Colorado State University, Fort Collins, CO.

Deffenbacher, J. L., Story, D. A., Brandon, A. D., Hogg, J. A., & Hazaleus, S. L. (1988). Cognitive and cognitive-relaxation treatments of anger. *Cognitive Therapy and Research, 12,* 167–184.

Deffenbacher, J. L., Story, D. A., Stark, R. S., Hogg, J. A., & Brandon, A. D. (1987). Cognitive-relaxation and social skills interventions in the treatment of general anger. *Journal of Counseling Psychology, 34,* 171–176.

Deffenbacher, J. L., & Thwaites, G. A. (1991, April). *Consequences of trait anger.* Paper presented at Rocky Mountain Psychological Association, Denver, CO.

Diamond, E. (1982). The role of anger and hostility in essential hypertension and CHD. *Psychological Bulletin, 92,* 410–433.

Fitts, W. H. (1964). *Tennessee Self-Concept Scale.* Nashville, TN: Counselor Recordings and Tests.

Hazaleus, S. L., & Deffenbacher, J. L. (1985). Irrational beliefs and anger arousal. *Journal of College Student Personnel, 26,* 47–52.

Hazaleus, S. L., & Deffenbacher, J. L. (1986). Relaxation and cognitive treatments of anger. *Journal of Consulting and Clinical Psychology, 54,* 222–226.

Hogg, J. A., & Deffenbacher, J. L. (1986). Irrational beliefs, depression, and anger in college students. *Journal of College Student Personnel, 27,* 349–353.

Jones, R. G. (1969). A factored measure of Ellis' irrational belief system, with personality and maladjustment correlates. *Dissertation Abstracts International, 29, 4379B* (University Microfilms, No. 69-6443).

Lopez, F. G., & Thurman, C. W. (1986). A cognitive-behavioral investigation of anger among college students. *Cognitive Therapy and Research, 10,* 245–256.

Moon, J. R., & Eisler, R. M. (1983). Anger control: An experimental comparison of three behavioral treatments. *Behavior Therapy, 7,* 493–505.

Novaco, R. (1975). *Anger control: The development and evaluation of an experimental treatment.* Lexington, MA: D. C. Heath.

Oetting, E. R., Swaim, R. C., Edwards, R. W., & Beauvais, F. (1988). Indian and Anglo adolescent alcohol use and emotional distress: Path models. *American Journal of Drug and Alcohol Abuse, 15,* 153–172.

Riley, W. T., Treiber, F. A., & Woods, M. G. (1989). Anger and hostility in depression. *Journal of Nervous and Mental Disease, 177,* 668–674.

Roberts, J. J., & Weerts, T. C. (1982). Cardiovascular responding during anger and fear imagery. *Psychological Reports, 50,* 219–230.

Schill, T., Ramanaiah, N., & O'Laughlin, S. (1984). Construct validation of a method for defining efficient and inefficient copers. *Psychological Reports, 54,* 969–970.

Schlichter, K. J., & Horan, J. J. (1981). Effects of stress inoculation on the anger and aggression management skills of institutionalized juvenile delinquents. *Cognitive Therapy and Research, 5,* 359–365.

Schwartz, G., Weinberger, D., & Singer, J. (1981). Cardiovascular differentiation of happiness, sadness, anger, and fear following imagery and exercise. *Psychosomatic Medicine, 43,* 343–364.

Spielberger, C. D. (1966). Theory and research on anxiety. In C. D. Spielberger (Ed.), *Anxiety and behavior* (pp. 3-20). New York: Academic Press.

Spielberger, C. D. (1972). Anxiety as an emotional state. In C. D. Spielberger (Ed.), *Anxiety: Current trends in theory and research* (Vol. 1, pp. 24-49). New York: Academic Press.

Spielberger, C. D. (1983). *Manual for the State-Trait Anxiety Inventory (Form Y)*. Palo Alto, CA: Consulting Psychologists Press.

Spielberger, C. D. (1988). *State-Trait Anger Expression Inventory*. Odessa, FL: Psychological Assessment Resources.

Spielberger, C. D., Gorsuch, R., & Lushene, R. (1970). *Manual for the State-Trait Anxiety Inventory (Self-Evaluation Questionnaire)*. Palo Alto, CA: Consulting Psychologists Press.

Spielberger, C. D., Jacobs, G., Russell, S., & Crane, R. (1983). Assessment of anger: The State-Trait Anger Scale. In J. N. Butcher & C. D. Spielberger (Eds.), *Advances in personality assessment* (Vol. 3, pp. 112-134). Hillsdale, NJ: Lawrence Erlbaum Associates.

Spielberger, C. D., Johnson, E., Russell, S., Crane, R., Jacobs, G., & Worden, T. (1985). The experience and expression of anger: Construction and validation of an anger expression scale. In M. A. Chesney & R. H. Rosenman (Eds.), *Anger and hostility in cardiovascular and behavioral disorders* (pp. 5-30). New York: McGraw-Hill.

Spielberger, C. D., Krasner, S., & Solomon, E. (1988). The experience, expression, and control of anger. In M. P. Janisse (Ed.), *Health psychology: Individual differences and stress* (pp. 89-108). New York: Springer-Verlag.

Stark, R. S., & Deffenbacher, J. L. (1986a, March). *Reactions of high and low trait anger individuals when provoked*. Paper presented at Colorado Psychological Association, Fort Collins, CO.

Stark, R. S., & Deffenbacher, J. L. (1986b, April). *General anger and self-concept*. Paper presented at Rocky Mountain Psychological Association, Denver, CO.

Stark, R. S., & Deffenbacher, J. L., (1987, April). *General anger and personality*. Paper presented at Rocky Mountain Psychological Association, Albuquerque, NM.

Story, D., & Deffenbacher, J. L. (1985, April). *Trait anger and irrational beliefs*. Paper presented at Rocky Mountain Psychological Association, Tucson, AZ.

Story, D. A., & Deffenbacher, J. L. (1986, April). *A test of state-trait anger theory*. Paper presented at Rocky Mountain Psychological Association, Denver, CO.

Tavris, C. (1982). *Anger: The misunderstood emotion*. New York: Simon & Schuster.

Watson, D., & Clark, L. A. (1984). Negative affectivity: The disposition to experience aversive emotional states. *Psychological Bulletin, 96,* 465-490.

Zwemer, W. A., & Deffenbacher, J. L. (1984). Irrational beliefs, anger and anxiety. *Journal of Counseling Psychology, 31,* 391-393.

Author Index

A

Abramson, E. E., 96, *110*
Accoce, J., 32, 34, 39, 52, 54, 57, *72, 74*
Adorno, T. W., 65, *72*
Ahmed, S. M. S., 105, 106, *110*
Ainlay, S. L., 2, *22*
Albert, S., 127, *139*
Alexander, C. N., Jr., 102, *110*
Alexander, I. E., 117, *125*
Allison, J., 120, *125*
Almagor, M., 144, *151, 152*
Almeida, D., 153, 156, *167*
Ames, M., 98, *110*
Ames, S., 79, 80, *111*
Andrews, T. G., 28, 30, *72*
Antonnovsky, A., 1, *22*
Arnold, P. D., 141, 142, *151*
Arsuaga, E. N., 6, 8, 9, 12, 13, 15, *22*
Athanassopoulu, M., 3, *25*
Averill, J. R., 186, 192, *199*

B

Baile, W. F., 156, 157, 158, 165, *167*
Bairey, C. N., 157, *168*
Ball, S. L., 178, 189, 194, *199*
Ballestra, A. M., 153, *168*
Bane, A., 180, *199*
Bariaud, F., 31, 32, 34, *72, 74*

Barnes, B. D., 90, 104, *114*
Barnes, R. D., 85, *110*
Barrera, M., 2, 9, 13, *22*
Barrera, M., Jr., 1, 2, 3, 4, 20, *22, 25*
Barrett, J., 13, *24*
Barrett, R. K., 141, *151*
Barrett-Lennard, G. T., 9, *22*
Barry, J., 15, *22*
Bash, I. Y., 135, 137, *139*
Basham, R. B., 9, *25*
Baughman, E. E., 127, 130, *140*
Beatty, J. R., 104, *115*
Beauvais, F., 190, *200*
Beck, A. T., 13, *22*, 194, 196, *199*
Beggs, J. J., 102, *110*
Beitman, B., 153, *168*
Bell, N. J., 85, *110*
Ben-Porath, Y. S., 142, 144, *151*
Benton, A. L., 127, 137, *139*
Berger, D., 80, 91, *112*
Berger, R., 153, 156, 158, *167*
Berkeley, M. H., 28, *75*
Berkowitz, L., 195, *199*
Berman, D. S., 157, *168*
Biaggio, M. K., 179, *199*
Biagini, A., 153, *168*
Biberman, G., 82, 98, 103, *110*
Bietendorf, J., 157, *168*
Birren, F., 118, *125*
Blatt, S. J., 120, *125*

Bloom, R. W., 101, 105, *110*
Blow, F. C., 157, *167*
Bogart, K., 89, *110*
Boster, F. J., 78, 83, 84, 105, 106, 107, 108, *113*
Boulanger, G., 13, 17, *22, 23*
Bourassa, M., 153, 156, 158, *167*
Bradley, M. T., 90, *110, 113*
Brandon, A. D., 181, 182, 185, 195, 197, 198, *199, 200*
Breen, L. J., 82, 83, *114*
Breme, F. J., 29, *72*
Brengelmann, J. C., 57, *72*
Brengelmann, L., 57, *72*
Brimlow, D., 156, 158, *167*
Brimlow, D. L., 157, 158, 165, *167*
Brinker, J., 156, 157, 158, 165, *167*
Broughton, R., 79, 80, *116*
Brown, B. B., 92, 104, *111*
Brown, E. C., 92, *111*
Brown, S. L., 117, *125*
Bruehl, D., 82, *115*
Budner, S., 101, *111*
Budnitzky, S., 87, *111*
Buglione, S. A., 5, 6, 7, 8, 14, 15, 16, 18, 20, 21, *24*
Bunyan, M., 58, *73*
Burch, S., 92, *111*
Burgoon, M., 92, *111*
Busse, P., 40, 43, 52, 57, 60, *72*
Butcher, J. N., 141, 142, 144, 149, *151, 152*
Byington, R. P., 156, *167*
Byrne, D., 15, *22*

C

Camille, D., 141, *152*
Campbell, S., 50, *73*
Cannon, R. O., 153, *167*
Caplan, G., 1, 2, 3, *22*
Caplan, R., 3, *25*
Carlisle, A. L., 127, 135, 137, *140*
Carp, A. L., 127, *139*
Carroll, J. L., 29, *73*
Cartier, A. M., 50, 58, *73*
Cassel, J., 2, 3, *22*
Cattell, R. B., 28, 69, *73*
Chaitman, B., 153, 156, 158, *167*
Cherulnik, P. D., 79, 80, *111*
Chierchia, S., 153, *168*
Chodoff, P., 13, *24*
Chonko, L. B., 96, 97, 99, 103, *111, 113*

Christie, R., 77, 78, 80, 81, 82, 83, 84, 85, 86, 87, 88, 89, 91, 93, 94, 96, 97, 100, 101, 102, 103, 104, 105, 106, 107, 108, 109, *111, 112*
Chupp, B., 98, *113*
Ciftci, H., 34, 37, 39, 40, 52, 59, 60, *73*
Clair, D., 5, 6, 11, 14, 18, *22*
Clark, L. A., 194, *201*
Clayton, M. B., 85, *111*
Cliff, N., 160, *167*
Cloetta, B., 52, *73*
Cobb, S., 1, 2, 3, *23*
Cody, M. J., 106, 108, *114*
Cohen, J., 9, *23*
Cohen, P., 9, *23*
Cohen, S., 2, 4, 9, 21, *23*
Comer, J. M., 82, 103, *111*
Conover, L. J., 131, *140*
Cook, S. W., 81, 82, *116*
Cookerly, J. R., 141, 142, *151*
Cooper, C., 84, 86, 106, 108, *111, 113*
Cooper, S., 89, *111*
Cormier, L., 153, *168*
Costa, P. T., 156, 157, 158, 165, *167*
Coyne, J. C., 17, *24*
Crane, R., 177, 178, 179, 192, 193, 194, *201*
Crits-Christoph, K., 6, 7, 8, 10, 11, 14, 15, 16, 18, *23, 24*
Crockett, W. H., 85, *111*
Cronbach, L. J., 127, 130, *140*
Crowne, D. P., 15, *23*
Cutrona, C. E., 3, *23*

D

Dahlstrom, W. G., 136, *140*, 142, *151*
Dalstrom, L. E., 136, *140*
Daum, I., 38, 40, 41, *74*
Davis, K., 153, 156, 158, *167*
Deanfield, J. E., 157, *167*
Deffenbacher, J. L., 178, 180, 181, 182, 183, 184, 185, 186, 189, 190, 191, 192, 194, 195, 196, 197, 198, *199, 200, 201*
Delia, J. G., 85, *111*
Demm, P. M., 181, 182, 185, 195, 197, 198, *199*
DePaulo, B. M., 90, *111*
Derogatis, L. R., 13, *23*
DeSanctis, R., 156, *168*
Diamond, E., 195, *200*
Diamond, G. A., 153, *167*

Dien, D. S., 89, *111*
Diener, E., 46, *73*
Dietch, J., 92, *111*
Dietch, J. T., 92, 104, *111*
Dingler-Duhon, M., 92, 104, *111*
Distante, A., 153, *168*
Dodson, M., 3, *23*
Dohrenwend, B. P., 3, *23*
Dohrenwend, B. S., 3, *23*
Domelsmith, D. E., 92, 104, *111*
Drory, A., 93, *111*
Duffey, N. S., 85, *110*
Durkin, J. E., 103, *111*
Duszynski, K. R., 129, 130, *140*

E

Eastman, K., 98, *113*
Easton, K., 127, 135, 137, *140*
Eckenrode, J., 3, *23*
Edgecomb, J. L., 157, *167*
Edwards, R. W., 190, *200*
Egendorf, A., 13, *23*
Ehrenstein, W. H., 64, *73*
Eisenberg, E., 84, 96, 108, *115*
Eisler, R. M., 197, 198, *200*
Eiswerth, L. E., 181, 184, *199*
Eiswerth-Cox, L., 182, 184, 185, *199*
Elias, M. F., 157, *167*
Emmons, R. A., 46, *73*
Engel, B. T., 156, 157, 158, 165, *167*
Epstein, S., 153, *167*
Ertel, S., 64, *73*
Everist, M., 157, *168*
Exline, R. V., 89, *111*
Exner, J. E., 117, *125*, 127, 128, 130, 135, *140*
Eysenck, H. J., 28, 32, 50, 52, 63, 65, *73*

F

Falbo, T., 79, 90, 92, *112*
Falloon, I. R. H., 20, *24*
Faschingbauer, T. R., 13, 15, *23*
Feigenbaum, K., 127, 135, 137, *140*
Feldman, M. J., 127, 135, 137, *140*
Ferraro, L., 4, 5, 6, 10, 11, 14, 15, 16, 18, 20, *23*
Fisher, L., 153, 156, 158, *167*
Fiske, D. W., 127, 130, *140*
Fitts, W. H., 191, *200*
Flachmeier, L. C., 82, 85, *114*

Fleg, J. L., 157, 165, *167*
Flessas, A., 157, *168*
Folkman, S., 2, *23*
Ford, G. G., 6, 8, 13, 14, 15, 16, 18, *23*
Forrester, J. S., 153, *167*
Forsyth, D. R., 90, *112*
Fortune, J. C., 82, 99, *115*
Fosberg, I. A., 127, *140*
Fox, H., 127, *139*
Frank, C. W., 158, *167*
Frenkel-Brunswik, E., 56, 65, *72*, *73*
Freud, S., 30, 66, *73*
Friedman, J., 157, *168*
Friedman, L. M., 156, *167*
Friedman, L. N., 108, *112*
Frigon, M. J., 6, *23*
Fry, W. R., 91, *112*
Fujisawa, H., 89, *111*
Furnham, A., 58, *73*

G

Gable, M., 99, 103, *112*
Galli, I., 82, 83, 87, 88, *112*, *114*
Gazes, P. C., 153, *167*
Geis, F., 88, 89, 91, 94, 103, 104, 108, *110*, *112*
Geis, F. L., 77, 78, 80, 83, 85, 88, 90, 91, 93, 96, 100, 102, 103, 104, 109, *111*, *112*
Gemmill, G. R., 97, 98, 99, *112*, *113*
Gerbing, D. W., 78, 83, 84, 105, 106, 107, 108, *113*
Gill, M. M., 120, *125*
Gillespie, R., 130, *140*
Gillies, J., 50, *73*
Giokas, J. A., 80, 95, 102, *115*
Glasgow, M. R., 50, 58, *73*
Glasser, S. P., 157, *168*
Gleason, J. M., 93, 104, *112*
Gluskinos, U. M., 93, *111*
Gold, A. R., 108, *112*
Goldstein, M. J., 20, *24*
Goodwin, T., 17, *26*
Goodwin, W. H., 179, *199*
Gore, S., 3, *23*
Gorsuch, R. L., 13, *25*, 87, *115*, 179, 182, 186, *201*
Gottlieb, B. H., 21, *23*
Gottman, J. M., 13, *24*
Gough, H. G., 13, *23*, *24*
Graham, J. R., 128, 136, *140*, 142, 144, *151*

Graley, J., 127, 135, 137, *140*
Greene, A. F., 157, 159, 163, 164, 165, *167*, *168*
Grey, C., 5, 6, *23*
Griffith, J. C., 86, *115*
Gross, A. C., 95, *113*
Grossman, W., 153, *168*
Guinta, D. M., 5, 6, 7, 8, 10, 11, 14, 15, 16, 18, 20, 21, *24*
Gumpert, P., 89, *111*
Guterman, S. S., 81, *112*
Guy, R. F., 92, *111*

H

Hafner, R. J., 141, *151*
Hakstian, A. R., 86, *112*
Hall, M. L., 153, *168*
Hamburger, C. D., 160, *167*
Hancher-Kuam, S., 5, 6, 8, *24*
Hanson, D. J., 78, *112*
Hare, R. D., 86, 88, *112*
Harken, D., 153, *168*
Harpur, T. J., 86, 88, *112*
Harrell, W. A., 89, 94, *113*
Harris, R. E., 145, *151*
Harrison, D., 3, *25*
Harrison, E. E., 157, 159, 164, 165, *168*
Hartnagel, T., 89, *113*
Hathaway, S. R., 13, *23*
Hazaleus, S. L., 186, 195, 196, 197, 198, *199*, *200*
Hazelton, V., 103, 105, *116*
Heberden, W., 158, *168*
Hegarty, W. H., 89, *113*
Hehl, F. J., 31, 32, 33, 34, 35, 36, 37, 38, 39, 40, 41, 42, 43, 44, 45, 46, 47, 48, 49, 50, 52, 53, 54, 55, 56, 57, 60, 61, 62, 63, 64, 65, 66, 69, *73*, *74*, *75*
Heineman, C. E., 87, *113*
Heisler, W. J., 97, 98, 99, *112*, *113*
Heitzmann, C. A., 4, 18, *24*
Heller, K., 1, 2, 3, 4, 5, 6, 8, 9, 10, 11, 12, 14, 15, 18, 19, *24*
Henry, E. M., 137, *140*
Hershberger, K., 98, *113*
Herzog, T. R., 29, 32, *73*
Hestrin, L., 157, *168*
Hickam, D. H., 153, *168*
Hickey, C. B., 89, *111*
Hilton-Chalfenm, S., 157, *168*
Hirsch, B. J., 1, 18, *24*

Hirschfeld, R. M., 13, *24*
Hjemboe, S., 141, 142, 144, 149, *151*, *152*
Hoberman, H., 9, *23*
Hogarty, G. E., 20, *24*
Hogg, J. A., 196, 197, 198, *200*
Hollander, E. P., 93, 104, *112*
Hollifield, M., 153, *168*
Hollon, C. J., 98, 99, 103, *113*
Horan, J. J., 197, *200*
Hornstein, H. A., 80, 95, 102, *115*
House, J. S., 4, 18, *24*, 92, *111*
Howarth, E., 80, 86, *113*
Howell, R. J., 127, 135, 137, *140*
Huber, V. L., 91, *113*
Hunt, S. D., 96, 97, 99, 103, *113*
Hunter, J. E., 78, 83, 84, 105, 106, 107, 108, *113*
Hurst, J. W., 155, 157, *168*
Hussey, M. A., 17, *26*
Hutter, A., Jr., 156, *168*
Hutto, D. B., 79, 80, *111*

I

Ickes, W., 85, *110*, *113*
Ingle, M. E., 17, *26*

J

Jackson, D. N., 13, 15, *24*, 85, *111*
Jacobs, G., 177, 178, 179, 192, 193, 194, *201*
Janisse, M. P., 90, *113*
Jansa, E., 38, 39, 40, 41, 52, 57, 59, 60, *73*
Jenkins, C. D., 153, 156, 157, *168*
Joachim, U., 40, 46, 47, 48, 52, 54, 61, 63, *73*
Johnson, E., 178, 179, 192, *201*
Johnson, J. H., 17, *25*
Johnson, P. B., 80, *113*
Johnston, L. K., 82, 85, *114*
Jones, R. G., 190, *200*
Jones, W. H., 81, 87, 92, *113*
Judkins, M. P., 153, 156, 158, *167*
Jung, C. G., 117, *125*

K

Kadushinh, C., 13, *23*
Kaemmer, B., 142, *151*
Kahn, M., 127, *139*
Kahn, R. K., 4, 18, *24*

Kanner, A. D., 17, *24*
Kaplan, R. M., 4, 18, *24*
Katon, W., 153, *168*
Kauffmann, D. R., 98, *113*
Kennedy, J. W., 153, 156, 158, *167*
Kerr, N. L., 95, *113*
Kessler, R., 3, *26*
Kidd, A. H., 98, *110*
Killip, T., 153, 156, 158, *167*
Kinder, B. N., 127, 130, *140*
Kischkel, K. H., 57, *73*
Klein, M., 153, *168*
Klerman, G. L., 13, *24*
Kline, P., 84, 86, 106, 108, *111*, *113*
Klohn, K. I., 90, *110*
Knight, P. D., 90, 104, *114*
Kohn, P. M., 84, *113*
Kolb, R., 157, *167*
Korchin, S. J., 13, *24*
Korioth, I., 53, *73*
Krampen, G., 83, *112*
Kranz, D. S., 157, *168*
Krasner, S., 177, 192, *201*
Kumar, R., 141, *151*
Kuo, H. K., 106, *113*

L

L'Abbate, A., 153, *168*
Lakatta, E. G., 157, 165, *167*
Langner, T. S., 13, *24*
Larwin, D. A., 29, 32, *73*
LaTorre, R. A., 87, *113*
Laufer, R., 13, *23*
Lazarus, R. S., 2, 17, *23*, *24*
Leary, M. R., 90, 104, *114*
Leary, T., 79, *114*
Lehmann, S., 84, 105, 106, 107, *111*
Leon, M., 153, *167*
Leonard, J., 38, 40, 41, *74*
Levenson, H., 83, *114*
Levenson, R. W., 13, *24*
Levine, H. M., 9, *25*
Levinson, D. J., 65, *72*
Levy, M., 89, *110*
Liem, G. R., 8, *24*
Liem, J. H., 8, *24*
Lindholm, L., 157, *167*
Lingoes, J. C., 145, *151*
Linker, W., 141, *152*
Litle, P., 58, 64, *73*
Lombardi, D., 92, *111*

Lopez, F. G., 193, *200*
Louis, E., 5, 6, 8, 10, 11, 14, 15, *24*
Lubin, B., 82, *116*
Luborsky, L. B., 28, *73*
Luescher, M., *125*
Lushene, R. E., 13, *25*, 87, *115*, 179, 182, 186, *201*
Lutz, J., 153, 156, *167*
Lyons, J. S., 5, 6, 8, *24*

M

MacAndrew, C., 149, *151*
Magarian, G. J., 153, *168*
Mahler, I., 83, *114*
Marlowe, D., 15, *23*
Maroldo, G. K., 82, 85, *114*
Marsella, A. J., 106, *113*
Martin, C. L., 79, *114*
Martin, L., 98, *113*
Martinez, D. C., 97, 104, 106, 108, *114*, *116*
Marzilli, M., 153, *168*
Masseri, A., 153, *168*
Maton, K. I., 2, *24*
Matthews, K. A., 165, *168*
May, J., 84, 86, 108, *111*
Mayer, J. L., 82, 85, *114*
Mayman, M., 118, *125*
Mayou, R., 153, 157, *168*
McClintock, C. M., 189, *199*
McCormick, I. A., 2, *25*
McCrae, R. R., 157, 165, *167*
McGhee, P. E., 30, 31, 32, 34, 35, 36, 37, 42, 49, 53, 54, 60, 61, *74*, *75*, 85, *110*
McIvor, G. P., 5, 6, 14, *24*
McKinley, J. C., 13, *23*
McLeoad, E., 87, *113*
Meehl, P. E., 147, *151*
Mehrabian, A., 80, *114*
Mehta, P., 81, *114*
Meisner, J. S., 137, *140*
Miklowitz, D. J., 20, *24*
Mittman, B. L., 127, *140*
Mock, M. B., 153, 156, 158, *167*
Molin, J., 98, *114*
Mones, G. A., 29, *74*
Moon, J. R., 197, 198, *200*
Moon, T. H., 90, 103, 104, *112*
Moos, R. H., 9, 18, *24*
Morell, M., 157, *168*

Murray, L. W., 81, *114*
Myers, I. B., 117, *125*

N

Nair, V., 141, *152*
Nastase, C., 141, *152*
Neale, M. A., 91, *113*
Nelson, C., 103, 104, *112*
Nelson, D., 15, *22*
Neron, C. A., 141, *152*
Nias, D. K. P., 45, 61, *74*
Nickel, T. W., 81, 87, 92, *113*
Nightingale, J. P., 85, *115*
Nigro, G., 82, 83, 87, 88, *112, 114*
Norman, R. D., 118, *125*
Novaco, R., 182, 184, 197, 198, *200*

O

Oetting, E. R., 190, *200*
O'Hair, D., 106, 108, *114*
Okanes, M. M., 81, *114*
O'Keefe, B. J., 85, *111*
O'Laughlin, S., 189, *200*
Osborn, E., 5, 6, *23*
Ott, C., 32, 34, *74*
Overton, M. N., 127, 135, 136, 137, *140*

P

Pandey, J., 93, 99, 104, *114*
Parodi, O., 153, *168*
Parry, C. H., 153, *168*
Pasternak, R., 156, *168*
Patterson, J. R., 52, 54, *75*
Patterson, M., 85, *113*
Patton, D., 141, *152*
Paulhus, D. L., 79, 82, 83, 98, 107, 108, *114*
Pedhazur, E. J., 130, *140*
Pepine, C., 157, *167*
Perrotta, P., 5, 6, 8, *24*
Perry, G. G., 127, 130, *140*
Peter, M. I., 82, 85, *114*
Peterson, C., 89, *111*
Pettigrew, C., 127, *140*
Pickering, J., 127, *140*
Pickering, T. G., 157, 165, *168*
Pien, D., 32, *74*
Pierce, G. R., 3, 8, 9, 12, *25*

Pinaire-Reed, J. A., 108, *114*
Poderico, C., 87, *114*
Powell, F., 84, *116*
Procidano, M. E., 1, 2, 3, 4, 5, 6, 7, 8, 9, 10, 11, 12, 13, 14, 15, 16, 18, 19, 20, 21, *23, 24, 25, 26*
Prociuk, T. J., 82, 83, *114*
Proudfit, W. L., 156, *168*

R

Rabkin, J. G., 1, *25*
Ramanaiah, N., 189, *200*
Ramsay, T. B., 2, 9, 13, *22*
Rapaport, D., 120, *125*
Rapkin, B. D., 1, *24*
Raps, C., 6, 7, 10, 11, 14, 15, 16, *26*
Rastogi, R., 93, *114*
Rath, S., 32, 33, 40, 48, 49, 52, *74, 75*
Ray, J. J., 78, 84, 86, 101, 103, 107, 109, *114, 115*
Regts, J. M., 141, 142, *151*
Regul, R., 39, 40, 43, 46, 52, *74*
Reidhead, S., 85, *113*
Reischl, T. M., 18, *24*
Reitan, E. J., 82, 85, *114*
Renshaw, S., 103, 105, *116*
Resser, K. J., 157, *168*
Reznikoff, M., 5, 6, 14, *23, 24*
Rice, A. P., 157, *167*
Richford, M. L., 82, 99, *115*
Richter, R. H., 118, 123, *125*
Rickels, K., 13, *23*
Rickman, R. L., 157, *168*
Riklan, M., 5, 6, 14, *24*
Riley, W. T., 179, *200*
Robbins, M. A., 157, *167*
Roberts, J. J., 183, *200*
Robson, K. M., 141, *151*
Rock, A. F., 13, *23*
Roe, A. V., 127, 135, 137, *140*
Rogers, R. S., 101, 104, *115*
Rogers, W., 153, 156, 158, *167*
Rokeach, M., 47, *74*
Rorschach, H., 118, *125*
Rose, G. A., 156, 158, *168*
Rosen, A., 147, *151*
Rosenthal, R., 13, 15, *25*, 90, *111*
Rosenthal, S. F., 91, *115*
Rosing, D., 153, *167*
Rothbart, M. K., 32, *74*
Rotter, J. B., 82, *115*, 137, *140*

Rozanski, A., 157, *168*
Ruch, W., 29, 30, 31, 32, 33, 34, 35, 36, 37, 38, 39, 40, 41, 42, 43, 44, 45, 46, 47, 48, 49, 50, 52, 53, 54, 55, 56, 57, 58, 59, 60, 61, 62, 63, 64, 65, 66, 69, *72, 73, 74, 75*
Rudd, J., 102, *110*
Russell, G. W., 82, 94, 95, *115*
Russell, K. L., 82, 85, *114*
Russell, S., 177, 178, 179, 192, 193, 194, *201*
Russo, J., 153, *168*
Ryan, T. J., 157, *168*

S

Sabadell, P. M., 181, 182, 185, *200*
Sandler, I. N., 2, 9, 13, *22, 25*
Sanford, R. N., 65, *72*
Saper, B., 29, *75*
Sarason, B. R., 3, 8, 9, 12, 19, *25*
Sarason, I. G., 1, 3, 8, 9, 12, 17, 19, 21, *25*
Savageau, J., 153, *168*
Savoia, M., 156, *168*
Schaefer, C., 2, 17, *23, 24*
Schafer, R., 120, *125*
Schill, T., 189, *200*
Schiller, P. von, 31, *75*
Schlichter, K. J., 197, *200*
Schmidt, A., 81, 87, 92, *113*
Schmiedel, J., 48, 49, *75*
Schocken, D. D., 157, 159, 163, 164, 165, *167, 168*
Schuchts, R., 98, *114*
Schugens, M., 38, 40, 41, *74*
Schul, Y., 3, *25*
Schwartz, G., 183, *200*
Scott, W. A., 118, *125*
Seaman, F. J., 93, 104, *112*
Seamons, D. T., 127, 135, 137, *140*
Selwyn, A. P., 157, *167*
Semin, G. R., 101, 104, *115*
Sereri, S., 153, *168*
Shaffer, J. W., 129, 130, *140*
Shapiro, D., 118, *125*
Shapiro, K. J., 117, *125*
Shapiro, S., 158, *167*
Shavzin, A. R., 127, *139*
Shea, M. T., 104, *115*
Shearin, E. N., 3, 8, 9, 12, *25*
Shelby, J., 92, *111*

Shepard, J., 178, *200*
Sheppard, B. H., 91, *115*
Shirey, E. K., 156, *168*
Shostrom, E. L., 13, *25*
Shrout, P. E., 3, *23*
Shultz, T. R., 31, *75*
Siegel, J. M., 17, *25*
Siegel, S., 82, *115*
Siegert, R. J., 2, *25*
Silverman, K. J., 153, *168*
Sims, H. P., Jr., 89, *113*
Singer, J., 183, *200*
Singer, J. E., 97, *115*
Singer, J. L., 117, *125*
Singh, P., 104, *114*
Sipps, G. J., 96, 103, 104, *116*
Skinner, N. F., 80, 81, 86, 87, 95, 102, *115*
Sloan, L., 13, *23*
Smith, C., 80, *115*
Smith, J., 13, *23*
Smith, R. J., 86, *115*
Snyder, D. K., 141, 142, *151*
Snyder, K. S., 20, *24*
Snyder, M., 85, *115*
Solar, D., 82, *115*
Solomon, E., 177, 192, *201*
Sones, F. M., 156, *168*
Spanier, G. B., 143, *151*
Spence, N. S., 141, *151*
Spielberger, C. D., 13, *25*, 87, *115*, 157, 159, 163, 164, 165, *167, 168*, 177, 178, 179, 182, 186, 192, 193, 194, 195, *201*
Stanford, J., 153, 156, *167*
Stanton, B., 153, *168*
Stark, R. S., 181, 183, 184, 191, 192, 194, 195, 197, 198, *199, 200, 201*
Steininger, M., 84, 96, 108, *115*
Stewart, R. A. C., 105, 106, *110*
Stiff, J., 108, *116*
Stokes, J., 3, *25*
Stokes, J. P., 2, *25*
Story, D., 181, 182, 185, 190, 194, 196, *201*
Story, D. A., 197, 198, *200*
Strachea, A. M., 20, *24*
Struening, G. L., 1, *25*
Suls, J. M., 31, *75*
Swaim, R. C., 190, *200*
Swan, R. J., 141, *151*
Sypher, B. D., 85, *115*
Sypher, H. E., 85, *115*

T

Tamborini, R., 108, *116*
Tardy, C. H., 4, 18, *25*
Tavris, C., *199, 201*
Taylor, A. J. W., 2, *25*
Tellegen, A., 46, *75*, 142, *151*
Tetzloff, C. E., 2, *25*
Thibault, G., 156, *168*
Thibaut, J., 89, *111*
Thomas, C. B., 129, 130, *140*
Thurman, C. W., 193, *200*
Thwaites, G., 180, *199*
Thwaites, G. A., 186, *200*
Tollefson, D. L., 28, 69, *73*
Tolsdorf, C. C., 2, *25*
Topol, M. T., 99, 103, *112*
Touhey, J. C., 81, 97, *116*
Treiber, F. A., 179, *200*
Trodahl, V., 84, *116*
Tuma, J., 127, *140*
Turnbull, A. A., Jr., 97, *116*
Turner, C. F., 97, 104, *116*
Turner, R. J., 3, *25*
Tyras, D. H., 153, 156, 158, *167*

U, V

Unterweger, S., 40, *75*
Vaux, A., 1, 3, 21, *25*
Vidmar, N., 91, *115*
Vielhaber, M. E., 85, *115*
Viglione, D. J., 130, *140*
Vinokur, A., 3, *25*
Vitaliano, P. P., 153, *168*
Vleeming, R. G., 78, 80, 84, 101, 102, 103, 104, 106, 108, *112, 116*

W

Wade, L. N., 6, 8, 11, *25*
Walkey, F. R., 2, *25*
Waring, E. M., 141, *151, 152*
Watson, D., 46, *75*, 194, *201*
Watson, R., 153, *167*
Way, J. H., 79, 80, *111*
Weerts, T. C., 183, *200*
Weinberger, D., 183, *200*
Weinblatt, E., 158, *167*

Weinheimer, S., 80, 91, *112*
Weinstock, S. A., 80, *116*
Welsh, G. S., 136, *140*
Wenger, N., 153, 156, *167*
Wertheim, E. G., 95, *116*
West, T. W., 157, *168*
Wetherington, E., 3, *26*
Whelton, J., 127, *140*
White, G. L., 103, *116*
Widom, C. S., 95, *116*
Wiggins, J. S., 79, 80, *116*
Wilcox, B. L., 3, *26*
Williams, C. L., 142, 144, *151*
Williams, M. L., 103, 105, *116*
Wills, T. A., 2, 4, 21, *23*
Wilson, Ch. P., 64, *75*
Wilson, G. D., 2, *25*, 50, 52, 54, 58, 65, *73, 75*
Winter, W. D., 118, 123, *125*
Wolf, F. M., 4, 5, 13, 15, *26*
Wolff, B. M., 6, 7, 10, 11, 14, 15, 16, *26*
Wolfgang, A. K., 82, *116*
Wolfson, S., 95, *116*
Woods, M. G., 179, *200*
Worden, T. J., 157, 159, 164, 165, *168*, 178, 179, 192, *201*
Wortzel, L. H., 95, *116*
Wrightsman, L. S., Jr., 81, 82, *116*

Y

Yarnold, J. K., 28, *75*
Yassa, R., 141, *152*
Yeaworth, R. C., 17, *26*
York, J., 17, *26*

Z

Zelles, P., 6, 9, *26*
Zenker, S. I., 82, *116*
Zillmann, D., 108, *116*
Zimbardo, P., 89, *110*
Zimet, C. N., 120, *125*
Zonderman, A. B., 157, 158, 165, *167*
Zook, A. II., 96, 103, 104, *116*
Zuckerman, M., 47, 58, 63, 64, *73, 75*, 82, *116*
Zwemer, W. A., 194, 196, *201*
Zyzanski, S. J., 157, *168*

Subject Index

3 WD (3 Witz-Dimension) humor test, 33, 35–72, *see also* Humor; Humor, assessment of
concerning humor structure, 48–61
construction of, 36
and individual differences, 45–48
psychometric properties of, 36–45
  characteristics of scales, 37
  intercorrelation between the scales, 43–45
  item statistics, 42–43
  means and standard deviations of, 38–39
  reliability, 37, 40–42
regarding humor content, 61–66
three humor categories of, 35–36
versions of, 35–36

A

Achievement
and Machiavellians, 80–81, 97–98
Adolescent Life Events Scale, 17
Age
and Anginal Syndrome Questionnaire, 163
appreciation of humor regarding, 37, 54
and conservatism, 54
relationship of to Perceived Social Support (PSS) scales, 7–8

Aggression
and Machiavellians, 81–82, 94–95
Anger, state. *See* State anger (S-Anger)
Anger, trait. *See* Trait anger (T-Anger)
Anger by Gender MANOVAs, 182, 187–188, 191
Anger Expression (AX) Scale, 178, 179–180, 182, 185–186, 189, 190, 193
Anger Inventory, 182, 184
Anger Situation Scale, 182, 184
Anger Symptom Index, 182, 184
Anginal Syndrome Questionnaire (ASQ), 153–167, 169–176
definition of, 158
development of, 158–164
  factor structuring, 160–163
  psychometric properties, 159–160
  relation to neuroticism and coronary artery disease, 163–164
  and multivariate analysis, 163–164
sample of, 172–176
three classes of symptoms used in the, 169–171
Angina pectoris (AP)
causes of, 153
classification of patients with, 155–156
and coronary artery disease (CAD), 155–158
criteria for diagnosis of, 153–154
definition of, 155

and gender, 154, 159–160, 161–166
and neuroticism, 157–158
symptoms of, 156–157
Angiography, 155
ANOVAs, 183, 184
Antisocial behavior
and Machiavellians, 94–95
Anxiety
and anger, 194, 198
anger suppression and, 179
and coronary artery disease (CAD), 157
influence on factor structuring of the
ASQ, 161
and Machiavellians, 87
Authoritarianism
and Machiavellians, 84–85, 88
and sexual humor, 65–66

B

Barrett-Lennard Relationships Inventory, 9
Behavior, Machiavellian, 88–100
Boredom Susceptibility (BS), 58–59
Buffering hypothesis, 15–17
Buss-Durkee Hostility Inventory (BDHI),
189

C

California Psychological Inventory (CPI),
9, 13
Cartoons. See Humor
Cheating
and Machiavellians, 89
Chest pain, 153–167, see also Angina Pectoris (AP); Coronary artery disease
(CAD)
classification patterns of, 155–156
Cognitive style
and Machiavellians, 85
Color preference, 117–125
Combat Index, 17
Consequence Rating Scale (CRS), 187
Conservatism, 64–65, 69
and appreciation of humor structure,
50–56
and aversiveness of, 55–56
funniness of incongruity-resolution humor, 53–54
funniness of structural basis in sexual
humor, 54–55

Conservatism, dynamic theory of, 50
Control, locus of
and Machiavellians, 82–84
Coping strategies
and trait anger, 182–183, 189–190,
195–199
Coronary artery disease (CAD), 153–154,
155–158, 160, 161, 163–165, see also
Angina pectoris; Chest pain
and gender, 159–160, 161–166
and influence of emotions on, 157
psychosocial risk factors for, 157
relation of ASQ to neuroticism and,
163–164
severity of, 155–157, 160
validity of angina pectoris as predictor
of, 156–157
Coronary Artery Surgery Study (CASS),
156
Coronary heart disease (CHD), 156–157, see
also Angina pectoris (AP); Chest
pain; Coronary artery disease (CAD)
Culture and Machiavellianism, 81
Cynicism and Machiavellianism, 84

D

Depression
and coronary artery disease (CAD), 157
and Machiavellians, 87–88
Dietch Self-Disclosure Inventory, 92
Disinhibition
and sexual humor, 63–64, 65
Dogmatism
and Machiavellians, 84–85, 88
Dyadic Adjustment Scale (DAS), 142,
143–144, 145, 148

E

Education. See Achievement
Employment. See Occupation
Ethics Position Questionnaire, 90
Ethnicity
and Machiavellianism, 83, 106
Experience Seeking (ES), 58–59
Extraverts
and color preference, 117–119, 122–124
and humor appreciation, 46–47
Eysenck Personality Inventory, 86

F

Factor analysis, 30–31, 32–33, 33–35
  of Anginal Syndrome Questionnaire
    (ASQ), 160–163, 165–166
  of Mach scales, 105–107
Faking Rorschach test, 127–139
Family
  Perceived Social Support from Family
    (PSS-Fa) scale, 1–22
  as sources of support, 18, 20–21
Family Environment Scale (FES), 9
Family Problems (FAM) Content Scale,
    142, 144–149
Feedback
  and social support, 2
Friends
  Perceived Social Support from Friends
    (PSS-Fr) scale, 1–22
  as sources of support, 20–21

G

Gender
  and angina pectoris (AP), 154, 156,
    159–160, 161–166
  and humor appreciation, 37
  and Machiavellianism, 81–83, 82–83, 86,
    87, 91–93, 97, 98
  and marital distress, 143, 148
  and trait anger, 180–181, 182–183, 184,
    186, 187–188, 192, 195

H

Heart attack. *See* Angina pectoris (AP);
    Coronary
  artery disease (CAD); Chest pain
Holtzman Inkblot Technique (HIT), 118,
    119, 123
Hostility, *see also* Anger; State anger (S-
    Anger); Trait anger (T-Anger)
  and Machiavellians, 81–82
Howarth Personality Questionnaire, 80
Humor
  content, 61–66
  development of taxonomy of, 33–35
  and dimensions of appreciation, 32–33
  incongruity-resolution (INC-RES), 31–32,
    35–36, 37, 43–44, 48–54, 55–59, 61,
    63, 64–65, 67–69

individual differences in appreciation of,
    45–48
  nonsense (NON), 31–32, 35–36, 37–41,
    43–45, 48–49, 50–52, 55, 56–57,
    58–61, 65–66, 67–68, 69
  and preference for different degrees of
    stimulation, 49–50
  sexual (SEX), 31–32, 35–36, 37, 43, 44,
    46, 54–56, 61–66, 67, 68–69
  state variance in appreciation of, 34–35
  structure, 48–61
  taxonomy of jokes and cartoons, 31–32
Humor appreciation, assessment of, 27–72
  conservatism and, 50–56
  current standard in, 30–31
  funniness vs. aversiveness regarding,
    33–72
  and individual differences, 45–48
  and intelligence, 61
  intolerance of ambiguity regarding, 56–57
  introverts vs. extraverts, 46–47
  and neuroticism, 47–48, 55
  seeking-avoiding stimulus uncertainty
    and, 60–61
  and sensation seeking, 58–60
  sexual, 61–66, 69
  tendermindedness vs. toughmindedness,
    47–48, 50–51, 54–56, 62–66, 69
  theory and research on the nature and,
    28–35
Humor tests
  3 WD (Witz-Dimension), 33–72
    construction and psychometric proper-
      ties of, 35–45
    and findings of studies involving, 45–66
    psychometric properties of, 68
  functions of, 27–28, 70–71
  IPAT Humor Test, 28–30, 69

I

Identity reframing, 198
Incongruity-resolution (INC-RES) humor,
    31–32, 35–36, 37, 43–44, 48–54,
    55–59, 61, 63, 64–65, 67–69
  conservatism and funniness of, 53–54
Individual differences
  in appreciation of humor, 45–48
  in humor, 30
Ingratiation
  and Machiavellians, 93

Intelligence
    and appreciation of humor structure, 61
Interpersonal space
    and Machiavellians, 79
Interpersonal Support Evaluation List, 9
Introverts
    and color preference, 117–119, 122–124
    and humor appreciation, 46–47
Intuition, 117–119, 121, 122
Inventory of Socially Supportive Behaviors
    (ISSB), 2, 9
IPAT Depression Scale, 87
IPAT Humor Test, 28–30, 69
    role in research, 29–30
    two forms of, 29
Irrational Beliefs Test, 190
Ischemia, 153, 157, 158

J

Jobs. *See* Occupation
Job satisfaction
    and Machiavellians, 98–100
Jokes. *See* Humor
Jung's typology, 117–119, 121–124

K, L

Kruskal-Wallis Rank Test, 130–131
Leadership
    and Machiavellians, 93–94
Life Experience Survey, 17
Luescher Color Test, 120, 121–122, 123–124
Lying
    and Machiavellians, 89–90

M

MacAndrew alcoholism scale (MAC), 149
Machiavellianism, 77–110
    cognitive style of, 85
    concept of, 77–78
    dogmatism-authoritarianism regarding,
        84–85
    hostility and self-reported aggression con-
        cerning, 81–82
    leadership and, 93–94
    and locus of control, 82–84
    locus of control concerning, 82–83
    and the need for achievement, 80–81
    and occupational choice, success, and
        satisfaction regarding, 95–100
    and perceived personality traits, 79–80
    personality correlates of, 78–88
    position in interpersonal space, 79
    prosocial and antisocial behavior regard-
        ing, 94–95
    psychometric issues concerning,
        100–110
    and psychopathology, 86–88
        anxiety, 87
        depression, 87–88
        psychopathy, 86–87
    regarding manipulation of others, 91–93
        ingratiation, 93
        persuasion, 91–92
        self-disclosure, 92–93
    relationship to self-monitoring, 85–86
    scales used in measuring, 100–110
    simulations regarding, 80
    and unethical behavior, 89–90
Mach IV & V scales, 77, 78, 100–110
    dimensionality and construct validity
        concerning, 107–109
    dimensionality of, 105–107
    factor analysis of, 105–107
    problems with, 101–105, 109
    reliability of, 103–105
    and socially desirable responding,
        100–103
    and tactics-views distinction, 106,
        108–109
Main effect hypothesis of social support,
    13, 20
Malingering of Rorschach test, 127–139
Manipulation
    and Machiavellians, 90–93
Mann-Whitney U Test, 131, 133
Marital Distress Scale (MDS), 141–151
    compared to other scales, 145–150
    development of, 143–144
    evaluating efficacy of, 145–150
    and importance of assessing marital rela-
        tionship, 141
    limitations of, 149–150
Marital Satisfaction Inventory (MSI) Global
    Distress
    Index, 142
Mental illness
    faking Rorschach test regarding, 127–139
Minnesota Multiphasic Personality Inven-
    tory (MMPI), 13, 128, 131, 136–137,
    138, 139, 141, 142–143, 144, 145,
    148, 149–150, 191

Multiple Affect Adjective Checklist, 87
Multivariate analysis
and Anginal Syndrome Questionnaire,
163–164
Myers-Briggs Type Indicator, 117, 118, 119,
121, 123, 124
Myocardial infarction, 156

N

Network, social, 1, 8, 19
Neuroticism
and appreciation of humor, 47–48, 55
and coronary artery disease (CAD), 157
influence of on factor structuring of the
ASQ, 161
and Machiavellians, 86
relation of ASQ to coronary artery disease and, 163–164
Nonsense (NON) humor, 31–32, 35–36,
37–41, 43–45, 48–49, 50–52, 55,
56–57, 58–61, 65–66, 67–68, 69
conservatism and funniness of, 55

O, P

Occupation
and Machiavellians, 95–100
Perceived Social Support (PSS) scales, 1–22,
see also Social support
construct validity of
and relationship to measures of stress,
17–18
and role of response bias, 15
and the buffering hypothesis, 15–17
relationship of PSS-Fa to PSS-Fr, 8
relationship of to personality and social
competence, 9, 13
and other social support scales, 8–9,
10–12
and symptomatology, 13–15
reliability
internal consistency of, 4–5
test-retest reliabilities for, 5
validity
of norms and contrasted groups, 5–7
role of age and, 7–8
Perception
and personality, 117–125
Personality
and angina pectoris, 153–167, 169–176

Machiavellian, 78–88
and perception, 117–125
relationship of Perceived Social Support
(PSS)
scales to measurement of, 9, 13
Persuasion
and Machiavellians, 91–92
Prosocial behavior
and Machiavellians, 95
Psychopath Checklist (PCL), 86–87
Psychopathic deviate (Pd), 86, 141–142,
144–147, 148–149
Psychopathology
and Machiavellians, 86–88
and trait anger, 191–192

R

Relaxation coping skills, 195–196, see also
Coping strategies
Reliability
of 3 WD (Witz-Dimension) scales, 37,
40–42
of Mach scales, 103–105
of Perceived Social Support (PSS) scales,
4–5
Response bias
relationship of Perceived Social Support
(PSS) scales to, 15
Rokeach Value Survey, 47
Role reframing, 198
Rorschach Inkblot Test, 119, 124
Rorschach test malingering, 127–139
general variables involved in, 131–134
instruments and procedures used in,
128–129
and response selection for data analysis,
129–131
and selection of statistical tests, 131
Rose Questionnaire, 156, 158, 161, 163,
166

S

Schizophrenia
faking Rorschach test regarding, 127–139
School. See Achievement
Seeking-avoiding stimulus uncertainty
and appreciation of humor structure,
60–61
Self concept
and trait anger, 191

Self-disclosure
  and Machiavellians, 92–93
Self-monitoring
  and Machiavellians, 85–86
Self-reports, 48
Sensation seeking
  and appreciation of humor structure,
    58–60
Sensing, 117–119, 121, 122
Sexual (SEX) humor, 31–32, 35–36, 37,
    43, 44, 46,
    54–56, 61–66, 67, 68–69
  appreciation of based on different struc-
    tures, 64–66
  and authoritarians, 65–66
  aversiveness of sexual content in, 66,
    67
  conservatism and funniness of structural
    basis in, 54–55
  and disinhibition, 63–64, 65
  funniness of sexual content in, 62–64
  and sexual libido, 65–66
  subdivisions of, 32, 44
  tendermindedness vs. toughmindedness
    regarding, 54–55, 62–66, 69
  three subdivisions of, 36
Social competence
  relationship of Perceived Social Support
    (PSS) scales to measurement of, 9,
    13
Social embeddedness, 1, 3
Socially desirable responding
  and Mach scales, 100–103
Social network, 1, 8
Social Network Questionnaire, 8
Social support, 1–22, see also Perceived
    Social Support (PSS) scales
  advantages and disadvantages in assessing
    perceived, 1–4
  definition of, 1, 2, 3
  Perceived Social Support instruments
    concerning
    construct validity of, 8–18
    reliability of, 4–5
    validity of, 5–8
Social Support Questionnaire, 9
State anger (S-Anger), see also Hostility
  definition of, 177
  predicting frequency of, 180–181
State-Trait Anger Expression Inventory
    (STAXI), 195

State-Trait Anger Scales (STAS), 178, 180,
    189, 190–191, 193
State-Trait Anxiety Inventory (STAI), 87,
    178, 182
State-Trait Anxiety (T-Anxiety) Scale, 179
Stealing
  and Machiavellians, 89
Stress
  adjustment to, 2, 3
  relationship of Perceived Social Support
    (PSS)
  scales to measurement of, 15–18, 21
  and social support, 3–4
Stress coping strategies
  and trait anger, 182–183, 189–190,
    195–199
Structure Preference Index (SPI), 59
Symptomatology
  relationship of Perceived Social Support
    (PSS) scales to, 13–15, 20

T

Taylor Anxiety Scale, 87
Tendermindedness
  and appreciation of humor, 47–48, 50–51,
    54–56, 62–66, 69
Test-retest reliability, 5, 18
Tests
  faking of Rorschach, 127–139
Toughmindedness
  and appreciation of humor, 47–48, 50–51,
    54–56, 62–66, 69
Trait anger (T-Anger), 177–199, see also
    Hostility
  and alcohol/drug abuse, 180, 189–190,
    199
  assessing consequences of high levels of,
    186–188
  clinical assessment and treatment of,
    195–198
  and comparing individuals with high and
    low, 181–186
  and gender, 180–181, 182–183, 184, 186,
    187–188, 192, 195
  physical vs. verbal antagonism concern-
    ing, 182, 184–186
  relation of to style of anger expression,
    178–180
  and stress coping strategies used,
    182–183, 189–190, 195–199

Trait-State Anger Theory, 178, 180–195
  additional correlates of trait anger concerning, 189–190
  concerning irrational beliefs, self-concept, and psychopathology, 190–192
  implications for and future research regarding, 192–195
  and prediction of anger frequency, 180–181
  tests of, 180–192
Trait-State Anxiety Theory, 177

U, V

Unethical behavior
  and Machiavellians, 89–90
Validity
  Mach scales regarding dimensionality and construct, 107–109
  of Perceived Social Support (PSS) scales, 8–22
  and the role of age, 7–8
  norms and contrasted-groups validity, 5–7